D1478715

SYSTEMS THEORY FOR SOCIAL WORK AND THE HELPING PROFESSIONS

Social systems occur in many contexts of social work. This book provides an easy-to-read introduction to systems thinking for social workers who will encounter social problems in their professional practice or academic research. It offers new insights and fresh perspectives on this familiar topic and invites creative, critical, and empathetic thinking with a systems perspective.

Through introducing systems theory as a problem-oriented approach for dealing with complex interpersonal relations and social systems, this book provides a framework for studying social relations. The authors present a strand of systems theory (inspired by sociologist Niklas Luhmann) that offers innovative, surprising, and practically relevant understandings of everyday social life, inclusion/exclusion, social problems, interventions, and society in general.

Systems Theory for Social Work and the Helping Professions should be considered essential reading for all social work students taking modules on sociology and social policy as well as students of nursing, medicine, counselling, and occupational health and therapy.

Werner Schirmer, PhD, holds a docent title in sociology from Uppsala University. He has worked at several universities in Germany, Sweden, the USA, and Belgium. Currently, he is working at the department of Sociology at the Vrije Universiteit Brussel, research group TOR. Schirmer has written several articles and book chapters applying systems theoretical thinking to topics such as interethnic relations, social work and social problems, inclusion/ exclusion, respect and tolerance, international relations, priority setting in healthcare, and loneliness among older people. His current research focuses on the impact of digital technologies on social relations.

Dimitris Michailakis, PhD, is Professor of Sociology and Chair Professor of Social Work. He is the author of several books and reports for national and international organisations. In his research, he mainly highlights two strongly correlated areas. The first area is political governance, with particular emphasis on how the welfare state has tried to control other social systems to become more responsive towards vulnerable groups. The second area is about modern society's strongest conflict, namely the one between a fundamental right to inclusion and steadily increasing exclusion.

SYSTEMS THEORY FOR SOCIAL WORK AND THE HELPING PROFESSIONS

Werner Schirmer and Dimitris Michailakis

Routledge
Taylor & Francis Group

LONDON AND NEW YORK

First published 2019
by Routledge
2 Park Square, Milton Park, Abingdon, Oxon OX14 4RN

and by Routledge
52 Vanderbilt Avenue, New York, NY 10017

Routledge is an imprint of the Taylor & Francis Group, an informa business

Published in Swedish by Studentlitteratur 2017

British Library Cataloguing-in-Publication Data
A catalogue record for this book is available from the British Library

Library of Congress Cataloging-in-Publication Data
A catalog record has been requested for this book

ISBN: 978-0-367-07689-4 (hbk)
ISBN: 978-0-367-07690-0 (pbk)
ISBN: 978-0-429-02210-4 (ebk)

Typeset in Bembo
by Taylor & Francis Books

CONTENTS

ILLUSTRATIONS

Figure

Table

PREFACE TO THE SWEDISH ORIGINAL

This book is the result of many years of cooperation between the authors in teaching, research, and writing of articles and book chapters. However, this book would not have taken on its current form without the valuable contributions of many other people. Without their help, this book would not have been written and would not appear as it does. That is why it is our turn to say thank you.

One of the seeds of this book is the positive response we received from students in our lectures and classes in social work and sociology. Their clever questions have challenged us, their genuine interest in a systemic perspective has surprised us, and their demand has convinced us that systemic thinking should get more space in social work education. All these things together have been key motivators for us to write this book. That is why we want to thank the social work students at the University of Linköping and University College of Gävle!

We also want to thank our colleagues in the Scandinavian systems theory groups whom we have met at several conferences, workshops, and other academic activities. The numerous interesting and instructive conversations we have had with them have contributed to our better understanding of and immersion in systems-theoretical thinking. Moreover, we have learned a lot from their many articles, books, and chapters, which in one way or another have affected our text. We thank Niels Åkerstrøm Andersen, Maria Appel-Nissen, Lars Clausen, Claus Hadamek, Roar Hagen, Gorm Harste, Holger Højlund, Jan Inge Jönhill, Morten Knudsen, Anders La Cour, Sverre Moe, Jens Rasmussen, Wendelin Reich, and Jesper Tække.

A book on systems theory in social work would hardly reach a certain level without a constant intellectual exchange with colleagues and researchers who are critical (or at best neutral) towards systems theory. Their input was at least as valuable as that of the advocates of systems theory for improving our argumentation and writing in a more pedagogical way. Therefore, we also want to thank those who have commented on previous versions of the manuscript or earlier papers on systems theory, conference presentations, and seminars. We thank Kamila Biszczanik, Berth Danermark, Peter Ekegren, David Ekholm, Kjeld Høgsbro, Anna Olaison, Apostolis Papakostas, Gunilla Petersson, Rudi Roose, Ian Shaw, Stefan Sjöberg, Peter Sohlberg, Mårten Söder, Sandra Torres, Javier Treviño, Kaspar Villadsen, and Karsten Åström.

Last but not least we want to express our gratitude to the editor Johan Lindgren, who invited us to write the book for Studentlitteratur, our technical editor at Studentlitteratur, Kajsa Persson, and the language editor, Sophia Lundquist. Furthermore, we want to thank Elisabet Lindquist for a very thorough reading of previous versions of the manuscript and her numerous good suggestions, which improved the text significantly. Werner Schirmer also wants to thank Anina Vercruyssen for support and inspiration during the harder phases of the writing process.

Despite all the help of the above-mentioned people, it is still our responsibility as authors to bear the full responsibility for the content of the book.

Stockholm and Ghent, May 2017
Dimitris Michailakis & Werner Schirmer

PREFACE TO THE INTERNATIONAL VERSION

After the book was released in Swedish for a primarily Scandinavian audience, some international colleagues approached us and asked us to re-publish the book in English. Kristina Karlsson, rights manager at our Swedish publisher, Studentlitteratur, generously gave us permission to take this step, for which we are very grateful.

During the process of translation from Swedish to English we scrutinised the manuscript and made several smaller amendments and changes to the text, replaced some Scandinavian examples with examples that work in an international context, and added a short section on social work as a reflection theory in Chapter 8. The translated manuscript was proofread by an English native-speaking professional, who improved the language substantially. Our gratitude goes to Chris Kennard and the firm Anchor English.

Furthermore, we want to thank Ian Shaw, who introduced us to our editor Claire Jarvis at Taylor & Francis/Routledge. Likewise, we wish to express our gratitude to Claire, who strongly encouraged this project and accompanied it from the beginning, to editorial assistant Georgia Priestley for her support during the production process, and the team at Bookbright Media for excellent copy-editing. We also want to thank the external reviewers commissioned by Routledge, whose evaluations were very positive and encouraging.

Finally, we need to mention that we changed the order of authors in the international edition to acknowledge the cooperative efforts by both authors when writing and translating this book.

Brussels and Stockholm, August 2018
Werner Schirmer & Dimitris Michailakis

INTRODUCTION

Social work serves as a link between general social policies of the welfare state and individual claims for help and support. The purpose of social work is to provide *organised* – and thus controllable – help and support for people who are threatened by different kinds of social exclusion. Help and support measures range from economic aid, counselling, and pro-active drug prevention to consultation for victims of domestic violence.

As an academic discipline, social work conducts research into the organisation of help and support, the means by which help and support are provided, which interventions are successful, and how help and support are distributed in terms of rights and duties. Social work research also examines the problems and frictions that arise in practice as well as the problems and frictions organised social help can trigger in other societal spheres, such as the economy, the political system, or the education system.

Central to this book, and at the core of both social work research and social work practice, is *social relations*. By "social relations" we do not mean only relations between individuals, for instance an alcohol addict and his family, a youngster and the criminal gang he ended up with, a prostitute and her pimp, or a welfare secretary and her client applying for economic support. Social work is also about relations between organisations, for example between social service agencies and the police, between social service agencies and schools, between social service agencies and psychiatric clinics. Social work is also characterised by social relations on a meta level, for instance the relations between the welfare state, party politics, and macro-social changes such as structural unemployment, liberalisation of markets, budget cuts in public spending, and migration crises.

One common denominator in all the examples given in the preceding paragraphs is the involvement of one or more *system(s)*. The term "system" refers to many different phenomena, from micro-organisms within the biological world to the globalised society. Within psychology and the social sciences, the concept designates phenomena as different as the mind, families, municipalities and social policy departments, the economy, science, religion, the internet, and social media – all of these are different kinds of systems. Social interactions such as counselling interviews with a client, a coffee break with colleagues, a drink with friends, or a verbal argument with one´s romantic partner are also systems. We are part of systems all the time, and wherever we are we use systems and we are defined by systems.

Within the first chapters, we will go into more detail about what the concept of the "system" can mean in social work and other helping professions. In very general terms, we can state that *systems are complex entities that consist of a number of elements and their relations*. The relations social workers enter and work with are *communication systems*. Typical fields of research and practice in social work include substance abuse, multi-problem families, domestic violence, poverty and homelessness, the integration of ethnic minorities, the fight against everyday racism, the resocialisation of ex-convicts, and the consequences of human trafficking. In all of these cases we deal with more or less complex social systems. Often, we even deal with relations between social systems, which (on a higher level) are systems, too.

In order to manage the complexity of social reality, social workers and other helping professions need suitable analytic models (Van Ewijk, 2018); they require theoretical frameworks that enable analysis and separate the wheat from the chaff of relevancy and, probably most importantly, frameworks that avoid falling for all-too-simple causal explanations (such as "it is the individual's fault" or "neoliberal society is to blame"). For a long time, the social sciences have been caught up in the dichotomy of society vs. the individual (Mortensen, 2004): either society is the cause of individual problems and the individual is the victim of structural conditions or the individual is responsible for her welfare, while the state, the education system, or ethno-cultural affiliation are not to blame.

In this book we present a theory that operates beyond the society/individual dichotomy, partly by focusing on systems (systems can exist on any level) and partly by combining realism and constructionism. Social reality is always too complex to be caught by a theory of this reality, to be represented by a social system, or to be grasped by the human mind. The term "complexity" refers to the circumstance that there are always more possibilities than can be realised, processed, or recognised (Van Ewijk, 2018). When consulting a substance user, a social welfare secretary has to deal with complexity on all fronts. Within the limited time she has at her disposal she cannot comprehend the whole prehistory of the case, cannot process every new problem the client has experienced since the last meeting, cannot control every piece of input from colleagues and supervisors; she has to *select* from the vast amount of information. This is one side of reducing complexity. Another side is the selectivity that happens within the minds (psychic systems) that the welfare secretary interacts with or the social systems that she is acting in (for example the frequently observed situation when the client refuses to talk about particular deep-rooted problems; another example is the overwhelming amount of other cases among which the department has to prioritise). We aim to show in this book that any such system is characterised by a momentum (*Eigendynamik*) that is difficult to grasp, limit, and control.

It is important to keep in mind the purposes that we use theories for. First, theories help in structuring the world. Not only researchers but also people in their everyday lives make use of theories. In their daily work, social work practitioners employ (scientific and folk) theories on clients' behaviour, the dynamics of groups, or the driving forces of social change. Without having theories in mind, they would not be able to do their work. We argue that social workers and practitioners in other helping professions can benefit from theoretical thinking. In this book we present a certain strand of social systems theory (more specifically the theory of social systems developed by Niklas Luhmann, 1995, 2012, 2013) that, as we argue, is well suited for this endeavour. In the German literature, there is a considerable body of work applying Luhmann's general theory of social systems to organised social help and the latter's relation to society (Baecker, 1994; Bommes & Scherr, 2000b; Fuchs, 2000). However, as there is scarcely any work published in international social work books and journals (among the exceptions are Scherr, 1999; Schirmer & Michailakis, 2015b; Villadsen, 2008; Wirth, 2009), one of the aims of this book is to provide a systematic introduction to the Luhmannian theory of society to an English-speaking audience. Naturally, we do not claim that this theoretical approach is the only one of relevance for social work. Neither do we claim that the conclusions drawn with the help of this systems theory represent the ultimate truth. But we do believe that systems theory offers unconventional, sometimes surprising, and practically relevant insights for professional and scholarly fields dealing with complex interpersonal relations.

Systems theory and systemic thinking are not exclusive to the social sciences. On the contrary, systems theory is an interdisciplinary paradigm that originates from the natural sciences. General systems theory (Von Bertalanffy, 1968) was developed when scholars from diverse disciplines such as chemistry, biology, and data science but also sociology, psychology, political science, and economics discovered peculiar similarities across disciplines in the theoretical puzzles they dealt with. Whether one considered biological cells, computerised facilities, self-steering apparatuses, political governments, families, minds, economic markets, or social groups, they all seemed to work according to some general, systemic principles. General systems theory was interested in finding and mapping these principles.

The particular ambition of systems theories in the social sciences is to provide theoretical toolkits for the analysis, understanding, and explanation of processes operating in today's complex world and to identify social problems and their solutions. In order to develop such a theoretical toolkit, systems theorists argue that it is not only beneficial but absolutely essential to consider and integrate scientific advances from other disciplines. The prerequisite for developing such a toolkit is a common conceptual framework, which comes at the price of a high degree of abstraction and which makes it appear inaccessible and unintelligible at first sight.

However, there is a tradition of systems-theoretical thinking within social work. The textbooks by Howard Goldstein (1973) as well as Allen Pincus and Anna

Minahan (1973) were the first ones to introduce systems theory approaches to a social work audience. Arguing against some strands of psychotherapy and methodological individualism, Goldstein emphasised that clients should be understood as parts of social systems in the same way that the relations between clients and social workers should be described as systems and not as an exchange between independent individuals. Pincus and Minahan pointed out the relevance of resource and support systems as well as their relations to clients. In addition to these textbooks, there is a long tradition of cybernetic and systemic approaches in psychiatric research, psychology, and family therapy that managed to gain some attention within social work. Since the works by Gregory Bateson (1972) and the Palo Alto Group around Paul Watzlawick (Watzlawick, Beavin, & Jackson, 1967) have been most influential in social work (see Kleve, 2007), we devote some attention to them in Chapter 1. Another example of systemic thinking in social work is the so-called "ecological model" of Urie Bronfenbrenner, which addresses the interplay between different subsystems from individual minds to the ecological environment. In this model the individual is situated in concentric circles that represent the subsystems that the individual is part of (Bronfenbrenner, 1979).

The common denominator in these different variants of systems theory is their insistence on comprehending human beings and their behaviour not in isolation but as elements in one or several systems. Working with a systemic approach implies the observation of connections and context, not of singular events. A systemic approach can see patterns of processes and can help to detect couplings between events that would otherwise go unnoticed. Hence, we can say that social work is about counselling or treating individuals, families, and groups *within a (social) context*.

Human behaviour requires the understanding of systems (context). In turn, systems cannot be understood by looking only at their constitutive parts. Thus, *it is the system that explains the parts* (or the function of the parts), *not the parts that explain the system*. For example, in order to understand a person's actions, we have to search for the explanation of this action in the interaction patterns (the system) of this person with other people – for instance family members, group members, colleagues, the partner, etc.

Because of the strong emphasis on the whole as the point of departure for the analysis, such an approach is sometimes called "relational" or "holistic" (Fuchs, 2001a; Shaked & Schechter, 2017). Instead of trying to explain phenomena and events by reducing them to an assemblage of separate entities that are allegedly researchable independent from each other, systems theories start at the level of the system as the encompassing unit and ask how it is organised.

Our ambition with this book is to strengthen and partly revive the already existing tradition of systemic thinking in social work and the helping professions. We want to open the door a little further for those students, scholars, and practitioners who are interested in becoming more deeply acquainted with this kind of thinking but who have not yet used it in their work. The book is primarily written for students, researchers, and practitioners of social work and other helping professions but also addresses readers with backgrounds in sociology and other social sciences who are ready for immersion in the "labyrinths" of systems theory (Kneer & Nassehi, 1993). While the latter is not meant to scare away potential readers we should mention now, early on, that systems theory (particularly Luhmann's) is situated on a high level of abstraction and complexity. Likewise, the terminology originates from interdisciplinary contexts and differs largely from mainstream social science vocabulary. This book is not a cookbook with guidelines for social work practice. Instead it is a theoretical book that offers new insights and unconventional perspectives on familiar subject matter. It can be read as an invitation to engage in creative, autonomous, and empathic thinking, all of which we consider key characteristics for good practice and research in social work and other helping professions.

Outline of the book

The book consists of eight chapters and a concluding section. Chapter 1 presents and explains the concept of communication as the key constituent of social relations. In mainstream sociology, social work, and even psychotherapy and pedagogy, it is common to understand social relations in an essentialist manner, starting with the individual and her properties or actions. Drawing on the psychological Palo Alto Group and sociological systems theory, we want to show that it makes sense to consider individual actions as elements of communication systems. We illustrate how communication systems have their own dynamics that often cannot be predicted or controlled by participants. Our book suggests that the social world should be understood as an arrangement of communication systems. Communication can be the key to successful interventions but can also be the very cause of the problems social workers and therapists set out to tackle. As a consequence, communication and its dynamics are at the heart of social work practice.

Chapter 2 demonstrates how social systems are embedded in their environments. The relations between systems and their environment can be complex and multifaceted. In this chapter, we discuss different types of social systems, such as face-to-face interactions and organisations, each one operating with logics and dynamics of their own that cannot be reduced to their elements or environments. Organisations define the framework for decision-making routines and guidelines and distribute rights and duties to their members. Interaction systems set the stage for system dynamics: who is present, who has said what in which way, how should it be interpreted, whose contributions need to be taken seriously and whose can be ignored? Practitioners are mostly employed by and represent organisations; their daily activities of counselling and street work happen on a face-to-face level. This chapter raises awareness of the fact that communication operates simultaneously on several system levels with sometimes-conflicting demands, dynamics, and rationalities.

Chapter 3 describes society as a social system. According to systems theory, modern society is a differentiated and multipolar unit that comprises diverse parts, such as politics, economy, religion, and science. These parts – function systems – operate with distinct functional logics, each with its own unique perspective on the world. A given phenomenon receives different meanings depending on different systems' viewpoints. For instance, a substance abuser can be seen as a person in need, as a cost factor, as a research object, as a legal infringer, as a bad parent, etc. In this chapter, practitioners get insights into the workings of modern society as a complex, heterogeneous entity differentiated into many rationalities and without a clear functional hierarchy. Social work is presented as a system with a particular function for society (the help system) but as one among many perspectives, which needs to compete with others.

Chapter 4 discusses the relation between human beings (individuals) and society from a systems perspective. Here we counter the common prejudice that systems theory has no real "place" for humans. We demonstrate how systems theory provides an appropriate conceptual apparatus for understanding the complex ways in which the individual is created by and participates in society. One key insight for social workers is that human beings are to a large extent formed into members of society by social systems, and by different systems differently at the same time. In modern society, function systems include people not as entities but as highly differentiated role holders (voters/politicians, consumers/traders, believers/priests, students/teachers, defendants/lawyers, etc.). The field of social work, here presented as the social help system, is discussed as a means to manage the inclusion and exclusion of individuals in social systems. Exclusion management by social work is a particular practice of inclusion and exclusion, too. In this chapter, social workers can learn why inclusion should not be confused with equality and why inclusion is not always good and exclusion not always bad.

Chapter 5 picks up the thread from Chapter 3 on society as a differentiated unit. In this chapter, we also argue that systems theory acknowledges the relevance of both the constructionist and the realist paradigms. Systems theory allows us to analyse how things are and how they behave – as complex phenomena with emergent properties. Social workers need to understand the workings of the systems they deal with in their practice. At the same time, systems are creators of their own realities. Hence, one consequence of societal differentiation is that different views on reality are anchored in different systems and that these views affect the actors operating in these systems. Within the perspective of social work, the actors see, evaluate, and experience different things than they would within the systems of politics, science, economy, or religion. We introduce the concept of *multiperspectivity*, which conveys the differentiation, co-presence, and incompatibilities between different viewpoints. In practice, multiperspectivity means that a good social worker should not impose his/her preferred perspective on the client without considering other relevant perspectives. Researchers and practitioners alike have to accept that there are several legitimate ways to describe a given problem, even if these descriptions can be (and often are) incompatible and contradictory.

Chapter 6 is more geared toward practice and deals with the issue of social problems. Here, we pick up the constructionism/realism distinction from the preceding chapter. Social problems have real, objectively existing components and socially constructed components. Adequate analyses of and appropriate solutions to these problems must consider both. Furthermore, we apply the concept of multi-perspectivity to social problems: from which societal perspectives (economic, political, scientific, etc.) do social problems look different in terms of causes, solutions, and responsible agents? The differentiation in several perspectives is a characteristic of pluralism, diversity, and modernity. Social workers can treat multiperspectivity as a resource, not as a burden, since it offers them a deeper understanding of the cases they deal with in their daily work and protects them from falling for pre-fabricated problem definitions by governments or particular interest groups.

In Chapter 7 we approach the issue of political steering from a systems perspective, which is relevant for anybody who is involved in social policy. Drawing on the preceding chapters we discuss the welfare state's dilemma when it is expected to steer what cannot be steered: other social systems. We demonstrate that function systems, such as the economy or healthcare, organisations, and people, cannot be steered as easily as governance or social policy intervention theories assume. We illustrate this with an example from our own research that deals with attempts at inclusion of people with impairment in the labour market.

Chapter 8 shows how systems theory is supported by a functionalist method that looks for latent, underlying problems behind cases. Social work researchers and practitioners have to explore the latent functions behind social and interpersonal problems that need to be analysed and substituted if they want their interventions to be effective. We illustrate the added value of such a functional analysis with examples from our own research on priority-setting in healthcare. Furthermore, we argue that systems theory is well suited for social criticism. In contrast to conventional critical theories, systems theory is not based on any particular political ideology. Seen from a systems view, the researcher is not critical by simply opposing certain societal conditions, but by pointing out the contingency of these conditions (things could be or be done otherwise), latent aspects of these conditions (what are the hidden agendas and interests behind dominating descriptions, what is not said in dominating descriptions) as well as multiperspectivity toward these conditions (how other actors look at things). All of this is social criticism, and that is what we consider central in a field such as social work. Finally, we discuss the role of academic social work as a reflection theory and thus as part of the social help system. Here we argue that as an academic discipline it also has to follow the normative requirements of the help system as well as the normative requirements of the system of science.

The book concludes with an emphasis on the value of thinking autonomously and critically, a key prerequisite for being a good social worker that can be fostered using systemic perspectives. Simply trusting what their employers, dominant colleagues, media, or authorities say is not a good starting point for social workers, since it means that they are not thinking autonomously.

1

COMMUNICATION

An answer we often get when asking first year students why they study social work is that they would like to work with people. What does "working with people" actually mean? Immediately one thinks of helping people, i.e. offering them counselling and supporting them in difficult situations, listening, mediating, providing safety and caring at women's houses, retirement homes, and other types of welfare agencies. Certainly, social work practice is much more than interaction with people in need of help (Shaw, 2005). In their daily work, social work practitioners are in constant need of coordination and negotiation with colleagues and supervisors within their own organisation and they exchange information with representatives from other helping professions, with teachers and pedagogues, with priests, with lawyers, judges, and police officers, with clients' relatives and friends, and many more.

All of this implies work with people, not only with the immediate recipients of help but also with those who make organised help possible in the first place. Naturally, there are differences in what the "daily work" entails, dependent on specific cases and interventions that range from finding living space for newly arrived and lonely refugee children or checking whether an ex-convict on probation behaves in accordance with the legal stipulations to discussing an action plan to improve a pupil's suboptimal performance at school with the parents. From all these examples we can distinguish a common denominator for what "working with people" actually means: working with people means *communication*. We have used formulations such as "provide counselling and support", "exchange", "interact", "listen", "coordinate", "negotiate", and "discuss", and all of them involve communication of one type or another.

Communication is a central aspect in this book because it is the foundational element of all social systems (Luhmann, 1995). We can even claim that any interaction between people – and this, of course, includes the interaction between social workers and clients or colleagues – either is a *system* or happens *within systems*. Expressed in general terms, communication is a social system, and inversely, every social system is a communication system. What we mean by this is what this chapter is about.

What people often mean by "communication"

Communication is a basic requirement for social co-existence, for technological and cultural development, and for human creativity. Both as a concept and a process, communication has been the object of interest for several disciplines: cybernetics, anthropology, humanities, psychology, sociology, linguistics, cognitive sciences, communication and media sciences, and others. There are, however, different ways to define what communication is. Among other things, the meaning of the concept of communication depends on the purpose inscribed to it. Ancient Greek philosophers such as Plato and Aristotle approached the phenomenon of communication through rhetoric. They understood communication as a process in which the speaker, equipped with linguistic skills, directed his utterances to an audience with the goal of achieving a certain result: to influence the audience's attitude toward certain subjects. We recognise this type of communication from politicians who give speeches, from department managers in their motivational talks with employees, from sales people who try to sell us merchandise we actually do not need, or from religious activists who try to persuade us to share their beliefs.

It is obvious that this type of communication is utilised when somebody tries to convince us to believe something we actually have no opinion about, do something we are wavering about, or to buy something we simply do not want, respectively. Here, communication works as an instrument to achieve tactical and strategic goals or to attain advantages at the cost of others, for example in bargaining situations. Sociologist and philosopher Jürgen Habermas (Habermas, 1991) has argued that such cases should rather be understood as instrumental action – even if they use language. Habermas explicitly distinguishes instrumental action from communicative action. The latter corresponds to communication as a dialogue in which the interlocutors take each other seriously as communication *partners*, rather than as potential adversaries or instrumental executors. If this type of communication has a purpose, then it is *mutual understanding*. Attempts at persuasion can be subsumed under this type of communication if there is dialogue and mutuality. It is, then, the factually (or sometimes morally) superior argument that determines the outcome, not the power position or social background of the interlocutors. In ideal cases, such communication is characterised by a "discourse free of dominance" (Habermas, 1991, 1992b) in which the better argument wins.

Everyday notions of communication are very close to this ideal type of Habermasian communication. We can see this in the ubiquitous situation of leadership in organisations. A typical claim is that the boss does not communicate but only "gives orders". Similarly, more traditional parental styles that entail reprimanding children for their wrongdoings are portrayed as showing a lack of communication. Even if some criticism may be justified in both cases, we consider this concept of communication as too narrow. Such a constricted concept only emphasises the "good", positive sides of the relation between people. The notion of "communication" becomes reserved for a very limited number of aspects of the complex social interplay, while commands, bargaining, and instrumental persuasion must be seen as different from communication. Thus, communication becomes a moral, value-laden expression, which in everyday language is not problematic.

This is a different story in professional – particularly pedagogical and therapeutic – contexts where a lack of conceptual precision can do harm. In the following paragraphs, we argue for the benefits of using a notion of communication that includes any interaction between people – the well-meaning and constructive interactions as well as the manipulating and antagonistic ones. In this chapter, we discuss communication as a social system and we describe how communication works in accordance with some systemic rules (not etiquette rules). These rules apply both to cooperation and conflict, to exertion of power and deliberations among equals, to cultivated conversations and the aggressive verbal exchanges preceding a fist fight, to small talk between strangers on a train and romantic love talk in a flirting situation. Communication can lead to the solution of a problem ("Great that we talked about this; now I understand you better!") but likewise it can be the cause or amplifier of a problem ("It was not nice of you to say these kinds of things. Could you just keep this to yourself next time?") and communication can point to problems the other does not want to know about, which more often than not can trigger conflicts.

The transmission model and its shortcomings

In order to understand what it means to say that communication is a system and that it complies with systemic rules, we have to discuss some folk concepts of communication. When we asked our students to write down words they associated with the word "communication", among the most common answers were "talk", "conversation", "message", "sender", "receiver", "medium", and "understanding". In everyday language, communication can have a positive or negative connotation although the positive ones are more common. But regardless of whether one associates communication with something positive (because it can lead to mutual understanding) or something negative (such as commands or insults), the common core is that communication refers to an *exchange* of thoughts, ideas, knowledge, experiences, or feelings. The notion of communication as exchange is based on the so-called *transmission model*.

It is called the transmission model because it is built on the assumption that communication is basically a transmission of information from a sender to a receiver. In the terminology of communication theory, one could say that the information to be transmitted must first be coded in such a way that the receiver can decode it successfully, i.e. understand the information. This model of communication is often associated with the mathematicians Claude Shannon and Warren Weaver (1972), who developed a solution in telecommunication technology for the problem of how a coded (or disturbed) signal can be decoded by a receiver in a way that gives him/her access to the transmitted information. Actually, the Shannon–Weaver model (as it is also called) is a mathematical model to be applied in technological contexts, mainly communication among machines. However, it has been applied to social relations (particularly media) because communication theorists in social sciences believe it to be very relevant for modelling communication among humans (Fiske, 1990).

Within the transmission model we can distinguish different means to code and different media or channels to transmit the information. One channel is oral transmission (for instance a dialogue in a theatre, a sermon, or a political speech); another is written transmission (for instance a letter, a printed book, or a website). All these cases are verbal to the extent that they utilise language. There are also, according to the transmission model, non-verbal transmissions of information, which include body language, gestures, Morse code, images, music, and dress style; even odours can be a medium for a message (Hall & Knapp, 2013; Mehrabian, 2007). When it comes to coding and decoding, non-verbal messages are much more difficult to understand because rules for decoding are much less clear and accessible than in verbal language. The latter only requires that both partners can speak the same language. Later in this chapter we will come back to this point when we discuss analogue and digital communication.

From a systems-theoretical perspective (Luhmann, 1992), the transmission model has a few shortcomings that limit its value for understanding and analysing social situations (and hence its value for application in the social sciences). One problem is the very image of transmission, simply because communication is not transmission. If I know something and want you to know it, too, I can tell it to you. Let us assume I know that a mutual friend is getting married, and after I tell you about it, you know it, too. However, this is not transmission. To transmit something requires that I have something (a virtual or real thing) that I give to you – something that I have first and then, after the transmission, you have it but I no longer do. Let us take a bank transaction as an example: my money goes to your account, which means it is gone from my account. In other words, after the transaction I have the same amount less money that you have more. Transmission in this meaning works fine in technical contexts (think of the cut and paste function on computers: you copy a file and transmit it from one folder to another, or from a USB stick to the hard drive). But this image of transmission does not correspond with information in social contexts. He who tells something does not lose this information. I still know that the friend is getting married after I tell you about it. What you want to inform about does not disappear; on the contrary, it is via communication that it becomes a social fact. Rather than cut and paste, the message from a sender through a channel to a receiver in social contexts seems to resemble file-sharing or copying of the information.

Strictly speaking, communicating is not the same as copying information either. This leads us to the next and even more serious issue with the transmission model, and that is the matter of coding and decoding. Not only does the sender not get rid of the information by communicating it; the receiver does not *get* the information either – at least not in the way the transmission model assumes. Let us consider a relatively mundane example. The sender feels that she is cold (information) so she codes it into the message "it's cold" and she says (utters) this to the receiver through regular oral communication. The receiver hears it, but it is anything but clear what information he has received: maybe that the weather is cold, but it could also be the case that the sender feels cold regardless of the factual temperature; the utterance could also be interpreted as an indirect request to have the heating turned up, to give her a blanket or a warm drink. Maybe the receiver has guessed but *not received* the intended information ("I'm cold" in contrast to the utterance "it's cold"). A possible objection to our argument could be made now: the sender coded the message the wrong way or chose the wrong channel and should instead have expressed herself more clearly by saying something like "I'm cold" or "Could you please turn up the heating?" Likewise, one could object that the receiver did not choose the "right" decoding routine and should (thanks to better decoding) have understood what the sender meant when she said she was cold, namely that she *actually* wanted the heating turned up.

Indeed, in contrast to communication between computers, in human communication receiving is not only decoding but also a process of *interpretation*. And when something requires interpretation this is so because the message is not unequivocal (Gadamer, 2004 [1960]). In this regard, the example of our friends' wedding mentioned earlier is misleading insofar as it assumes simplicity and unambiguousness that is often not given in our everyday communication. Often, communicating is more complex than simply uttering and spreading some news that can be received rather free from interpretation. The issue becomes yet more complicated when we think about how we communicate feelings and experiences. It is apparent that the latter cannot be transmitted, and in contrast to knowledge and news, they cannot even be sent or received. If I feel a headache and tell you about it, this does not mean you get a headache, too, does it?

The complexity of communication

From a systems perspective, the transmission model is not very suitable for describing human communication. The idea of a sender that sends a message to a receiver is not entirely wrong, but it is a coarse simplification that misses most of the complexity of communication. We have seen how the sender can mean or think something, try to find a good way to express this, and hope that the receiver comprehends it in exactly the intended way. It is precisely this expectation that guides much of the communication we participate in on a daily basis. And when people in everyday communication hear (or see) the receiver's reaction it is not uncommon that they wonder why the receiver does not understand correctly, why he does not do what is expected, why he does not reply with what they wanted to hear. In other words, the receiver actually did *not receive* the intended information but did something else. In the "I'm cold" example from the previous section we

demonstrated that the receiver does not receive but *interprets* the message. Therefore, "addressee" is a more fitting word than "receiver". A person that communicates does so in line with her own ideas, previous experience, assumptions,
values, cultural background, and a number of other variables. The same is true for
the addressee. What the addressee ultimately understands is neither random nor
arbitrary but on the basis of the previously mentioned variables it is less likely that
the message intended by the sender "comes across" at all.

On the other hand, sometimes the addressee "understands" something, but reads
something into the communication that was not intended by the sender whatso-
ever; sometimes the sender is not even aware of having "communicated" anything
in the first place. Imagine someone next to you starts coughing and you wonder
whether that was a signal directed at you to behave, for example to watch your
words, to close your fly, or to go away. So you ask, "What do you mean?" and
suddenly there is a dialogue:

A: What do you mean?
B: Mean what?
A: You coughed. What did you want to tell me?
B: Did I cough? I didn't realise, but I didn't want to say anything; why should I?

Quickly, such a dialogue can turn awkward or absurd. And if the other does not
admit that she wanted to convey anything by coughing you have no way to figure
out what this means. Was it a message or not? In any case, it was not the alleged
sender who started the communication (not even by the act of coughing) but it
was you, the alleged addressee who started the communication by interpreting the
behaviour of the alleged sender as an utterance and by replying. If we want to split
another hair, you were not even an addressee but only believed you were.

That is the crux of the matter regarding communication from a systems perspective: often communication comes into being not because somebody wanted to
utter something but because somebody else *understands* something as an utterance
and acts accordingly. But even if the sender wanted to say something, it is the
addressee, with his way of interpreting and understanding, who determines how
the communication will continue. The addressee's new interpretation takes place
guided by a few unknown factors, which in turn increase the momentum of
communication as a system. We will return to this a few pages on in this chapter.

We hope these examples have shown that communication does not work as
simply as the transmission model would have us believe: that a sender utters
something that contains particular information that an addressee receives. It gets
really complex when the addressee answers (after having understood or interpreted
the utterance) because then the roles switch and the addressee becomes the new
sender while the original sender becomes the new addressee, and in the following
turn, they switch again. In order to keep our text readable, we will from now on
call the first sender person A (she) and the first addressee person B (he). Thus,
when person A says something and person B replies with something, the same

principle is valid: A has to interpret and understand in her way what B meant with the answer, and it is this interpretation that determines how the communication continues. Again, it is not what the sender (B in this case) wanted to get across. We demonstrate this with another example in two variations. Here is the first one:

A: A cup of coffee would be nice now.
B: We can go to the café.
A: But it's raining.
B: OK, I can make some coffee here.
A: That would be nice.

Person A says something that could be interpreted in different ways and we do not know exactly what A actually wanted to express. Through B's answer we can infer how he interprets the utterance: namely that A wants some coffee. Accordingly, he suggests going out in order to accommodate her request. Her subsequent reply "it's raining", again, can be interpreted in several ways but in this context together with the previous two utterances it is likely that she takes his proposal as a partial mis-interpretation – coffee yes, going out no – and hence she makes her objection to going out more precise by pointing at the rain. At least this is how B interprets it, who now adjusts his proposal in accordance with the new interpretation. Only after A's final reply does B get the confirmation that A from the beginning meant that she wanted to have coffee in the house. If A aimed to maximise her chances of communicative success in making B understand exactly what A wanted, she should have said something like, "Could you make me a cup of coffee, please?" Since she expressed her request in a rather indirect and unclear way, B had to interpret somewhat freely, which includes the increased risk of interpreting something other than A intended. He could have wondered what rain has to do with coffee or he could have suggested, "Then we'll take the car" or "Then we'll take an umbrella along". Both replies would have handled the rain issue but not A's original desire to drink coffee without leaving the house. Thanks to B's communicative compe-tence, A and B achieved a shared understanding rather quickly. This goes the other way in the following example, which starts out the same way as example 1 but then takes a completely different turn.

A: A cup of coffee would be nice now.
B: I don't agree. People drink too much coffee and that's not fair.
A: Could I get coffee now, please?
B: It's unethical to drink coffee when workers on coffee plantations in South America get exploited by greedy corporations.
A: That's enough. I'm leaving.
B: Why do want to go out now? It's raining!
A: Because you won't give me coffee.
B: I didn't say that. I only said that coffee consumption contributes to injustice.
A: So you say that I shouldn't have any. But that's not up to you!

This case, regardless of how realistic it may be (outside of student collectives), demonstrates how communication can derail, i.e. it leaves the pathway person A intended and it probably does not mirror the intentions of B either. Basically, it is simple: A wants coffee and expresses this desire rather unclearly at first and more clearly later. For person B, coffee is obviously some moral issue that seems more important to him than accepting (or even understanding) A's request. We should not make the mistake of treating B's and afterward A's interpretations as wrongful decodings. Neither should we consider the communicative dynamic as showing one party's malicious desire to sabotage a successful communication. From a systems-theoretical perspective, rather, we see a situation nobody wanted to end up in but that happened anyway.

Before we describe what a systems-theoretical model of communication looks like, we have to remember the problems with the transmission model. First, the metaphor implies that the sender gets rid of something (the information) and the addressee receives it. Second, the transmission model focuses on the channel and how it is designed for the purpose of transmitting the message. This focus on the channel makes us overestimate the weight of the message. The model presupposes that the message the sender wants to transmit is the same one that the addressee receives. As we have shown in examples 1 and 2, such a correspondence is possible but not necessarily likely. Instead, communication is a system that has its own momentum and follows its own (not predefined) rules. Hence, communication should not be analysed as a process of successful or failed transmissions of information between a sender and a receiver but as an *emergent* reality.

What is emergence?

The concept of *emergence* is used across disciplines. It expresses a "gap" between complex phenomena such as organisms, cognition, language, and society, on the one hand, and their constitutive elements (such as particles, cells, words, communication etc.), on the other hand. A system is emergent if its characteristics, activities, and functionalities cannot be understood or explained by studying its elements and their characteristics. In order to comprehend what happens on a systemic level, the study of the constitutive parts and their properties is not enough; one has to keep an eye on the emergent properties of the system. As we have seen in the preceding section, the course and dynamics of communication cannot be explained by knowing individuals' thoughts, personal characteristics, or what they intend to express.

Emergence is a property that characterises any social system, but it is prevalent in many different systems in nature. In biology, we can look at cells as living systems that consist of a number of parts (for instance particles, chemical elements, molecules) and these have to be present in a certain quantity and be arranged in certain, very specific relations to each other. Life requires all of this but is something qualitatively different than the sum of its parts. Life is an emergent phenomenon. We recognise the same principle in chemistry. There are chemical elements (such as oxygen, hydrogen, sulphur) that, in a certain constellation, form molecules with emergent properties. It is safe to say that molecules are located on a higher level of emergence than their basic elements. The water molecule H_2O has emergent properties that hydrogen and oxygen (the constitutive elements of the water molecule) do not have. To make this picture more vivid, if water comes into contact with fire, the water extinguishes the fire or the water evaporates, depending on the quantities involved. If, on the contrary, you mix the elements of water, i.e. hydrogen and oxygen, and bring them into contact with fire you will have an explosion (and water as a result).[1]

Within general systems theory we can distinguish several levels of emergence. Molecules can constitute living cells, where life is situated on a higher level of emergence. Living cells can be brought together to form a complex organism (for instance a plant, an animal, or a human being), which is situated on a higher level of emergence than the cells. More complex organisms have a neuronal system built from nerve cells that transmit neuronal impulses. The network of neuronal impulses is situated on a higher level of emergence than the neurons themselves. On a yet-higher level of emergence – at least in organisms that are complex enough, such as human beings and great apes – there are minds, so-called psychic systems:[2] consciousness that generates perceptions, thoughts, and emotions. In all these cases, emergence means that the respective emergent system cannot be reduced to the next lower level of emergence: you cannot read people's minds by measuring the electric activity of their brains. The consciousness is situated on a higher level of emergence than neuronal brain activity.

Let us now return to the topic of this chapter. Communication takes place on a higher level of emergence than the mental activities that happen within our heads – thoughts, perceptions, emotions. Readers familiar with the writings of classic sociologist Emile Durkheim may recognise the idea of emergence from the term "social fact" (Durkheim, 2014 [1895]). Through "social facts" Durkheim aimed to describe the coercive forces that operate between people and that push them toward expectable behaviours and submission to norms and rules. If individuals attempt to resist social facts they have to reckon with different kinds of sanctions. Durkheim was eager to justify sociology as a discipline in its own right and in contrast to psychology by establishing, observing, and analysing social facts as emergent properties, i.e. as phenomena that are neither visible nor comprehensible with psychological methods. Durkheim regarded society as an entity comprising all social facts as a reality *"sui generis"*, which is exactly what we describe here as emergent reality.

Communication as system

So far, we have said a lot about communication as a system but now it is time to look closer at what it actually means to say that communication is a system. The definition of the concept "system" varies among different scientific disciplines, practical and technical contexts, and everyday language. Within scientific contexts the term refers to an arrangement between the system's elements and the relations among these elements (Easton, 1967; Luhmann, 1995; Parsons, 1951; Von Bertalanffy, 1968; Willke, 1991). In accordance with the idea of emergence, it is neither the individual element nor the individual relation that determines how the system works but the whole arrangement of elements and relations. By way of its operations (what the system "does") the system maintains a boundary to its environment. A system becomes and continues to be a system by constantly delimiting itself from its environment.

Put in abstract terms we can say that social systems are *operationally closed*, which means that they cannot, by means of their own operations, "stretch" beyond their own boundaries. Conversely, the environment – more precisely, other systems – cannot encroach on the system. In the examples from the previous section we had to deal with three operationally closed systems. In these examples, there were one *social* system (communication) and two *psychic systems*. The term "psychic system" refers to the things going on within the heads of people – perceptions, thoughts, feelings (such as joy, fear, anger, envy). To say "*within* one's head" is important for the understanding of the concept and phenomenon of "operational closure". The operational closure of psychic systems corresponds to the experience, well known from everyday life, that we cannot know what the other person wants, desires, or feels if the other does not communicate it; we cannot "read their mind". In the same way, we cannot feel their feelings, nor can we perceive their perceptions.

Keep in mind that with all of this we have not denied that we can have similar (and often even the same) thoughts, feelings, perceptions as our communication partners, for instance, "Did you also hear that strange noise?" What we refer to instead is the circumstance that we need to experience all thoughts, feelings, and perceptions *on our own*. If I feel a headache and tell you about it, this does not mean that you also get a headache, even if you, thanks to previous experiences, know what it's like to have a headache, and thanks to your empathy you may show understanding of my unpleasant situation. However, that is the whole point with operational closure: you *need to have understanding* just because you, at this moment, do *not feel* the pain on your own, because the feeling of pain "takes place" in another system (my psychic system) and there is no direct, telepathic link between your psychic system and mine. In other words, the feeling of pain cannot be transmitted or transferred like computer files from a USB stick to a hard drive.

This is the point of departure for communication. Communication emerges (or is utilised) just *because* person A cannot feel or perceive what happens within person B's head and vice versa. If A wants B to know about her headache she has to tell him about it; thus she must communicate. However, as soon as something is uttered, this happens through communication. Remember that communication is not a transmission. In accordance with the idea of emergence, communication "does" something with the elements (such as individual utterances) and thereby shapes the meaning of the elements.

In the previous examples we wanted to show that the meaning of statements can deviate vastly from the intentions of the involved agents who uttered them. If we conceive communication as a system, we see that there is an emergent order somewhere between two (or more) psychic systems. According to Luhmann (1995, 2008), communication is an operationally closed system insofar as it processes only communication – only utterances and the meaning that emerges through a sequence of utterances. However, communication cannot process thoughts, feelings, or perceptions. Put into a formula, communication cannot think and psychic systems cannot communicate (Luhmann, 1992).

We can express this in yet another way. Within psychic systems, different things (thoughts) happen than happen within social systems (communication). On the one hand, the meaning of an utterance can get corrupted during the course of the interaction if person B interprets it in a completely different way than person A intended and if B then feeds his interpretation back into the dialogue, which A then interprets in her way and replies accordingly. After some turn-taking, communication can have taken pathways that do not have much in common with the thoughts, hopes, and perhaps even persuasion tactics of the involved people.

On the other hand, there are always so many more things going on in psychic systems than communication can process. An individual can think so much more than she can utter to her conversation partner. The partner, in turn, can also think much more than can be represented in a communication system. Therefore, we cannot assume that communication is a copy or excerpt of what is going between involved psychic systems. Communication as an emergent system in its own right has a different dynamic, momentum, and history of events than those involved psychic systems. Let us revisit the first variation of the coffee example, this time with some "insight" into the psychic systems of persons A and B (Figure 1.1).

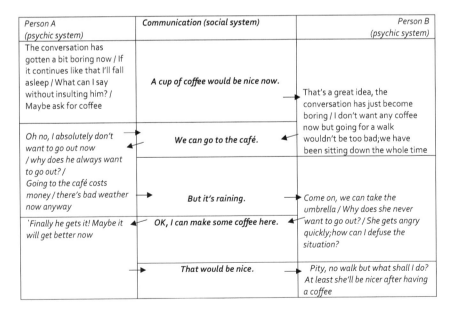

FIGURE 1.1 Communication and consciousness: how what we think and what we say are not the same

In the left column we see a number of possible thoughts in person A's consciousness. Likewise, the column on the right represents some of B's possible thoughts. The arrows indicate the course of time, thus first A's thoughts, then her utterance, then B's thoughts, then his reply, then A's thoughts again, etc. What is going on inside of the heads (psychic systems) of persons A and B is probably a caricature of what people normally think during such a trivial conversation but then again, who knows? By exaggeration we can at least demonstrate how communication (thus only what outsiders without mindreading skills can observe) gives a greatly reduced and sometimes very different image of what is going on compared to what the participants experience. At the same time, the conversation would have taken very different turns, and might even have become ugly, if the participants really said what they thought. It is part of good demeanour and interactional competence not to say what you really think!

In order to understand what "communication as a system" means we must treat all events within the course of this communication as the result of *selections*, i.e. conscious or unconscious choices between many possibilities. Utterances (communicative acts) are selections. Whatever A says refers to so many more possible connections than what Person B, by way of his understanding, can deal with in his reply. In Figure 1.1 there are always many more thoughts compared to what is actually said. So this is one aspect of the selectivity in communication. Another selection is related to how to say things. The very way of uttering is a selection, like the communication channel/medium in the Shannon–Weaver model, but intonation, choice of words, and so on are also involved.

When something (such as communication) is the result of a couple of selections, systems theorists like to speak of *contingency*. Something is contingent when it is neither necessary nor impossible. It can be like this but could also be different. We will revisit the concept of contingency in Chapters 6–8. What is important for now is that systems (psychic as well as social) constantly make contingent selections based on system-internal, not entirely predictable processes. Summarised in technical terms, we can regard communication as a system that is an operationally closed process of a series of contingent selections that, taken together, form an emergent order and maintain a boundary to their environment, in particular to the psychic systems that participate in the communication.

Systems theory, communication and causality

If we want to conceptualise communication as a system we need to abandon the transmission model and all of its implications. We also have to take into account that communication requires the involvement of two or more psychic systems that affect communication and, in turn, are affected by communication. Your thoughts affect what you say, and what you and others say affects your thoughts. This mutual affection should not be taken as a linear, cause-effect-chain. Rather, communication systems, like psychic systems, are emergent, momentous orders that cyberneticist Heinz von Foerster described as "non-trivial machines". This term originated in cybernetics, an interdisciplinary science that deals with the steering and self-steering of complex systems. Von Foerster distinguishes trivial from non-trivial machines (Von Foerster, 1984).

Trivial machines are mechanisms that transform a certain input into a determined, defined, and predictable output. A typical example is a coin-operated soft drink vending machine. There are options for input, such as a coin slot and a few buttons to select the drink. Operating the buttons requires the right amount and types of coins. Once you do everything the correct way, i.e. in line with how the trivial machine is designed, you get the drink as the output. Machines like this are trivial because they can be described with simple causal relations, i.e. relations with clearly delimited causes and effects. Among the causes are the money, the operation of buttons, and the internal mechanism. The effect is the delivery of the soft drink. Once you know how the mechanism works and what input is required you can precisely predict the output, which in this case is a drink, not cigarettes, train tickets, or sweets. If the desired effect does not occur this is an indicator that the machine is broken. This is what is meant by "trivial": you can tell exactly when the machine works and when it is broken.

A more modern example of a trivial machine is an app on a smartphone or computer. If you do not succeed in buying a ticket with a ticketing app although you followed every step according to the instructions, it is because the app has a "bug", a programming error. Trivial machines can be described in such precise ways only if all of their components and the interplay between them are known. The relation between the parts is designed; it is not emergent.

Non-trivial machines, by contrast, are not predictable. Social systems, psychic systems, organisms, biological ecosystems, and many other types of systems are non-trivial machines. As we said earlier, they are emergent orders. If I say that I want coffee now to a coffee maker with artificial intelligence (AI) and speech recognition, I will get a coffee. If I say that I want a coffee now to a human being, I might succeed and get coffee. However, it might also happen that I get caught up in a political discussion instead.

While a trivial machine remains in the same default state (unless it is broken, or the stock of drinks is empty), non-trivial machines change their internal state after every new input. One and the same input (a coin) will produce the same output (drink). After the fourth or fifth time within a few minutes, the machine will not refuse the service and state that I have had enough cola now. However, using the same input into a communication system, for instance, the question "How are you?" will have completely different effects due to ever-changing states of communication systems and the involved psychic systems. Every input changes the whole system. Imagine the following example:

A: How are you?
B: I'm fine, thanks. How are you?
A: How are you?
B: I just said that. Aren't you listening?

A: How are you?
B: Are you making fun of me?
A: How are you?
B: Shut up now!

This example only shows the social system, i.e. the communication, but we do not know what is going on in the respective psychic systems. We can, however, guess what must be going on the mind of B. This is more difficult with A because she, to say the least, is behaving strangely. She is behaving rather like a trivial machine, for example a computerised AI-assistant or an automaton. For human beings, such conversations feel uncanny and annoying.

The fact that communication systems change their internal states all the time means not only that they are unpredictable, but also that they are very difficult to steer. As emergent orders (and in accordance with the assumptions of cybernetics), communication systems mostly steer themselves. When we have to deal with such systems (by participating or by trying to intervene), it is not wise to expect clear-cut, linear cause-effect relations. More often, causality in non-trivial machines is circular rather than linear. This means that a cause can be both cause *and* effect, and likewise effects can also be causes. The Dutch artist Maurits Cornelis Escher expressed this circularity in many of his drawings. For example, in his "Drawing hands", it is impossible to determine which hand is the cause (the drawing hand) and which hand is the effect (the one that is drawn). In fact, both draw (and thereby constitute) each other at the same time. Another good example is his "Print gallery", where we see a boy looking at a picture in a gallery while at the same time this picture displays the town in which the very gallery including the observing boy are situated. What is the cause (the image the boy is looking at) and what is the effect (what is displayed in the picture)? Again, we cannot discriminate between cause and effect.

Escher's drawings are paradoxical and certainly offer an extreme view of circularity. Nevertheless, the causal relations in non-trivial machines are circular to some extent. Within trivial machines, causality can be described like this: A leads to B, B leads to C, C leads to D, etc. Hence, trivial machines are deterministic in the sense that if A, then always B, C, and D. In non-trivial machines, by contrast, B, C, and D can also affect A, thereby changing it into future A, future B, future C, and changing the foundations of the whole system. In cybernetics, one speaks of "feedback" when the output of a system is a new input. In causal terms, the effect is a new cause of change in the system's state (new effect), which is a new cause for changed system operations (newer effects).

The concept of feedback is used for describing a mechanism that can be found in nature, in the body, in the mind, in society, and in complex technical systems (Bateson, 1972). Cyberneticists distinguish between positive and negative feedback (Ashby, 1962). Positive feedback means that the unchanged output of a system is directed back into the system and thereby adds to the existing state. Positive feedback leads to change in the same direction of the original state and tends to accelerate and escalate very fast until it encounters natural limits. Imagine a technical system that produces sound. The positive feedback adds the sound of the output (speaker) as input into the system (microphone). The sound from the speaker gets picked up by the microphone and sent to the amplifier back to the speaker, and from there back (and louder) into the microphone. The sound system reacts with a very loud, sharp, and unpleasant noise. An example of positive feedback in the social sciences is the capitalist economic system. Interest rates on an investment are fed back into the investment. The capital thus gained will produce higher returns of interest, which increase the capital. Positive feedback also works in the opposite direction. If you want to borrow money but lack your own capital or have only a little income you have to pay higher interest rates, which in turn increases your debt and reduces your creditworthiness.

It should have become obvious at this point that positive feedback does not mean something positive or something good but only that something is accumulated as in mathematical addition (more of the same). Whereas positive feedback leads to escalation, negative feedback has a balancing function. Instead of escalating and getting out of equilibrium such a system remains stable. A prime example is a thermostat that measures and regulates the room temperature. If the current temperature is below the target value, the heating is turned on automatically until the target is reached. Then the heating is turned off until the temperature sinks below the target again, which turns on the heating, and so on. To understand these workings, imagine for a second a thermostat that operates (wrongly) with a positive feedback loop. When the temperature is below the target, the heating would be turned off, which leads to an even colder temperature. In turn, when the temperature is above the target, the thermostat would turn the heating on (instead of off, as you would expect from a working thermostat) and would thereby raise the temperature ever higher until the machine broke or the user pulled the plug. An instructive example of negative feedback in society is financial redistribution through taxes and subsidies.

Communication theorist Paul Watzlawick and his research team have stressed the importance of feedback loops and circularity for the analysis of communication systems (Watzlawick, Beavin, & Jackson, 1967). They describe a situation of a married couple, in which the husband is often passive and withdrawn while the wife often nags. We learn that the husband withdraws *because* the wife nags. But we can also observe that the wife nags *because* the husband tends to be passive and withdrawing. The cause is the effect and the effect is the cause, almost like in Escher's "Drawing hands". In a causal scheme it appears that the husband withdraws because the wife nags, and the wife nags because the husband withdraws. Watzlawick's point is that, regardless of who started it, the circularity is eye-catching. Mostly it is not even important who started the process, because after the system has stabilised, its circular causality is maintained.

This pattern is also well known from armed conflicts, for example in the classical case of the "security dilemma" (Herz, 1950). Country A is compelled to invest in arms because it feels threatened by the military of country B. A's arms investment then raises the alarm with B, which sees the need to increase its military spending as a reaction to A, and so on. Watzlawick and his associates were interested in this kind of relational conflict because both parts tend to describe the other part (their adversary) as a cause and their own reaction as an effect, albeit diametrically opposed. In the same way they that justify their own actions (as legitimate reactions), they condemn those of the other. The husband experiences his withdrawal as a legitimate response to the wife's ongoing complaints, thus as an inevitable effect of her actions. If she did not nag and complain about his withdrawal all the time, he would not have to withdraw in the first place. For the wife the situation is the same, just mirrored. She sees her complaints as a legitimate response (effect) to his passivity and withdrawing behaviour (cause). If he did not withdraw all the time, she would not have to complain.

Who is right? Watzlawick argued that in such situations there is no clear-cut right or wrong because both parties are right in seeing themselves as victims, and both are wrong because it is their very actions that make the other a victim. Both parties "punctuate" differently, i.e. they cut the (in principle) infinite causal chain at different moments. Therefore, they can always experience the other's action as a cause and their own action as a response. For both parties, the other appears as either evil or crazy. It is easy to see how people can get stuck in such pathological situations. According to Watzlawick, frustration in the short term, and mental illness in the long term, are possible.

Metacommunication and the five axioms of communication

In order to escape from pathological situations like the one the married couple was trapped in, either help from outside is necessary (for instance from a couples therapist who, from a neutral vantage point, can observe the destructive patterns) or the couple can break through the communicative structures by using *metacommunication*. Metacommunication is communication outside the "regular" communication and it has the "regular" communication as the subject. One talks about *how* one talks. Taking place outside the "regular" communication means that the rules of this "regular" communication do not apply. Rather, the rules for the "regular" communication can be altered at the level of metacommunication. If they can get there in the first place, the couple can use metacommunication in order to discuss their pathological patterns and their opposed "punctuations", to explain their perspectives on how the situation evolved, and to consider how they could improve their future communication.

Unfortunately, metacommunication is not always possible. Either people are not aware of this option, so it does not appear on the radar, or people cannot establish mutually accepted rules for metacommunication and for how to execute the switch from the "regular" to the "meta" level. Within sado-masochistic sex games there are "safe words" agreed upon beforehand that can be used to indicate that one of the partners wants to end the game. Such sex practices are often characterised by radical dominance and submission, so a simple "no" or "stop" will not suffice because it could be interpreted as part of the role play. In order to work as a safe word, the agreed-upon word or phrase must be something so entirely different that it cannot be confused with words and phrases normally used in the role play.

Outside of sex games, it also happens frequently that attempts to switch to metacommunication fail because they are understood as part of the "regular", conflict-laden communication. Think again about a conflict affecting a married couple. One partner attacks the other verbally, and the attacked person complains that he does not want to be treated in a certain way. This could be taken for metacommunication and induce a reaction such as "Sorry, I shouldn't have said that," or it could be taken as a counter-attack in the symmetric conflict situation, which would trigger a reaction such as "Don't tell me how to express myself!"

What makes metacommunication more complicated is the fact that it does not only define the rules for "regular" communication; it also defines the relationship between the partners. An attempt to use metacommunication can be understood as questioning an established relationship between the communication partners. While it is a continuous struggle to define the relationship between partners in a romantic couple, the situation is much more rigid in institutionally predefined relations of superordination and subordination. In such relationships the power-holder can hinder or forbid metacommunication because it poses a threat to his/her authority, particularly in totalitarian political systems, in religious sects, or at the workplace. The same can happen and have serious consequences within social work practice or in psychotherapy. Whatever the client says, whatever attempts she makes to use metacommunication, can always be interpreted as yet further proof of her mental disorder or resistance to cooperating.

Paul Watzlawick and his fellow researchers (1967) claim that any communication bears a small metacommunicative element regardless of whether or not the participants are aware of it. This is so because communication always has a content aspect (*what* is communicated) and a relational aspect (*how* the content is communicated). The way I utter something defines the relationship between me and the other, and is therefore also metacommunication. The utterances "Coffee now!" and "Could I have a cup of coffee, please?" share the same content but the relationship between speaker and addressee is defined very differently. The former relationship appears as a hierarchy in which the addressee is not respected as an equal but instead has to obey – politeness seems unnecessary. This is metacommunication insofar as it sets the framework for how the message is supposed to be understood. If the addressee executes the command without objection, he tacitly agrees with the speaker's definition of their relationship. It is not always possible to openly question the relationship without facing sanctions.[3] Explicit metacommunication ("That was not nice of you. If you want coffee you should ask me in a polite way!") would be taken as an insult because it enforces a redefinition of the relationship from hierarchical to egalitarian, which disrespects the authority of the speaker. In this case, the relationship is not only redefined by the content aspect of the metacommunication (which can be interpreted as "Don't talk to me like that") but it also has its own relational aspect (which can be interpreted as "I have to teach you manners and appropriate behaviour"). The simultaneous presence of content and relational aspects is expressed in one of five axioms (i.e. unprovable but well-founded assumptions) that, according to Watzlawick and his associates, characterise communication. Table 1.1 gives an overview of all five of the axioms in the order presented in their book (Watzlawick et al., 1967). We have to deal with them in a slightly abridged order.

In the previous section we have already encountered the axiom that participants tend to punctuate differently: they describe cause and effect in opposing ways. We have not yet dealt with the most important of the other axioms, which says that in the co-presence of other people one cannot *not* communicate. Activity or inactivity, words or silences – everything can be interpreted as communicative behaviour. For instance, a passenger on a train who takes his book out of a bag communicates, whether intended or not, that he does not want to talk or be talked to. Conversely, any behaviour affects co-present people, and they, in return, cannot avoid interpreting this behaviour as communicative behaviour and reply with the same (communicative) behaviour, as in our example with the coughing person. While in everyday life most of this is routine, it can sometimes lead to awkward situations, for example when a short exchange of smiles could be understood as flirting, and hence an invitation to continue the interaction, or as a polite way of expressing that one does not want to talk right now.

This leads us to the fourth axiom, which states that communication can be *digital* or *analogue*. In this context, "digital" and "analogue" have nothing to do with the type of medium, e.g. computer, internet, or smartphone vs. talk, print, or handwriting. Instead, "digital communication" means everything that can be expressed by using letters, digits, or words, for instance names. Digital communication enables precise messages and can utilise a formal logic through word pairs such as "yes/no", "with/without", and "more/less" but also words with grammatical-syntactical functions such as "and", "or", "where", or "why", all of which have no referent in the real, physical world, and which cannot be expressed by means of analogue communication.[4] Analogue communication is a way to convey perceptions and feelings. Typical means are facial expressions, body language and movements, gestures, and intonation.

TABLE 1.1 Axioms of communication, according to Watzlawick et al.

Axiom 1 One cannot not communicate (in the presence of another person)

Axiom 2 Every communication has a content and relationship aspect, such that the latter classifies the former and is therefore a metacommunication

Axiom 3 The nature of a relationship is dependent on the punctuation of the partners' communication procedures

Axiom 4 Human communication involves both digital and analogue modalities

Axiom 5 Inter-human communication procedures are either symmetric or complementary

By being able to distinguish analogue and digital communication we gain insight into why things that appear meaningful in one type cannot be translated (without loss) into and understood the same way through the other type. By means of digital communication, we can express that the coffee was "good", but this could mean anything and does not represent the real smell and taste of the coffee. How would you express this? You could say something like "the well-rounded smell of freshly brewed, dark-roasted bean coffee, with subtle notes of cocoa and a crisp finish". Skilled poets, belles-lettres authors, and copywriters are better at catching these analogue things within the confines of digital communication than is the average bureaucrat or accountant. The rising popularity of emoticons on social media and in internet communication is an indicator of a need to integrate analogue expressivity into the realms of written language.

Inability to keep apart analogue and digital communication and react adequately according to their perks and limits can easily give rise to misunderstandings. This is particularly true for communication with a certain level of emotional weight. An artist paints an abstract image and the audience (believing themselves to be art experts) read anything and everything into the painting but fail to grasp the essence of what the painter felt when he created his work. A romantic couple ends up in a fight because one of them (A) sighs deeply. The other (B) wonders what the sigh meant and asks, by digital communication, "What happened?" A replies, "It's nothing; it's OK," but the intonation, facial expression, and body language point to the opposite. Another example of the gap between analogue and digital communication is the following, which one of us found in a newspaper ad by a florist: "A flower says more than thousand words". But what does the offering of a flower actually convey – an apology, a declaration of love, congratulations? In line with the content and relational aspects, digital communication corresponds to the content while analogue communication corresponds to the relation. We will see in the next section what can happen when digital and analogue communication are not "congruent", i.e. do not fit together, and how this becomes highly relevant in the practice of helping professions.

The fifth and final axiom postulates that the relationship between communication partners can be symmetric or complementary. Symmetric communication tends toward establishing or restoring a certain equality between partners. Complementary communication establishes/reproduces an unequal relationship based on a power or status differential, such as in manager–employee, parent–child, or supervisor–intern relationships. Furthermore, communication as a system almost automatically maintains the (symmetric or complementary) relationship. As soon as a person in a symmetric relationship says or does something that would elevate or lower her position toward the other, the latter is led to restore the balance. If I give you a present and you say, "Thank you", then maybe you will give me something in return the next time, for which I will thank you. If I, in a symmetric relationship with you, criticise your efforts or performance, you either defend yourself or question my competence.

The same, but in reverse, happens in communication in complementary relationships. Every attempt to diminish the complementarity is responded to by restoring the gap. When the person with the lowest status starts talking before being asked to do so, this will be taken as an insult and will be responded to with a punishment that puts the violator back in his place. If my boss does not encourage me to make critical remarks, my (unasked-for) criticism will be interpreted as disobedience and my boss will make me feel that I was wrong as a means to restore the complementarity.

Pathological communication: the practical relevance of systems theory

Watzlawick and his co-authors worked together in a research group at the Mental Research Institute at Stanford University. The group is known as the "Palo Alto Group". Among the founders of this group were psychiatrist Don Jackson and polymath Gregory Bateson, who was an anthropologist, cyberneticist, and psychologist. The Palo Alto Group had enormous influence on the many branches of "systemic thinking", i.e. systemic and systems-theoretical approaches in psychology, family therapy, social work, and social pedagogy. With the application of his anthropological works to questions in clinical psychology and psychiatry, Bateson (1972), more than any other, paved the way for a systems-theoretical approach to communication. The five axioms of communication are largely based on Bateson's findings and ideas. According to the Palo Alto Group, traditional psychiatry was (and still is) built on problematic assumptions because it locates the root of deviant behaviour, mental disorders, and mental illness in the individuals' brains (for instance genetic defects or lack or overproduction of certain hormones). For the Palo Alto researchers, the individual and his disorders need to be put into a context of different levels of interaction with other people, and here particularly, the family. In other words, the Palo Alto Group locates individuals in a *system*. Correspondingly, Watzlawick speaks of their approach as the "interactional view" (Watzlawick & Weakland, 1977).

If we look at an individual with a mental disorder isolated from her *social* context, we are likely to locate the disorder and its roots isolated from *any* context, and accordingly, the therapy will happen on the level of the individual, decoupled from the social environment (by prescribing a cocktail of pills). In some way, this reminds us of the shortcomings of the transmission model: the systemic dynamics are missing in the analysis. The Palo Alto Group argues that if we see the individual as a part of an arrangement of several social systems with their own communicative patterns, we would possibly find pathologies on a system level that account for some of the disorders observed in the individual. Think again about the married couple and their continuous fight (complaints and withdrawal). The partners are neither mentally unstable nor emotionally cold (individual explanation); rather, the disorder lies in their communication pattern. So the relationship could be improved by an intervention addressing the communication pattern, thus at the systemic level. Traditional, individualistic approaches would attempt to treat the individuals separately (hopefully not with pills!).

Ideas like this were revolutionary in their day, but have become common knowledge within psychology. Together with two colleagues, Bateson and Jackson put out the most provocative proposal of that time. They argued that traditional explanations of schizophrenia should be discarded and replaced by an explanation grounded on systems theory (Bateson, Jackson, Haley, & Weakland, 1956). According to them, originally mentally healthy people can develop symptoms of schizophrenia if they are exposed to certain pathological and communicative patterns that exert force on the individual for a long time. Under such conditions, schizophrenia is regarded as a (possible) way out of the otherwise untenable coercive situation. We should add that systems theory does not *per se* regard the individual with the disorder as ill but rather as a "symptom bearer". Apparently, something in their behaviour is not "normal" but this can be an expression of systemic (i.e. social) and not individual (i.e. physiological or psychiatric) pathologies.

In their theory of schizophrenia Bateson and his co-authors argued that the symptom bearer is trapped in the inferior position of an unequal relation. They developed their theory mainly by observing communicative pathologies in mother–child relationships. There was an incongruence between digital and analogue communication, for instance when the mother says, "I love you", while her body language and facial expressions shows disgust and repulsion (this can happen when the child reminds the mother of the violent father). The mother's communication to the child conveys mixed messages and the child ends up in a "double-bind": the content aspect of the communication expresses one thing, while the relational aspect (metacommunication) expresses something that logically contradicts the former. Sometimes such contradictions are built into one and the same sentence: "I demand that you are autonomous!" If the child tries to obey in line with the relational aspect and do what the mother demands, the child is not autonomous (because he/she obeys, which is the opposite of autonomy). The only way to be autonomous in this situation (to obey) is to not obey, but this, of course, contradicts the content aspect of the demand to be autonomous. Neither can the child decide to do nothing because, in line with the first axiom of communication, the child cannot *not* communicate. To do nothing could be interpreted both as a disobedience and an expression of reluctance to communicate with the mother. Whatever the child does, it is classified as disobedience and the child risks punishment.

It is not hard to imagine how such situations can confuse the child and trigger doubt and mental tension. If something like this happens once in a while, it should not do much harm. However, constant exposure to such communication patterns can have harmful consequences if the child, being in the inferior and dependent position, neither has the right to metacommunication ("Stop questioning me!") nor the ability to withdraw from the relationship (and thereby avoid the double-bind). Normally a child is dependent on his/her parents, and thus cannot simply avoid communication with them. Because the child is trapped in this pattern and will not be able to see through the pathology in this communication, he/she may develop a negative self-image and search for the flaw in him/herself (What am I doing wrong? Am I not good enough? Why can I never make mommy happy?). In order to handle such an untenable situation the child can, according to Bateson and colleagues' (1956) theory, develop psychopathological behaviours that can be classified as schizophrenia (the child may question his/her own existence, develop a split personality, imagine living somewhere else, exhibit self-destructive behaviour, etc.).

One of the most important insights of the Palo Alto Group was that communicative double-binds – as dangerous they may become if one is exposed to them for a long period – can be useful as therapeutic tools. Watzlawick (1993) gives an example of a therapeutic double-bind in a case where a patient was unable to say "no". This patient ended up in a number of situations where she had to help other people or do errands she actually did not want to do (like in the comedy *The Yes Man*, with Jim Carrey). No matter what she tried to solve her problem, nothing worked. Hence, her therapist convinced her to participate in a group therapy session. Because she was unable to decline, she had no choice but to participate. In the session, the therapist created a paradoxical situation for her. He informed her that the other participants would make requests of her and her task was to say "no" to each of them. Of course, she could not do that because she was not able to say "no" at all. That was her problem in the first place, wasn't it? So she became angry, rejected the task and said, "No!" Without noticing, she had broken her own pathology. This is a classic communicative double-bind because the patient could either comply with the therapist's command and say "no" to everybody else (which would resolve her problem) or she could decline the task and thereby say "no" to the therapist (which also would resolve her problem). After this barrier was overcome, the therapist could finally deal with the underlying psychological problem that made her refuse to say no in the first place.

Very related to the therapeutic double-bind is another communicative technique called *symptom prescription*. Watzlawick executed this technique most keenly in his book *Anleitung zum Unglücklichsein* (*Manual to being unhappy*; Watzlawick, 1983a).[5] This book is written as a parody of happiness guidebooks.[6] The point of departure for symptom prescriptions is an undesired emotional state or a pathological behaviour that occurs spontaneously, i.e. is uncontrolled. One worries, gets sad, gets performance anxiety, has difficulty saying no, etc. Sometimes the condition can become so strong that it blocks an individual's interest in almost anything else in life, and so that state becomes untenable. According to Watzlawick's "manual" a symptom prescription can help: the individual is prescribed to intentionally cause her own misery (i.e. the symptom). The book gives a number of "hints" for what the reader can do to avoid feeling too good, for example by intentionally misunderstanding compliments as attacks, by sticking to a glorified past that makes the present and future seem pale in comparison, or by assuming that everyone wants to harm her and acting accordingly.

In this case, symptom prescription as a technique means that the symptom is the frequently occurring experience of misery, and the prescription entails that the "client" him/herself has to create situations that conjure up the (actually undesired) state. Another example can illuminate this: a therapist can suggest to a person who tends to worry too much that worrying is actually quite okay, but maybe instead of worrying all the time, the client should only worry at a certain hour. So the therapist prescribes the client to worry every evening between six and seven o'clock. Between these hours, the client is not allowed to do anything other than worry. Once the client has gotten used to this procedure of worrying on command at a certain hour, it will sooner or later become annoying, and finally unbearable, to worry during this period. During this phase, change occurs. Without being aware of it the client gains control over the behaviour and the feeling. The worry is no longer spontaneous but self-inflicted. From this moment onward, she can get a grip on the worries more easily if they occur spontaneously.

The principles of symptom prescription and therapeutic double-binds work in very many cases. The point is always the same: to break through gridlocked behavioural or communicative patterns from which an individual, a couple, or a family cannot escape. By means of communication, the client should be put into paradoxical situations that lead to untenable, albeit artificial, states that help them break the pathological state and win back control.

Notes

1 One of the key influences of symbolic interactionism, George Herbert Mead, also refer-red to the distinct properties of the water molecule and its constitutive elements when explaining *emergence* (Mead, 1962 [1934], p. 198).

2 The word "psychic" is a direct translation from Luhmann's original works in German "*psychische Systeme*", which refers to the mind and consciousness and thus has nothing to do with paranormal abilities.

3 In Chapter 2 we demonstrate that the relations within a social system are often pre-defined by institutional rules derived from an overarching system.

4 From an evolutionary perspective, analogue communication is a primordial form that certain animals are capable of, whereas digital communication only evolved with the more sophisticated brain capabilities of human beings.

5 This book has been published in English with the title, *The situation is hopeless, but not serious*. While this title is funny in its own right, it unfortunately misses the point of symptom prescription (Watzlawick, 1983b).

6 This kind of literature gives a vast number of (good and bad) suggestions on what to do to feel better, with countless examples of formerly unhappy people who have succeeded after following advice from the respective books. This, however, has the paradoxical effect that the readers who do not succeed feel worse than they did before reading the books. This is so because the reading forces the readers to compare themselves with all those people who are now happy, and if the readers do not make progress (for example because the reported cases are anecdotal), they have even more reason to doubt themselves.

2

SYSTEM AND ENVIRONMENT

Communication is the backbone of any social system. We can also say that communication is the basic, constitutive element in any social system, or in yet other words, that any social system is a form of communication system. One consequence of this conceptualisation, difficult to grasp at first sight, is that human beings are not part of the social system. In Chapter 1 we argued that the boundary between psychic and social systems is essential. The human being with body and consciousness (i.e. thought, perceptions, memories, feelings) belongs to the *environment* of social systems. In Chapter 4 we will demonstrate how human beings, as parts of the environment of social systems, can participate in society anyway. Now, in Chapter 2, we will take a closer look at the relation between communication systems and their environment, or to be more precise, their different environments, since every system has its own environment. System and environment are mutually exclusive; the environment is thus everything that a specific system is *not* (Luhmann, 1995). The environment of a specific system comprises anything from the eco-system to other social systems, human beings, animals, the material world, etc. Assuming that there is a large variety of systems in the world – a vast number of social, psychic, neuronal, organic, and other systems – this means that every system has a different environment that contains everything except the specific system itself. So the environment of a certain system is, so to speak, system-specific.

If our system is a simple interaction system – for example the discussion about coffee from Chapter 1 – the participating psychic systems (including their thoughts, perceptions, and feelings) belong to the environment of this interaction system. Conversely, communication – the emergent order that is generated by the interplay of the participants – is an environment to each of the individual psychic systems. For person A (psychic system) both person B and the interaction system itself are then part of the environment. In Chapter 1 we described extensively how what individuals say belongs to one system (communication) and what they think belongs to another system (psychic), each with different emergent properties. It is the systems themselves that draw their own boundaries between system and environment by discriminating between what is happening inside and what is happening outside, for example the boundary between what participants say during a conversation and what they (only) thought but kept to themselves. What we think but keep to ourselves implies a demarcation between what remains part of the psychic system and what is uttered and thereby becomes part of a communication system.

The distinction between systems and environment is not simply an academic question without any practical relevance. On the contrary, this distinction makes us aware of system-specific relativity, i.e. it helps in keeping apart phenomena that belong to (or take place in) different systems, which has consequences for the analysis of problems and causes, attribution of responsibilities, and the possibility of finding solutions and alternatives for steering and intervention. The diagnosis will appear vastly different if the cause is attributed to the system or to its environment. The system of politics detects and approaches problems in a different way than the system of science or the economic system does. For example, from a political perspective, youth unemployment can be attributed to the government's policies (system) or the recessive internal economic climate (environment). The relativity in causal explanations and the diversity of systemic perspectives will be the topic of Chapters 5–7, in which we describe different opportunities and limits for social workers and therapists to direct, enlighten, or treat their clients. Furthermore, we will demonstrate how the same underlying principle also applies to policy-makers who, on a macro level, try to direct society and work against the negative effects of social problems.

Systems do not operate in isolation from each other. Instead every system operates in the context of other systems in its environment. Sometimes a system is part of an encompassing system, where the latter functions as a sort of inner environment. The prime example of this is society. Within Luhmannian systems theory, society (*Gesellschaft*) is defined not as an assembly of human beings, a political or moral community with shared values, language, or cultural background (like traditional and folk concepts of society); Luhmann, by contrast, suggests conceptualising society as the overarching and encompassing social system, i.e. the social system that comprises every other social system (Luhmann, 2012). Every social system, from simple interaction systems, social movements, and organisations to complex function systems (such as science, politics, or economics) are encompassed in a global societal system. Society, therefore, is a system that functions as an internal environment for every other social system.[1]

Interaction systems

As *systems-in-an-environment*, social systems – despite their operative autonomy – are not decoupled but are in some ways dependent on each other; they observe, react upon, and affect each other. A simple interaction system between two people requires language, behavioural rules, and a whole inventory of meanings that are provided by society's internal environment. Without these prerequisites, the interaction system could not work properly. If I ask a passer-by on the street for the way to the metro, we do not first have to agree what I mean by this question, why I want to know this, and what the metro is, but we can (mostly) presuppose that both of us understand what I mean because it takes place within the wider internal environment of society, from which we gather a shared understanding of the metro and ways to describe directions. Nevertheless, it is very obvious where the boundaries of this small system are: other conversations taking place near us in the street do not belong to our interaction system. Neither do other social systems that the passers-by or I belong to, nor do any of our psychic systems.

Another important aspect of understanding the conditions for how an interaction system works is whether the interaction takes place within the context of an encompassing social system (on a lower level than the all-encompassing society) or outside it. The encompassing system can dictate rules, topics, expectation structures, and role definitions of the interaction partners, and more. For example we can imagine two people having lunch together at a restaurant. What they talk about, thus what happens in their small interaction system "lunch", depends greatly on the social context, i.e. the context within other, larger social systems. First, the "lunch" system takes place in the context of a social system "restaurant". But even if the interaction takes place within the walls of the restaurant as a building, their interaction system is not part of the "restaurant" social system. The latter is an organisation, i.e. a social system that reproduces by membership rules and decision-making structures (Højlund & Knudsen, 2003; La Cour & Højlund, 2008; Luhmann, 2000b; Nassehi, 2005; Seidl & Becker, 2006).

Normally within organisations there are specific member roles that are arranged in a certain, mostly hierarchical, relationship. There are the owner(s) and manager (s), the chef, kitchen assistants, bartender, maître d' and waiters, cleaning personnel, and others. Furthermore, there are more or less clearly defined rules about who is expected to do what and who has the right to determine what the others are supposed to do and what they are not. We will get back to the topic of "organisation" in the following section. For our little "lunch system" the restaurant (the organisation) is certainly a relevant environment because the interaction partners must talk to the waiter and maybe the maître d' in order to get their table, to order, and to pay. Naturally, this affects the "lunch system" and its two participants insofar as the organisation dictates some rules to them and expectations that differ greatly from a lunch interaction at home. For instance, the guests are prohibited from entering the kitchen, have to adhere to a certain dress code, and are not allowed to make too much noise or insult the personnel. By having their lunch at the restaurant, our interaction partners assume the social role of "guest", which is defined by the organisation (and the societal institution "restaurant" in general). But guests are not members of the "restaurant" organisation like the waiters and the managers are. Consequently, the restaurant personnel cannot dictate what they can and cannot talk about.

Notwithstanding, the "lunch system" can be one part within another, encompassing system that can very well define what this interaction should be about. It makes a big difference whether the two lunch partners are friends, a married couple, love-seekers on a date, a manager and his employee, representatives of two corporations meeting for negotiations, or a social worker catching up with a former client who "has made it".[2] How a business lunch looks is very much defined by the firm (organisation) and the participants' role and position in the hierarchy. Two co-equal colleagues would usually mingle in a more relaxed way than a manager and his secretary, particularly if the lunch is supposed to be "spontaneously relaxed" on command (like the double-binds from Chapter 1).

At the same time, the "lunch system" as an interaction system is – to a certain degree – autonomous from the overarching system. Interaction systems are autonomous insofar as they are emergent orders; what people talk about cannot be determined through the organisational structure (to the despair of managers!). The "lunch system" can be affected by something going on at the neighbouring table. For example, our lunch guests might become witnesses to an interesting conversation or see celebrities or otherwise remarkable people and start talking about these instead of their original topic. Or they might study what the other people are eating and also want this food.

All of this can radically change the course of the interaction, while it hardly affects the foundations of the overarching organisation system. Expressed in systems-theoretical terminology, this is so because the organisation as an overarching system is also relatively autonomous from the interaction – "relatively" because what happens during an interaction can have a great influence on the future of the organisation, for instance if the negotiations with the investor or trade partner fails and potential profits are lost. In that case, typical characteristics of interaction systems can have a huge impact. In all other regards, organisations are much more rigid and stable than interactions, while interactions are more dynamic, flexible, and of shorter duration. As sociologist Erving Goffman (1963, 1967) has shown repeatedly, interactions can emerge very quickly when people encounter and perceive each other. Interaction systems emerge all the time but often they dissolve just as quickly (like my inquiry about the metro). You meet a friend in a shopping mall, greet each other, and start talking; you meet a colleague at the copy machine in the corridor and start small talk until your copy job is done.[3]

Interaction systems require that the participants are co-present and perceive each other mutually (Luhmann, 1995). Hence, interaction systems are very dependent on the participants and, by extension, on how the participants' psychic systems are affected by their environment. When the participants become hungry, angry or stressed, happy or unhappy, this can affect how they behave during the interaction. The interaction system can, therefore, quickly change from positive, cooperative, and nice to confrontational and hostile. Conversely, the interaction system generally affects the involved psychic systems much more strongly and in much more immediate ways than other social systems in the environment. Think how communication can console a sad person or unintentionally upset her (which happens

more often than we might like, particularly in communication between participants of different genders or cultures).

Interaction systems are less complex than other social systems and they do not
have the capabilities to handle or build up higher levels of complexity. The inevitable dependence on personal presence[4] and mutual perception reduces the capacity to handle complexity, with the result that communication takes place much
more slowly than thoughts are processed in the involved participants' minds. We
can perceive and think so much more than we can express.[5]

In order to remain meaningful, communication in interaction systems has to
build a temporal order, one sentence after the other, and one speaker at a time.
When participants start talking at the same time or cut each other off it is typically
an indicator of disturbance (or that we are watching a political discussion on TV).
The flow of information is hampered severely. Furthermore, communication in
interaction systems often takes places in the shape of what conversation analysts call
"adjacency pairs". Examples are questions and answers, greetings and returns,
"Thanks" and "You're welcome" (Garfinkel, 1967). Adjacency pairs are systemic
structural properties that facilitate communication, but like any structure (see more
on that in Chapters 3 and 7), they constrain the possibilities for what, when, and
how something can be said. Thus, structures delimit the capacity for building up
complexity. Compare the polite phrase "How do you do?", which does not
express a specific interest in the other person – nobody expects a real answer, only
a return of the same question, maybe supplemented by a "Fine, thanks".

The topic of the conversation is another example of structure in the interaction
system. It is difficult for interaction systems to deal with more than one topic at a
time without ending up in a similar mess as when several people speak at once. Of
course, we can imagine an interaction system with more than two or three participants, in which subsystems within the overarching interaction system can differentiate, and each of these subsystems deal with their own topic. This works well in
teaching situations with several groups working at the same time in the same
classroom, but it requires institutional precautions that are normally backed up by
organisational structures beyond the interaction system, for instance the school or
the university.

Organisation systems

For those who have read this far it should not come as a surprise that we, when
using a systems-theoretical framework, do not consider organisations as assemblies of
human beings who aim to fulfil a shared goal (Ahrne, 1994; Wagner-Tsukamoto,
2003). Granted, starting an organisation requires human beings and most likely the
founders will have defined a purpose. But in the same way that society comprises all
communication and interaction systems form a reality *sui generis* between psychic
systems – a so-called emergent order – organisations consist of communications that
follow defined rules. In saying this we are not making a statement about what an
organisation *is*. Hence, we do not claim that scholars who regard organisations as

collectives of human beings are wrong and systems theorists are right. It is a matter of definition. Systems theorists *define* social systems, particularly society and organisations, in a different way than the mainstream in social sciences (Andersen, 2003b). Naturally, anybody can define anything in any way they like but the relevant questions are always: How far do you get with a certain definition? Which definitions can be integrated into an existing conceptual framework without contradictions and incoherencies?

In accordance with its conceptual framework, Luhmannian systems theory defines the organisation as a specific type of communication system. Communication within organisations is formalised by a more or less complex arrangement of decisions and decision premises and it distinguishes members from non-members (Luhmann, 2000b; Nassehi, 2005; Seidl & Becker, 2006). Decisions and membership are the lowest common denominators for any type of organisation system. It is these features that make the boundary between organisation systems and their environments more distinct than is the case for interaction systems. As for the latter, in the restaurant example we may wonder under which circumstances the conversation at the adjacent table in the restaurant is also included in our "lunch system" the moment the people start talking to our lunch guests.

In organisation systems, by contrast, there are clearly defined rules that determine who is a member and who is not (mostly in written form and by contract). Every organisation has defined criteria for membership and these criteria vary depending on the type of organisation. If the organisation is an association or political party you can apply for membership and then pay a yearly fee in order to keep your membership. In other organisations you can become a member by birth (for example citizenship in states) or by initiation ceremonies, such as getting baptised.

The most common membership in modern society is through employment, i.e. through a labour contract that determines that an individual is hired for a certain period or until retirement, with the purpose of executing defined work in exchange for defined compensation. Here, membership is connected to an agreement that the individual will fulfil specific tasks and receive a wage and/or other privileges (e.g. stock options, discounts) for the work done. Organisations are often a vehicle to make contact and participate in society. Via different roles or functions people are included as members of several organisations simultaneously – employer, church, leisure and interest associations, etc. To a large extent, modern social life is organised, and organisations are prevalent in more and more realms of life.

Membership is assigned by means of decisions. Decisions are the core element in organisations. The concept "decision" refers to a communication of intentional choices between alternatives, for example to hire person A (instead of person B or nobody), to invest in one country (instead of another country or omitting investment), to raise a tax (instead of lowering it or leaving it untouched), to place a child in a foster home (instead of letting him stay in a multi-problem family), to grant a refugee asylum (instead of deporting him). A system that operates on the basis of decisions is capable of operating in a goal-oriented manner but flexibly so because decisions are reversible. If changes in the environment require adjustments, these can be achieved by new, more appropriate decisions; hence we can argue that decisions are a way for organisations to master contingency.

Systems theorists claim that organisations cannot be understood appropriately if we look at the intentions of individual members or the system as a whole. Instead, systems theory proposes focusing on decisions and the structure of decision-making. As we will demonstrate, the intentions of individuals represent only one of many premises on which decisions are made. Which decisions are made, i.e. which choices are made, is not (entirely) arbitrary but (largely) contingent on a set of *decision premises*.[6] Luhmann distinguishes three types of decision premises: communication channels, programmes, and personnel (Luhmann, 2000b; Seidl & Becker, 2006).

Communication channels refer to the formal structure of an organisation, i.e. which departments there are, who is superior to whom, who has to report to whom, who is entitled to make which decisions, who is accountable for what. By "who" we do not mean a human being but a position. To be sure, this position has to be inhabited by a real human being, but this real human being is replaceable and can be substituted with somebody else who fulfils the formal criteria (specific competencies and skills, legal status, gender, age, etc.), as was pointed out by Max Weber in his classical studies on bureaucracies (Weber, 1968). Communication channels are mostly arranged in a hierarchical manner, with few on top (executives), some on the middle levels (middle management), and the most on the lower levels (workers). Once an organisation reaches a certain size, it will be divided into a number of departments dealing with particular functions. A business corporation is divided into a buying department, as well as production, research and development, human resources, and marketing departments, etc. A government has a number of departments that focus on specialised political fields (foreign affairs, economy, defence, social affairs, environment, education, labour, etc.). A university is arranged in several faculties comprising different academic disciplines.

The second category of decision premises, *programmes*, determines how decision-makers make their decisions. Luhmann derived one of the semantic meanings of the word "programme" from the world of computers. Programming the computer means providing the machine with precisely formulated instructions (algorithms) governing how they function when a user gives a specific input. Fed with a number of variables, the computer, by following the instructions, calculates a number of results. These results depend on the variables and algorithms, but apart from that, they are completely predictable. Algorithms are the very program. Within some boundaries we can apply this principle to organisations. Programmes within organisations mean instructions for how to make decisions under pre-determined conditions. According to systems theory, two types of organisational programmes can be distinguished: *conditional programmes* and *goal programmes*. Conditional programmes are decision routines defined by the interplay of internal rules, on the one hand, and variable environmental conditions, on the other hand. Like computer programs, the results of the decision are contingent on the values of the environmental variables. For example, *if* a rule prescribes that a client is entitled to raise a certain claim only at the age of 18 or above, *then* the social secretary grants the claim only if, factually, the client is at least 18 years old. Expressed in a way that resembles digital code, if variable age = 0–17 then deny; if variable age ≥ 18 then grant. The same is true if the formal requirement is EU citizenship. The social secretary is not allowed to accept the claim if the applicant is not a citizen in an EU country. In cases where it is easily and unequivocally possible to determine what is correct, organisations equipped with conditional programmes function like trivial machines. Tax agencies and a number of other public authorities can work very well by following this principle.

The complexity increases once we consider the other type of programme in organisations: goal programmes (*Zweckprogramme*). Here, the underlying principle is to subordinate the choice of decision algorithms to a certain goal. The goal is the variable. A goal programme can take on a form like this: if the goal is to reduce costs, the decision is made according to alternative A (for instance fewer fresh hires, increased number of work hours, fewer privileges for the personnel). If, by contrast, the goal is to achieve an improved working environment, the decision is made according to alternative B (an upper limit on overtime hours, more new hires, improved privileges, extended options for parental leave and flex-work). Here, the trivial machine approach does not work, not least because there will be many goal conflicts and internal fights, and a number of collateral effects and unintended consequences. Research shows that decision-making in organisations is characterised by unclear, ambiguous, and unstable goals (March & Simon, 1967) and that different agents within the same organisation can strive for opposing goals.

This is where the third decision premise enters the scene: *personnel*. In a pure, ideal type of bureaucracy, according to Weber's classic description, all employees are replaceable. The personnel represent a kind of cog in a big machine. This cog does its job on the whole but if it breaks or does not work as it is supposed to, it will be replaced with a new one that fulfils the function as planned. Expressed in a radical way, the personnel (the piece of human beings behind the task) are neutralised so much that it does not matter who inhabits a certain position as long as she/he has the required competencies and skills. In reality, however, it makes a huge difference for most organisations (and outside pure bureaucracies) which person occupies a position, particularly when the job description entails right-brain, creative work. Within the helping professions, such as psychotherapy, social work, and pedagogy, the person is more important than the programme because the cases are usually so complex and unique that standardised methods can only be applied within very limited boundaries (in contrast to the tasks at the health insurance office). The debates on evidence-based practice have shed light on the conflict between standardisation of methods and the uniqueness of cases that require professional discretion (Høgsbro, 2011; Vandenbroeck, Roets, & Roose, 2012). Within the helping professions the tasks are very ambiguous; they require relationships of trust between client and practitioner that take a long time to establish and that thereafter always carry the risk of breaking down (Abbott, 2014; Nevo & Slonim-Nevo, 2011; Webb, 2001). The less regulated a certain task is, and the more background variables are in play, the more personal scope of action there is for the executor. The greater the scope of action a decision-maker has, the greater his/her impact is in setting premises for decisions; which decisions are made and how they are made, then, depends on the actual personnel that inhabit the position, not the conditional or goal program. Within certain limits, different people in the same position make different decisions.

Differentiation of system levels: interaction, organisation and society

Interaction systems can exist outside or inside organisation systems, as we demonstrated with the "lunch system" earlier in this chapter. Beyond this there are interaction systems right on the boundary of the organisation and its environment, for example when a private person calls the customer service of a telecommunication corporation in order to file a complaint. The customer service personnel represent the organisation while the private person only represents herself. If the customer service worker does not agree with the complaint, the private person may get angry and express her discontent about the corporation or the specific agreement; the customer service worker, however, cannot lose his temper but has to remain polite and friendly because it is not his own but the organisation's reputation that is at stake (Goffman, 1952). Likewise, the customer service worker needs to adhere to the rules of the organisation while the private person is not constrained by them; being a private person, she may follow rules of politeness and demeanour but otherwise she is not bound to anything other than the customer agreement.

This is a situation social workers know all too well. In their work with problematic clients they represent municipal social services, a school, or a private social care agency and have to act in accordance with social law and other legal regulations. They must be able to control their temper and act professionally while at the same time finding ways to handle situations in which they receive insults, ridicule, or threats. Sometimes it is not the clients themselves but family members or peers who make the lives of social workers troublesome (Lloyd, King, & Chenoweth, 2002).

The last two examples highlight an important difference between a human being as an organisation member and the same human outside the organisation. The person working in the customer centre or social service is addressed as representative of the organisation, not as a private person. Hence, the anger of the customers or clients is actually directed at the organisation, even if that organisation is embodied by a concrete human being. In Chapter 4 we return to this issue, the complex relation between human beings and social systems. For now, we focus on the relation between social system and environment. The boundaries between the organisation system and its environment cut right through the human being working for the organisation, which means that human beings (with their minds and bodies) are not part of the system, but their membership and concomitant role expectations are part of the system. What the customer service and social service workers do in the name of the organisation (handling customers' complaints, working with clients) is at the same time a reproduction of the organisation as a system because this activity leads to or makes decisions on the basis of decision premises. Whether the customer service worker offers the customer some new privileges or discounts to convince her not to switch operators, rejects the customer's complaint without giving a reason, or promises to send a technician to the customer's home, all of these are decisions made in the name of the organisation, reproducing the very organisation as a social system. In a similar manner, the social worker makes decisions for his organisation when he documents the client's ability to work, defines measures of intervention, contacts fraud investigators, etc.

While these talks with customers or clients reproduce the specific organisation, they are – at the same time – interaction systems, including all characteristics of interactions, such as less capability to handle complexity, more dynamics, and sensitivity to the current states of the involved psychic systems (anger, irritation, desperation).

A key characteristic of modern society is the enormous number of social systems that exist simultaneously. There are infinite interaction systems that occur spontaneously and disappear just as quickly; numerous organisation systems that are founded later fuse with others or are closed down. Society as an all-encompassing communication system has existed since our early human predecessors started communicating. From the beginning until today, society has increased its complexity and changed its shape several times. Within a systems-theoretical framework, societal change is identified on the level of societal differentiation in subsystems (not at the level of the composition of human beings). By this, we mean that the major constitutive elements of society and their relations in between have changed from heterarchical tribes and clans to hierarchical relations of strata or castes to functional subsystems such as the economy, politics, and law. In Chapter 3 we deal with societal differentiation at length. In the remainder of Chapter 2 we have to consider another type of change human society has gone through in the course of its history: the increasing differentiation of interaction systems and society as an all-encompassing system.

As pointed out previously, systems theory defines society as the system that comprises all other systems; thus interaction systems take place within society. Logically, an interaction system is a part of society on the one hand, while on the other hand, (the rest of) society is the environment for this interaction system. There is an important operative difference between interaction systems and society, and this difference is easier to grasp in our present times, which are characterised by the ubiquity of new communication media. Today, we have no problem understanding the gap between interaction systems and the many parts of societal communication that take place in ways other than face-to-face interaction. So-called dissemination media (Lee, 2000) such as books and the printing press, the telegraph, telephony, radio and TV, the computer and internet, and for the last decade, social media have changed communication patterns and opportunities radically. Dissemination media have enabled a huge increase in social complexity that was not possible in oral, pre-literary societies for the simple reason that communication had to pass through the bottleneck of interaction systems, such as co-presence, turn-taking, time limitations, limited mental attention, etc.

One obvious effect of dissemination media is the preservability of communication (Havelock, 1996). If I say a sentence to you the sentence is gone after it was uttered. Now, if you and I forget the sentence, it is gone forever. Even remembering exactly what I said, or who said what in a dialogue – for instance if the interlocutors want to recapitulate how the conversation went off the rails – can be difficult and unreliable, and even more so if the participants' emotions are heated.

Now that we live in a time in which social media and giant search machines connected to even more giant databases have become an essential part of our everyday lives, it is not oblivion that is the problem but the lack thereof: everything once uttered in the digital is saved forever (Orlik, 2016).[7] Thanks to almost unlimited server capacities, all sorts of data are stored. This is another important consequence of dissemination media for the differentiation of interaction systems from society. In contrast to face-to-face interactions, dissemination media do not only include those who hear me uttering my words (conversation partners and bystanders alike) but communication through, say, social media, includes anyone who now or at any later time gets access to my stored utterances.[8] This has severe and unintended consequences. It has happened numerous times that compromising pictures from parties shared on social media have broken promising careers (Ross & Lester, 2011). Information on the internet is difficult to have deleted and it is impossible to avoid spreading when it is so easy to share. When anybody can find the information on the web and make free associations and interpretations in contexts completely different from those in which the information originated, much harm can be done.

If I have written down text on a piece of paper, everyone who is literate and understands the language can have access to the information. My presence is not necessary. That is the principle of written communication, of letters, and since the invention of the printing press, also of books and newspapers. Thanks to mass production of newspapers and books, an author's text can reach masses of recipients (largely) independent from the point of time in which it is written. The great thing about printed text is that it can be read a long time after it has been written; the author may have been dead for hundreds of years. Today, we can read Aristotle's descriptions of ancient Greece.[9] Likewise, we can benefit from the systems-theoretical writings of Bateson, Watzlawick and Luhmann although these authors have been dead for a few decades. While this thought may seem trivial today, it is not so at all when keeping an eye on the differences between interaction and society.

Precisely because of the decoupling between a text and its author, more and more information can be stored, collected, combined, remixed, and developed. This is one of the prerequisites for the development of a system of science. It is hard to imagine the system of science as a continuity of a chain of interaction systems. Many big breakthroughs have occurred after researchers have gained novel insights by reading, comparing, and combining findings from innumerable sources from a diversity of fields of different eras.

A less obvious but equally profound consequence of society's increasing differentiation from the level of interaction systems, enabled by the dissemination medium of writing, is relief from the pressure to say "yes". Throughout history, there was a tendency to reward the messenger lavishly if the message was positive (for instance the message that the king's army had won a battle against an adversary). Conversely, the messenger may be punished hard, and sometimes was executed if the message was negative.[10] Politicians and business leaders are often in a similar situation as the messengers when they have to convey bad news (for instance, increased unemployment, a drop in the quarterly profits) and are criticised for the results, whether it is their fault or not (Kahneman, 2011). It is easy to understand the motives of messengers of bad news who keep it to themselves or make up fluffy formulations that erode the core of the message.

Returning to the thread from the beginning of this section, unpleasant decisions are often conveyed by letter or email in order to avoid exposing personnel to negative reactions by clients and customers. Since the arrival of the SMS about 20 years ago, it has become more common to end a romantic relationship by SMS in order to avoid the awkward (and possibly painful) situation of seeing the other person sad and hurt – emotions that could be expected in face-to-face interactions (Turkle, 2011). That way, the emotional pressure can simply be transferred to the dumped person, while in a face-to-face interaction both parties have to share the emotional burden.

The reduced pressure to say "yes", or to suppress negative news, is anything but trivial. It has huge effects on the development of society. If "no" is socially possible (without fear of punishment), it means that it is possible to challenge the existing, to question the status quo. A "no" makes visible the contingency behind everything: it does not have to be as it is. At least in theory, it could work in another way; it could be better, more effective, or more just. All grand utopian philosophies (such as neoliberalism, Marxism, multiculturalism) are built upon this assumption. To be able to say "no" without the risk of punishment enables social change and progress. It means increased legitimacy for social deviance, increased tolerance toward other groups, other lifestyles, and other ways to think. Once more, a healthy system of science requires the possibility of expressing deviant thoughts, in particular against religious or political doctrines, such as creationism and any ideology that claims moral superiority. The Heterodox Academy movement founded by social psychologist Jonathan Haidt is a good example for initiatives aimed at protecting pluralism in science.[11] We return to this in Chapter 8, when we deal with the topic of "social criticism with systems theory".

If we go back in time and imagine a small tribal society consisting of about 150 people who do not know about computers, phones, or writing, we can understand how society could only work as an interaction system. There are, of course, other, smaller interaction systems within such a tribal society. Not everyone talks at the same time. In order to be preserved, information needs to be conveyed orally from situation to situation, from generation to generation. Such societies are, according to classical sociologists Émile Durkheim (2012 [1893]) and Ferdinand Tönnies (Tönnies & Loomis, 1964 [1887]), characterised by strong internal bonds, relatively low degrees of role-differentiation (unless between sexes and generations), strong similarities in behaviour, and hardly any toleration of deviant behaviour or opinions concerning creed and worldview. Durkheim describes "mechanical solidarity" as a way of keeping such tribal societies together. Within systems theory we would, complementarily, describe a lack of differentiation between interaction systems and society, which was not possible without dissemination media. In the next chapter we demonstrate how modern society is characterised by a high degree of differentiation.

Notes

1 Two other examples of system-internal environments are the market within the economic system (in which we find all important economic actors and organisations that observe and affect each other's decisions; Luhmann, 1988) and the international order within the global political system (in which states and political organisations observe each other's activities; Schirmer, 2007).

2 Be aware that the manager and the employee could also be on a date together, or it could be an ambiguous situation between work-related and private, which can lead to very awkward or sensitive situations (for instance: sexual offence) if one of the participants interprets the situation differently than the other. From a systems-theoretical perspective, this would be an overlap of system rationalities with conflicting expectations.

3 Or you pretend not to have seen each other and omit the greeting. In line with the first axiom (one cannot not communicate in the co-presence of others) people may see through this and – paradoxically – interpret this as communication (I don't want to communicate with you), so sometimes it is less costly to quickly say "hi".

4 Presence in the physical space, but also by phone or video call or social virtual reality.

5 This is true both for oral and written communication. Everybody who ever tried to write a meaningful text has experienced the fact that many thoughts are required before succeeding in writing a sentence that expresses these thoughts in a good way; in the meantime the thoughts have moved on!

6 The brackets indicate that there is often at least some arbitrariness involved. Research has shown repeatedly that organisations do not always adhere to what is written down in their rule set. There is a lot of nepotism, irrationality, coincidence, and fraud (think of Enron and Volkswagen) but the organisation puts effort into appearing legitimate, lawful, moral, and in line with public opinion (Meyer & Rowan, 1977). In a classic study well worth reading, organisation researchers Bensman and Gerver (1963) showed how the employees of all levels in an American firm that produced military airplanes were more or less compelled to cheat in order to achieve their predefined goals. The fraud was serious because it entailed forbidden procedures that undermined the safety of the planes. The study found that the fraud was accepted unofficially on all executive levels, even if the firm officially had to look like the fraud was fought with rigour.

7 Interestingly, there is one social media platform, Snapchat, whose operative principle is oblivion by design. Every sent message disappears after a while, which fosters a digital communication style that, within limits, resembles oral culture (Soffer, 2016).

8 This is different for communication technologies such as the telephone, radio, and TV, where utterances are as ephemeral as with regular face-to-face interaction. The ephemerality can be circumvented by using storage media such as magnetic bands, vinyl discs,

or digital memory devices (discs, CDs, hard- and flash-drives, or online in the "cloud"), which then allow for a certain independence from time.

9 Havelock (1996) showed that the Greeks in the Homerian era highly valued simple and monotonous messages because newly acquired knowledge had to be repeated constantly or otherwise it would be forgotten in an oral culture. After the transition from oral to literary culture, human minds evolved as radically as society. Because of the impact the new communication medium of writing had on the human brain, it also allowed for the formation of new, more abstract concepts.

10 The Spartans threw Xerxes' messenger into a well because they refused to capitulate without battle. After Xerxes sent another messenger to Athens with the demand to capitulate, Themistocles sentenced this messenger to death, for "he had dared to use the Greek language to express Barbarian commands" (Munn, 2006).

11 It is apparent how saying no is easier in written communication (such as blind peer review) than orally; this is all the truer when other factors that irritate the course of face-to-face interaction come into play, such as authority, gender and age.

3

MODERN SOCIETY AND FUNCTIONAL DIFFERENTIATION

In Chapter 2 we demonstrated how different levels of social order are connected to each other. We mentioned three such orders:

1. Interaction systems characterised by a sort of ad hoc order that requires immediate real-time coordination between involved psychic systems;
2. Organisation systems characterised by a formal order through decision premises and rules;
3. Society as the encompassing social system, i.e. the highest level of social order and the most inclusive social system; inclusive here means that society includes every other social system.

Within Luhmannian systems theory, interaction, organisation, and society have long been considered as the most important levels of social order. In the meantime, however, systems theorists have shown interest in networks, groups, and social movements as social systems in their own right. None of these latter types can be represented through interactions or organisations (Fuchs, 2001a; Nassehi, 2008b; Schirmer & Michailakis, 2018a). On the one hand, these types of sociality are more complex than interaction systems and they require neither co-presence nor communication in real-time. On the other hand, they are much less formalised and operate in much more of an ad hoc way do than organisations.

The division in levels of social order can be seen as one type of *differentiation*. Within a systems-theoretical framework, the term "differentiation" means that systems are separated from other systems; they delimit each other. What happens in one system is different to what takes place in other systems. We have seen how interaction systems lack the ability of differentiation; organisations, by contrast, can differentiate in an array of divisions, departments, work groups, etc.

A short history of societal differentiation

Next to differentiation in levels of social order, i.e. types of social systems, there is also a process of differentiation on the level of society. By this, we mean that the encompassing social system, society, is differentiated into a number of *subsystems*. These are called subsystems in order to express that they are subordinated to the main system society. The subsystems can coexist in several constellations or relations. For example, subsystems can be similar or dissimilar; they can be in a hierarchical or co-equal relation to each other.

Throughout history, there have been different sorts of societal subsystems and so-called forms of differentiation (*Differenzierungsform*). Tribes, clans, and villages are examples of age-old subsystems (Durkheim, 2012 [1893]). They were similar to each other and did not stand in a specific and stable hierarchical relation, even if some of them were bigger or, at a given time, stronger or richer than others. In this context, we speak of *segmentary differentiation*; the subsystems are segments of a higher order.[1]

Ancient civilisations such as Egypt, Babylon, and Greece already operated in another form of societal differentiation that emphasised the hierarchy, inequality, and heterogeneity of the subsystems. Here, the subsystems consisted of strata, classes, or castes with very rigid and hardly permeable boundaries that would not allow the entry of "alien" elements. In such societies a very small stratum on top (for instance the pharaoh, his family, and staff) dominated all other groups, and this layer determined the prevailing social order, i.e. what counted as moral or immoral, sacred or profane, lawful or unlawful, and how wealth and privileged social positions were to be distributed. This upper stratum had a different status and function than, say, peasants and slaves, who belonged to lower subsystems that provided all physical labour and the material reproduction of society. Societies with this type of differentiation, i.e. *stratified differentiation*, dominated in medieval Europe under the label "feudalism" and in early-modern Europe as "absolutism". Instead of the pharaoh and his followers, it was the nobility with a selection of royal families on top of the hierarchy. A number of socio-cultural developments undermined this form of differentiation. Social activities that historically suffered from the stranglehold of a repressive political order legitimised by religious dogma, such as economics and science, gradually started to crystallise into separate and autonomous systems.

Within the frame of these societal changes, the differentiation of the political and religious spheres deserves special attention because it implied the liberation of political power from religious dogma. After several armed disputes between the Catholic church (which was then a mixture of a pre-modern organisation and a parallel image of society under clerical leadership) and the monarchies, political power no longer depended on religious legitimacy (as was the case with the king "by grace of God"). This struggle, which went on for several centuries, ultimately undermined the union of politics and religion and led to their operative differentiation into separate societal subsystems. The modern nation state – whose shape originated at the end of the Thirty Years' War in 1648, the so-called Westphalian order (Harste, 2004)[2] – received its legitimacy from mundane ideas such as "nation" or "people", but no longer from a godly world order.

Simultaneously, another development occurred in the realm of the economy. A capitalist economic system came into being in which the accumulation of wealth was transformed from a means (accumulating enough money to secure future survival) to an end in itself. In his ground-breaking study, Max Weber showed how the rise of capitalism was related to a protestant creed (Weber, 2009 [1904]). Protestantism is a branch of Christianity that emphasises the individual fate of people much more strongly than does Catholicism. Next to its emphasis on individuals, Protestantism, particularly in its more radical forms, such as Calvinism, allowed and encouraged the striving for financial wealth, for example to collect interest for lent money – something that was strictly forbidden in almost any other religious congregation. After some generations, the religious roots lost their significance while striving for wealth became the prevailing attitude. Originally economic activity was founded upon religious activity, but the economy ultimately developed a type of rationality in its own right.

These events happened at the same time as other societal realms began to free themselves from the ideological social order defined by religion. For instance, science began to develop as an alternative pathway to knowledge beyond what priesthood, theological charters, scripts such as the Bible, and writings by church fathers had to offer. The difference between scientifically ascertained and proven truth, on the one hand, and religiously prescribed dogma, on the other hand, became more and more apparent. Technological progress, which was so important for industrialisation (Mumford, 2010), meant strategic advantages for progressive kings and their armies. Scientists were often sentenced to death or prison for blasphemy when they tried to understand natural laws and spread their findings. Ultimately, religion began losing its authority to speak about universal, worldwide wisdoms when the clergy continued preaching things that did not correspond to scientific findings.

These brief examples should suffice to indicate the enormous change that started in the late Middle Ages and went on until the beginning of the 20th century, when the development stabilised on a global level. Politics, science, economy, and other social spheres started developing and differentiating from each other, and, in particular, from religion. They formed their very own rationalities, which could no longer be subsumed under the same roof. What is economically rational (to focus on short-term profits) is not synonymous with what is rational in science (to spend much time studying something with highly uncertain results), or vice versa. In this new social order of different sub-spheres with their incongruent rationalities – where religion has lost the grip it previously had on former societal formations and has been degraded to one societal realm among others – stratification is no longer the core ordering principle of society. Instead it is the diversity of different, inhomogeneous spheres that fulfil specific functions for society. In modern society, societal differentiation is built upon functions that give rise to specific rationalities.

Around these rationalities, specific systems have formed. It was sociologist Parsons at first, and after him Habermas and Luhmann, who called these subsystems of modern society *function systems*.[3] The political system, the economic system, the legal system, religion, science, media, art, social help, and the system of medicine are examples of function systems (see also Roth & Schütz, 2015). The societal order built by or upon function systems is called *functional differentiation*. The term was introduced by Durkheim (Durkheim, 2012 [1893]), one of the most influential theorists of societal differentiation in classical social science.

Societal differentiation by the classics of social science

We believe that the theory of societal differentiation can be integrated into a larger and more coherent framework. However, the concept of societal differentiation was not devised by systems theorists. Let us, therefore, take a look at how the idea of societal differentiation was established in the social sciences, and what insights we can gain to further our attempt to present a systems theory for social work and helping professions.

During the 19th century, scholars who worked on understanding and explaining the vast social changes that came with industrialisation were influenced by Charles Darwin's monumental classic of evolutionary biology, *The origin of species* (Darwin, 2011 [1859]). The traditionally dominant view of a stable order of things, which had its foundation in religion, started to loosen up and little by little was replaced by secular thought about a world experiencing constant change and development. Social philosophers such as Henri de Saint-Simon and Auguste Comte saw society as a malleable system under ongoing evolution. According to Darwin's evolutionary theory, more complex species are characterised by a higher degree of internal differentiation than primitive species – an idea that had great influence on social thought. Many theorists of that time regarded modern society with its higher degree of differentiation as a new evolutionary stage that could be distinguished from earlier traditional and, in general, more primitive societies. Social change was perceived as causing an increase in the complexity of social relations and an increase in societal differentiation.

In the light of societal differentiation, the relation of the differentiated parts to each other and their integration into the whole (society) have been core issues for classical social theorists such as Spencer, Durkheim, Tönnies, Weber, and Simmel. For instance Spencer understood evolution as a transition from a vague homogeneity to a strictly defined and mutually related heterogeneity (Spencer, 2010 [1876]). In Spencer's theory, strongly influenced by Darwin, the degree of differentiation of heterogeneous parts of society and their integration into a functioning entity – which Spencer compared to an organism – was an important indicator of societal development. Spencer assumed – wrongfully, as we know today – that the weight of cultural and blood bonds in the village community would decline and ultimately disappear.

In his work on the rationalisation of the occident, Max Weber took up the idea of societal differentiation as a sign of modernisation. The concept rationalisation stood for an organisation of economic life according to principles of efficiency, profitability, and controllability, grounded on technical and scientific knowledge (Weber, 1968). In more general terms, rationalisation is a way of thinking and practice in which everything is subsumed under means–end calculations. Weber demonstrated throughout several studies how rationalisation had advanced in different societal spheres, in economy, science, law, music, romantic love, and politics.[4] For Weber, society was differentiated into these autonomous spheres (he called them "value spheres"), which worked according to their own logic or rationality.

Émile Durkheim claimed that societies with a low degree of differentiation were held together by a strong concordance of values and worldviews, a collective consciousness that comprised everyone and that was supported by strict sanctions directed at potential deviations. He called this form of cohesiveness "mechanical solidarity" (Durkheim, 2012 [1893]). Influenced by Spencer, Durkheim noted that the unitary norm systems of earlier societies over the course of time were scattered into a number of diverse and specified norm systems fulfilling specific functions. In societies with a developed division of labour, norm systems and worldviews cannot be as unitary as in traditional societies. The diversity of norm systems also vastly increases the tolerance for deviance. When integration and coordination are not possible through shared norms and values, it is the functional interdependence through division of labour that creates a new form integration through what Durkheim called "organic solidarity". Durkheim's studies on societal differentiation are particularly relevant for contemporary systems theory insofar as Durkheim distinguishes societies with *segmentary differentiation*, which are characterised by the homogeneity of the parts (communities with mechanical solidarity), and *functionally differentiated* societies, whose characteristic is the heterogeneity of the parts through division of labour.

Influenced by Darwin and the previously mentioned social theorists who emphasised differentiation as an aspect of modernisation, Talcott Parsons (Parsons, 1951, 1963; Parsons & Smelser, 1956), in his sociological systems theory, interpreted societal development as a result of the "adaptability" of diverse social systems. According to Parsons, this evolution took place over many generations and has led to species becoming better adapted to the environment they live in. A social system's ability to survive depends on its adaptability to its environment. For Parsons, the subsystems of a functionally differentiated society pursue specific rationalities that each solve a particular problem for society as a whole. These subsystems are called *function systems* because the term "function" in the functionalist paradigm is used with the meaning "solution to a particular problem" (Knudsen, 2010). For example, the problem of scarce, finite resources is solved by an economically rational allocation of resources/money. Different subsystems are integrated into the whole because of the function they fulfil for it.

The differentiation of society according to systems theory

This brief overview has shown how classical social scientists described modernisation as a process of differentiation. Modern society, in contrast to archaic societies, is not a defined, unitary entity (such as the village) but an entity that is decomposed into a diversity of heterogeneous parts; these parts are social spheres that can be distinguished by the function they fulfil for modern society as a whole. Systems-theorist Luhmann argues that it is precisely this structural characteristic that marks modern society as functionally differentiated (Hagen, 2000; Luhmann, 2013). Function systems pursue their very own rationality and operate in a distinctive, function-specific way. Within a functionally differentiated society, none of these systems can take over the function of another system. Politics cannot be substituted for the economy (as advocates of neoliberalism claim); neither can the economy be substituted for politics (which became painfully visible during the planned economy experiments in the Soviet bloc of the 20th century and in Venezuela in the 21st century).

Function systems are not receptive to each other's logics and specific ways of organising communication, as Weber had already pointed out in his discussion of incommensurable value spheres, for example science and politics (Weber, 1946, 1958 [1922]). Communication produced within one system cannot be part of or fused with communication in another system. The function systems are operationally closed in regard to their logics and rationalities: the economic system cannot deal with justice, truth, or beauty; only the legal system can deal with justice, the scientific system with truth, and the system of art with beauty.

Stratified societies had a centre and an apex, from which those in the highest social position in a pyramid-like order (pharaohs, kings, tyrants, emperors, sultans, etc.) made the important decisions that determined the fate of society. In a functionally differentiated society, by contrast, there is no apex, nor is there a centre (Luhmann, 1989a). There are "only" a number of co-equal function systems that each experience themselves as the centre and society as "the other". For function systems, this "other" serves as a sort of internal environment. For example from a political perspective the state is the centre (with the government on top) and society is the "civil society" or the "population", thus a collective subject that "expects" something from the state or that needs to be kept quiet through material or symbolic concessions. From the viewpoint of the economy, the market appears as the centre while society is seen as a potential source of irritation, mainly through governmental attempts to intervene in the market or the legal limitations of free trade. Similar dichotomies between the very centre of the function system and (the rest of) society can be found for other systems: religion, with its transcendental powers and clerical representatives in the sacred centre, and the "secular", profane society; science and the unilluminated society (of "alternative facts"); art and the tacky, tasteless society.

In any of these dichotomies, the result is always the same: a society that appears as something else, contingent on the function system's perspective describing society. There is no privileged position from which it could be determined whether a legal rationality is better or more important than a political or religious rationality. Society is the encompassing system, but in itself it represents nothing. It is a unity and entity but this entity is "multipolar", without a centre that is shared by all function systems.

What does "functional differentiation" actually mean?

The process social theorists tried to capture with the term "functional differentiation" is a remarkable evolutionary achievement. It is about a development that has gone on for such a long time that it is hardly noticeable. This process is systemic in its nature; no single agent, no single movement, and no single organisation can claim to have brought it about. It is helpful to avoid the association of "functional" with "useful". Function systems are not planned institutions that society (or any actor within it) created on purpose to serve certain interests or to ensure an actor's own survival (Nassehi, 2008a).

Except for some elementary role differentiation according to parameters such as gender, age, function, and rank, segmentary and stratified societies did not allow for more division of labour than was necessary for solving the complex issues that population growth, technological progress, Christian reformation, and a number of other factors had caused. Ultimately, functional differentiation has been victorious over other forms of differentiation because of its greatly increased possibilities to handle social problems. With distinct function systems, society can deal with problems such as the scarcity of resources, the need for new knowledge, how to make collectively binding decisions for large populations, etc.

In contrast to a society that is not functionally differentiated, such as a theocracy, in a functionally differentiated society no system can steer another. The subsystems are not in a hierarchical relation to each other. What is deemed attractive in the economic system (for instance low taxation on corporations) cannot be dictated or imposed by the political system. Conversely, a policy effort on subsidies for activating the dormant work force under certain conditions will not automatically lead to new jobs in the economic system. Because of the lack of a central agency with authority, a functionally differentiated society will always be torn by conflicts about boundaries of meaning, disputes about the right to define problems, etc.

Nobody and nothing can represent modern society as a whole (Schirmer & Hadamek, 2007).[5] In this regard, function systems are co-equal. However, this equality between function systems should by no means imply the claim that we live in a society free from inequality. More precisely, modern society is more *and* less equal than pre-modern societies. On the one hand, functional differentiation abolishes the primary inequality between people from different classes, ethnic, or religious groups, men and women, and elders and youngsters. The status of a person now depends much less on the background of the family and much more on individual track records within different function systems. On the other hand, functional differentiation makes possible new types of inequality between people and groups (see Chapter 4), even if the inequality has to be legitimised on different grounds than in stratified class societies, where power holders could refer to a natural, divine order that should not be questioned. After society has transitioned from a primarily hierarchical structure to a structure founded in the functions of different subsystems, individuals are no longer locked up in a particular social position and activity, and new types of inequality can occur as long as they are in line with the legitimising semantics of this new order.

The development captured by the term "functional differentiation" does not exclude a co-presence of mixed forms of differentiation. Functional differentiation is the *primary* differentiation form, but we can (still) see several *secondary* differentiation forms of stratification and segmentary differentiation (Luhmann, 2012, 2013; Schirmer & Michailakis, 2008). Much of today's social inequality is not a "divine order" but the co-product of function systems (see Chapter 4). There are also new segmentary differentiation forms, such as the differentiation between states in the international system, between ethnic groups within one state, or between groups that identify themselves by religion rather than political ideology. However, functional differentiation is the dominant form in globalised, modern society (Luhmann, 1997a; Stichweh, 2000).

Function systems: some examples

After this introduction of functional differentiation as the structuring principle of modern society, we will now look more closely at some function systems. As mentioned earlier in this chapter, function systems are social systems that have differentiated within society as solutions to specific societal problems. The economic system deals with questions regarding the efficient allocation of resources under conditions of scarcity; the political system deals with the question of how decisions bind whole collectivities (for example, legislation) and can be made and pushed through (using the monopoly of violence). Science deals with questions regarding how new knowledge about the world can be attained and proven; religion deals with questions regarding the meaning of life and explanations of the "unexplainable"; the social help system deals with questions about problematic inclusion and exclusion of people.

By means of specialisation toward societal problems, function systems are receptive to certain events, while they are blind to or ignorant of others. Thus, functional differentiation can handle a much higher degree of complexity than can previous societies because every one of its subsystems reduces the vast complexity of social reality to a small, relevant section. Function systems subsume everything that exists and happens in the world to their own function-specific rationality. In the following paragraphs, we give the examples of the economy, law, science, medicine, religion, education, medicine, politics, and the social help system.[6]

Economy

For the *economic system*, the world appears as a place full of merchandise that can be bought and sold for a certain price on a certain market. Things, events, and services become economically relevant as long as they can be considered as a target for investment or a cause of profits and losses. Human beings become relevant as market participants who compete and bargain, but also as resources and sets of skills and competences that can be bought or hired on the labour market. Economic communication comprises negotiations, trade with merchandise, services, insurance, values, investments, payments – in short, everything for which money is used as a medium of interchange.

Law

The *legal system* (system of law) reduces the vast complexity of society to the question of whether something is lawful or unlawful. The legal system does not necessarily deal with justice understood as fairness. Whether a weapons deal is financially risky for one of the trade partners, whether it is morally dubious, breaks with God's will, or evokes political resistance is irrelevant for the legal system as long as it does not violate any law, and the reverse – if it is illegal it becomes irrelevant whether it is economically profitable, etc. Likewise, the legal system cannot treat the open online trade of a new chemical drug as a felony as long as this drug is not classified as an illegal substance. It is only after contractual terms or trade embargos are broken, licences expired, or products delivered to illegitimate recipients that the legal system becomes active. As long as they are acting in accordance with the law, governments can spy on the private lives of their own and other countries' populations; rental fees can be raised to levels so high that tenants cannot afford them any longer; experiments with animals can be conducted; refugees can be sent back to their home countries; and firms can continue with creative accounting at the expense of staff and small shareholders.

Hence, the societal function of the law is not to achieve fairness (as a moral concept) but to ensure stable expectations about what can be done without sanction and what will be punished when detected.[7] The only relevant question is what is, according to prevailing jurisdiction, allowed and what is not. Or, to be more realistic: if something is actually forbidden, do we need to handle it in such a way that nobody detects it, or so that once it is detected nobody can prove that we have done it? The legal system communicates through the application of prevailing law, prosecution, and trials but also by the consultation law firms provide.

Science

Because the function of science is to find and provide reliable knowledge, the *system of science* reduces the complexity of the world to questions of objective truth. Everything is viewed as a potential research object that can be studied, analysed, and explained if only we have the right method at our disposal. From its beginnings, science has tried to understand the natural laws that govern the world, but by doing so it has contributed to what Max Weber meant by "disenchantment": the rational analysis of a formerly sacred object. Today, we can understand how extremely impertinent late-medieval and renaissance scientists must have appeared to be in the eyes of clerical powerholders when they questioned the divine order of earth (such as the geocentric world system).

The quest for truth requires quality criteria, such as validity and reliability in the methods used as well as theoretical coherence in order to ascertain that research results and the produced knowledge correspond to the truth. There are clear rules for how to review the validity (or invalidity) of claims in order to qualify as scientific truth or be disqualified as pseudoscience or politicised opinions that hide behind scientific jargon (Sokal, 1998). The debates on evidence-based practice that have shaken up a number of academic disciplines affiliated with the helping professions (medicine, pedagogy, social work) are very instructive for how a scientific approach differentiates itself from its social environment (Blom, 2009; Gambrill, 1999, 2001; McNeece & Thyer, 2004; McNeill, 2006; Otto, Polutta, & Ziegler, 2009; Shaw, 2005; Thyer, 2008; Webb, 2001).

Medicine

The *system of medicine* deals with questions of health and illness (Luhmann, 2005a [1990]; Michailakis, 2008; Michailakis & Schirmer, 2010). Within this system, human beings become relevant as bodies (organisms), not primarily as personalities (Saake, 2003). From a medical viewpoint, the body is scrutinised for potential pathological deviances from the norm in the workings of organs. Deviations from the norm are diagnosed as illnesses, disorders, functional impairments, syndromes, etc. Medical treatment is restricted to deviations from defined standards of what is conventionally regarded as good health (according to physiological, biological, behavioural, and psychological criteria). It is the "medical gaze" (Foucault, 2002 [1963]) that determines which deviations are recognised as illness and which therapies will be applied, but this is highly contingent on other social systems (such as advances in related natural sciences), organisational decisions on how scarce resources should be distributed (Michailakis & Schirmer, 2010; Schirmer & Michailakis, 2014), technological advances, the experience and observational capacities of doctors, ethical considerations, and ecological changes. Accordingly, the definition of what is good health and what is illness changes over time. There are several examples of conditions that in earlier times were recognised as illness – particularly within psychiatry – but that today are considered as part of the variation in human behaviour or bodily state (e.g. homosexuality, hysteria, nostalgia), or that have received a new explanation or label (e.g. stroke, cancer). There are also conditions that were not defined as illness until new knowledge and technology allowed for their discovery (such as Crohn's or Alzheimer's diseases).[8]

Religion

The *system of religion* once had a strong standing as one of society's most important systems. Until the end of the Middle Ages, the church dealt with questions of the legitimacy of education and the search for new knowledge, social integration, and social cohesion. Since the Renaissance, throughout the Enlightenment and the Industrial Revolution until now, religion has, little by little, lost its strong foundation in Europe and considerable parts of the British Commonwealth of Nations. How-ever, if we keep in mind the millions of people who currently are members of reli-gious congregations and the involvement of religious parishes in social movements, it would be premature to ignore the religious system when studying social problems in contemporary society.

In addition to religion's modern function of providing meaning with strong complexity-reducing worldviews (here, religion competes with secular political movements driven by nationalist, xenophobic, or social–romantic worldviews), religion can offer something no other function system can: the ability to deal with paradoxes. Religion can explain the unexplainable, observe the non-obser-vable, determine the indeterminable, give meaning to the meaningless. It is therefore the case that religious communication is more ambiguous, vague, and unclear than communication in other function systems (Beyer, 1998, 2009; Laermans & Verschraegen, 2001).[9] Central to any religious communication is the reference to something transcendent, beyond the twilight, regardless of whether we call it God, a spirit, a force, or the sacred.

Education

The rise of the modern *system of education* can be traced back to the 18th century. The societal reference problem of education is the desire to cultivate in individuals the capabilities that are needed for mastering their own lives within the normative foun-dations and expectations of society (such as discipline and punctuality, basic math and reading/writing skills, and other competences capitalist corporations demand). These are deemed too important to leave them to socialisation within families and peer groups. Expressed in a different way, the problem the system of education deals with is to *school* individuals to autonomously live up to social expectations. Communication within this system strives to change individuals through education, to form psychic systems through communication.

Politics

If one listens and reads carefully one can find several references to transcendental forces within communication of the *system of politics* (particularly in the USA and in Arab countries). Despite more or less frequent allusions to God and community, the political system and its organisations (for example state, government, parlia-ment, parties) mostly revolve around power (Luhmann, 1990c, 2000a; Mik-Meyer & Villadsen, 2013).

Power is required to fulfil the functions of the political system, to make and push through decisions that are collectively binding. The term "collectively bind-ing decisions" primarily refers to law and administrative rules. Carrying out such decisions requires a power-based infrastructure (Willke, 1992), i.e. an arrangement that can credibly threaten the use of sanctions if (parts of) the collectivity do not abide, taxes are not paid, or territorial borders are not respected. For this reason, states maintain the legitimate monopoly of violence through the military and police (Weber, 1946). According to constitutions in parliamentary democracies, physical force against the civil population is only legal in very specific states of emergency, such as riots or violence against the police, although historically, there are many examples demonstrating that state violence against the civil population has been exerted in less legitimate cases (such as violence against protestors or racial and sexual minorities).

In a modern welfare state, collectively binding decisions cannot be arbitrary but depend on legitimacy provided by public opinion. Typically, in its self-descriptions (often shared by mainstream social scientists and journalists) the political system regards itself as the centre and apex of society, equipped with the capability and normative pretence to steer other function systems, mainly the economy (reflating the market, reducing unemployment). As a flipside of this, the welfare state faces claims of all sorts by interest organisations, social movements, and individuals. Despite the operational logics of functional differentiation, the (welfare) state is expected to protect its population from anything ranging from military invasion to economic pauperisation to unfair distribution of resources to natural disasters and medical epidemics and, more generally, it must tackle social problems and safeguard basic civil rights (Schirmer & Hadamek, 2007). All these things together render political communication very sensitive to currents in public opinion. It makes established politicians avoid calling an obvious spade a spade and instead utter media-optimised and streamlined standard phrases that will appease the broad mass of voters, journalists, and other political observers.

Systems theory can warn that the central role a political system ascribes itself has to be treated as modified truth because politics is one (co-equal) function system among others. It does not inhabit any elevated position that allows for an Archimedean fulcrum,[10] standing for society as a whole, and the belief in omnipotence.

Social help

Because this book is mainly targeted at readers active in the field of helping professions, in particular social work, we discuss the *social help system* more extensively than the other function systems. In contrast to everyday help, communication in the help system is about organised help provided by public and private social services for people whom the system identifies as needing help (Moe, 2003). The help system maintains a set of mutual expectations (between provider and recipient) that are written in law (Baecker, 1994; La Cour, 2002; Scherr, 1999). Therefore, the help organised through the help system has a completely different role than the help given in pre-modern societies. In archaic societies, help was organised through unspecified reciprocity: people helped one another and, when needed, expected help in return. The key to reciprocity is to not specify the type, moment, and scope of previously given help. In stratified societies, help was an expression of moral and religious expectations. Help was considered as charity, i.e. a good deed which the giver regarded as his/her duty as, for example, a good Christian.

The commonality between help in pre-modern and modern societies is that both societies depend on the circumstance that help is provided to those who need it. Historically, the modern help system has evolved as a hybrid of two different traditions of social intervention: pedagogy and welfare by Christian charity. Depending on the viewpoint, the "social question" appears as an issue of socially organised education beyond family and school (pedagogy) or as a means of compensation for social, mainly economic, inequalities and poverty (welfare tradition). Because modern, functionally differentiated society cannot be integrated with religious and moral commandments and such integration is even less possible through reciprocity, other forms of help are needed (La Cour & Højlund, 2008; Luhmann, 2005b [1973]). Accordingly, the help provided by the help system differs from other forms of help. It is something other than the help given in everyday life, such as helping friends move or watching the neighbour's dog.

Moreover, organised help is different from charity because both the relation between providers and recipients and the criteria for the help given are *formalised*. The development toward the differentiation of a specific function system responsible for parts of the population (who suffer from injustice and cannot take care of themselves) goes hand in hand with the development of a professional knowledge base, professional competences, and a professional ethical code.

The function of the help system needs to be understood against the background that function systems include and exclude people (more on this in Chapter 4), which can lead to cumulative exclusion from one sphere to the next – from the labour market, from the family, and from the housing market. Cumulative exclusion is a subsequent problem (*Folgeproblem*) of functional differentiation (see Chapter 6), and the rise of the social help system can be regarded as a functional way for society to deal with this problem. The help system identifies, addresses, and strives for management of those effects that cannot be resolved by the standardised support provided by the welfare state (i.e. the political system), such as compensation for unemployment, early retirement benefit, and benefits for functionally impaired people.

The societal function of the help system can best be described as *social exclusion management* (Bommes & Scherr, 2000a, 2000b; Miller, 2001). Social exclusion management can occur in different forms: prevention, inclusion mediation, and exclusion administration, depending on the individual situation of clients. In Chapter 4, we deal in more detail with this issue (section "Social work as exclusion management"). The help system handles issues of aid and support in an organised manner, which logically implies that help is given as the outcome of *decisions*. The system needs criteria, prescribed by law, that allow determination of which of the claims raised by people in need of help are valid and which are not. Without such a rule system, the agency (and in practice, social secretaries) mediating the provision of help would be exposed to pressure to accept the demands of unentitled clients – particularly if the clients were backed up by the loyalty of their extended family. This would lead to arbitrary decisions or clientelism.

Social welfare organisations, such as municipal social services, determine whether individual claims-makers are entitled to help or not. To the extent that communication around these issues can develop towards an autonomous function system – and not be just a tool for the welfare state or the legal system – it is the system itself that defines what is a case requiring social help and what is not (Schirmer & Michailakis, 2015a). In this way, the system can focus on actually helping those in need and not just labelling them as "deviant cases". The latter was often brought forward as criticism against social work practice, not least by Habermas (1992a). However, such a criticism builds on a confusion between the function of a system (solving a particular problem for society) and its performance, i.e. the system's relation to other function systems (giving aid to other systems). While the function of exclusion management has a feedback effect on society (and its members) as a whole, the performance differs from function system to function system. The economic system, for example, needs competent and reliable people who offer their workforce in exchange for some compensation; the education system needs pupils who are able to sit still, not disturb the others in the classroom, and focus on given tasks; and the political system needs "good citizens" who do not threaten the public order. What the help system offers these function systems is to help, support, and re-socialise – in other words, to "correct" people who for one reason or another do not fit into the respective expectation schemes of the function systems (again, more on this in Chapter 4).

The difference between function systems and organisation systems

In Chapter 2 we presented the vertical differentiation between different levels of emergent orders among social systems (interaction, organisation, and society). Now we want to combine this vertical differentiation with society's horizontal differentiation in function systems. Here it is important to avoid confusing function systems and organisations, which frequently are mixed up – particularly in the media and in politics but also in research that uses its concepts sloppily.

Organisations and interactions in the context of function systems

It is crucial to distinguish function systems from organisations. Organisations operate within the context of one or more function systems. Function-related interactions can take place within or outside of organisations, but they always take place *within* the respective function system. Since this may seem hard to grasp, let us look at a number of examples. Among the most relevant organisations in the context of the political system are the state, the government, the parliament, authorities, parties, etc. Typical interactions that take place within these political organisations are, for instance, negotiations for a new law proposed by the government, or a parliamentary debate. A spontaneous rally induced by a recent event or outrage on social media are examples of social interactions outside of political organisation but within the function system (and in contrast to a demonstration that was organised by an authoritarian government).

In the context of the function system of science we can think of organisations such as the university or private research institutes but also academic publishers and journals. Scientific interactions within organisations take place at conferences or research seminars, or outside when researchers sit together in a bar discussing theory or planning the design of an experiment.

National churches are organisations in the context of religion. Examples of interactions within the church are services, baptisms, or wedding rituals. Private religious practices such as praying together are cases of religious interaction outside organisations.

Within the context of the educational system, prime examples of organisations are schools and colleges. Accordingly, lessons, seminars, and lectures are examples of organised interaction, whereas informal study groups or private tuition are educative interactions beyond organisations.

The social services, private care agencies, and homes for functionally impaired people are examples of organisations in the context of the help system. Counselling talks, control visits, or family therapy sessions are cases of organised interaction. An example of helping interactions outside organisations is voluntary workers visiting lonely older people.

In all of these examples we see how the societal function of the function system more or less determines the context for organisations and interactions. It is rather easy to tell the difference between, say, discussions in natural science and negotiation on the price of a used car. This is so not only because of the content of the interaction but also because the discussions refer to distinct function systems and their rationalities. While the former, clearly, takes place in the context of science, with reference to truth, methods, theories, etc., the latter occurs in the context of the economic system, where prices, value, money, etc. matter.

In contrast to function systems, organisations share an important property: they can act as (collective) agents. Organisations have a formalised (mostly hierarchical) structure, and this gives them a communicative address (Fuchs, 1997; Luhmann, 2013; Schirmer, 2007). In the same way that individual people can act and be held accountable for their actions, organisations can act and be held accountable for their decisions. When someone within the organisation (CEO, manager, press spokesman) can speak in the name of the organisation and communicate with other organisations, we can, (speaking simplistically), say that the organisation said or did this or that. We cannot say corresponding things about function systems or interactions. A function system can be understood as an abstract arrangement or chain of communication, a rationality, a logic that *operates*, but does *not act*. A function system cannot be held accountable; it cannot be addressed. Certainly, we can raise our voices against "the economy" that perpetuates the cleavage between rich and poor, against "science" that undermines the essence of humankind, against "religion" that incites people to hatred and intolerance, or against "education" that produces mindless abiders, but we would not succeed in finding a specific address, someone who can speak up and be held responsible for the whole function system and its function. We cannot even hold "capitalists" responsible for the way the economic system operates, as Marx was well aware.

Polyphonic organisations

There is another reason why we have to keep function systems and organisation systems apart. As has been pointed out by a number of scholars working the Luhmannian systems theory, it is not exactly clear "where" organisations actually operate (Andersen, 2003b; Kneer, 2001; Roth, 2014). When we look at the economic system (function system) we can immediately think of a number of organisations that are associated with it: banks, consulting firms, stock exchanges, venture capitalist firms, trading organisations, etc. They are associated with the economy because their main operations have to do with the influx and outflow of money. But if we take a closer look, we notice that any organisation with the essential purpose of earning money and distributing some of it to its shareholders (publicly listed companies as well as family businesses) is actually associated with the economic system. Regardless of which merchandise they produce or which services they offer, the whole organisational structure is aligned with the purpose of making profits.

Organisations such as courts, hospitals, churches, or social welfare agencies do not exist for the purpose of earning money but (can) have idealistic purposes. An obvious purpose of courts is to maintain law and order; hospitals offer healthcare; churches provide meaning and solace; social welfare agencies organise help for people in need; etc. The purposes of these organisations are subsumed to the function of "their" respective function system: law, medicine, religion, social help, etc. Nevertheless, they also need to consider their financial budget, make do with scarce resources, pay wages and social security premiums for their employees, etc. At same time, they also need to observe the law regarding employment, contracts, privacy and confidentiality, etc. Therefore, it is safe to say that communication in organisations is associated with more than one function system. An organisation can, for instance, switch quickly from economic to legal rationality, i.e. it can make decisions that make use of several criteria (economic, legal, scientific, etc.) for one and the same decision. According to systems theorist Niels Åkerstrøm Andersen (2003b), organisations are *polyphonic*, which means that they simultaneously operate with plural voices (read: functional logics). Even if a corporation mostly operates within the economic system with the main purpose of generating profit, it usually has a multitude of departments associated with the logics of other function systems (such as the legal department, the R&D department, the communications department, etc.). Similarly, a research institute mainly operates within the system of science. In their communications, researchers apply valid and reliable methods and verified theories in order to acquire new knowledge[11] but they cannot do so unless their organisation has enough financial resources and takes care of legal agreements.

In both of these examples the function-systemic rationalities are subsumed to the organisational rationalities and purposes. A corporation that conducts research with the goal of producing innovative products and gaining a competitive edge on the market does so in order to achieve its ultimate goal of maximising profit. In this regard, it is clear that organisations do not represent "their" function systems. Banks and corporations are not "the economy", a national research council is not "the science", and the Church of England is not "the religion". Sometimes organisations can even go against the rationality of "their" function system; for example there may be political parties that manipulate their member numbers in order to receive more financing, a financial rating agency that is partial (or nationalist) in its reviews, a research council that grants research projects according to political opportunity or ideological preferences, or a religious sect that uses collected donations for the personal benefit of its leaders.

Notes

1 Still today we can see a parallel to the archaic segmentary differentiation in the international political system. Nation states, despite their individual differences regarding territorial and population size, wealth, power and influence, and reputation, are similar and, *de jure*, co-equal units in the international community. This condition is formalised by political sovereignty and the right to vote in the United Nations (see Schirmer, 2007). This segmentary differentiation into nation states is not society's primary and most important differentiation but a specific characteristic of the function systems of politics, law, and, to some extent, media.
2 The name originates from the peace treaty that ended the Thirty Years' War, which entered the history books as the "Peace of Westphalia". The agreement signed in the Westphalian towns of Münster and Osnabrück forged the modern political system of independent states with the trinity of sovereignty, territoriality, and legitimacy.
3 In his well known AGIL scheme Parsons distinguished four functions that any system had to fulfil in order to survive: adaptation (A), goal attainment (G), integration (I), and latent pattern maintenance (L). Applied to the level of society, these functions correspond to the function systems of economy (A), polity (G), societal community (I), and the fiduciary system (L) (Parsons, 1951). In Habermas' theory, there are two function systems: politics/administration on the one hand, and capitalist economy, on the other hand. Together, these two make up the "system" in the pair system/lifeworld (Habermas, 1992b).
4 The positive side of rationalisation is that it enforces efficiency through introducing new action patterns built upon calculations of goals, means, secondary consequences, and values. However, Weber saw many downsides to rationalisation, such as dehumanisation, emotional coldness, or bureaucratisation, which degraded human beings to cogs in a societal machine. The driving forces for rationalisation – in Weber's romantic and pessimistic worldview – are science and technology.
5 In terms of decision-making and coordination, the centralisation in segmentary societies (with their internal hierarchies) and stratified societies (with their external hierarchies between the social strata and internal hierarchies within the upper strata) had its advantages.
6 There are other function systems, such as art, media, love and family relations, and sports, that we do not discuss here. The status of these as "function systems" is contested. See the debate by Roth and Schütz (2015), among others.
7 Laws are designed and made through a political process. Like other non-legal issues, matters of justice will be acknowledged and may have significant impacts. When it comes to application of the law in force, it is the law, but not matters of justice, that determines whether an action was legal or illegal.
8 For the changing definition of illnesses, see Foucault's brilliant study "The birth of the clinic" (Foucault, 2002 [1963]).
9 Maybe with the exception of postmodern jargon in certain academic disciplines.
10 In physics, a lever arm together with a fulcrum can multiply the mechanical force toward an object. When Archimedes calculated the length of the lever arm in relation to

the object and the support point, he shouted out "Give me a lever long enough and a fulcrum on which to place it, and I shall move the world!" In order to do this, however, he would require a fulcrum outside the world.

11 This, of course, is an ideal type description of science. Numerous works in the field of science and technology studies have shown that scientific practice in the lab can be very messy (Knorr-Cetina, 1983; Latour & Woolgar, 1979).

4

SOCIETY AND THE HUMAN BEING

On inclusion and exclusion

The concept "person"[1]

From a systems-theoretical perspective, society is decomposed into many different social systems in particular function systems. As we saw in Chapter 1, human beings, with their bodies and thoughts, feelings, and memories, are not parts of society. However, there are "parts" of human beings that do belong to social systems. In contrast to their bodies and their psychic systems, these "parts" are products of social systems because they are addressed by social systems. In figurative language, we can say that social systems "baptise", "call", or "label" these parts of the human being.[2] This is a somewhat simplified image but for now we can stick with it because it will be helpful for what comes next.

In Chapter 1 we talked about "emergence". In line with the idea of emergence, the human being consists of many different systems: chemical molecules, a complex biological organism, a neuronal system, consciousness, etc. Consciousness, i.e. the psychic system, is of particular importance because it is the only system that can come into contact with social systems. If someone insults me, I may feel this as figurative punch in my stomach or pain in my heart, but this only happens mediated through my psychic system, which processes the information of the insult – presupposing that my psychic system understood the utterance as an insult in the first place – and forwards the negative interpretation through my neuronal system into my body. To say that social systems consist of communications means that they are situated on a higher level of emergence than psychic systems (the registry of the insult) and the neuronal and organic systems (the pain in my stomach).

The theoretical manoeuvre of placing human beings outside social systems and into their environment has given rise to many misunderstandings and sharp criticism among sociologists and social workers. To "displace" the human from society is regarded as anti-humanist and for disciplines affiliated with helping professions this can come across as ridicule (Kihlström, 2012; Klassen, 2004). Social work researchers Bardmann and Hermsen (2000, p. 90) commented somewhat ironically, "This has not only been regarded as an unnecessary complication of the theoretical landscape; it has primarily been evaluated as an 'unforgivable' attack on the individuality of the human subject". A common objection from critics is that society is inconceivable without human beings. The strange thing about objections against the idea that human beings of flesh and blood are not part of society is that systems theorist Luhmann (who introduced the operative distinction between psychic and social systems) never claimed that a human society can exist without human beings. On the contrary, Luhmann (Luhmann, 1992, p. 253) argues that communication is impossible without the body and the psychic system. Yet he adds, "It is also impossible without carbon, without moderate temperatures, without the earth's magnetic field, without the atomic bonding of matter." In the same way, the human being is a prerequisite for the existence of society. However, if the human being in its totality is said not to be part of society, we have to ask in what ways people appear in (the context of) society instead.[3]

Two of these ways need mentioning here. We discussed the first, and most obvious, answer already in Chapter 1, and partly in Chapter 2: human beings participate in the context of social systems through their psychic systems. Keep in mind, though, that psychic and social systems are environments for each other. A social system cannot think; a psychic system cannot communicate. Accordingly, no transfer is possible between a psychic and a social system and vice versa, i.e. no perceptions can enter communication (Brunczel, 2010): "...one must also be aware that the systems are opaque to each other" (Luhmann, 1992, p. 258). As we have demonstrated with the examples in Chapter 1, opaqueness implies that "[o]ne can neither confirm nor refute, neither interrogate nor respond to what another has perceived. It remains locked up in consciousness and non-transparent to the system of communication as well as to every other consciousness" (Luhmann, 1992, p. 258).

The second answer to the question of the ways in which people appear in society can be approached with help of the concept *person*. In contrast to the human being as body and mind, the "person" is part of social systems. Human beings enter, or are identified, by social systems as persons. "Person" is a system's construction of a concrete human being that serves as a point of reference in communication in order to distinguish who says something and who is just passively involved (Luhmann, 2000a, p. 375). In order to operate, communication needs authors and addresses, i.e. senders and receivers of messages. Persons are the addresses that specific communications can be attributed to. This concept enables determination of who said what and allows the attribution of actions to one individual and not another. Seen from that perspective, the difference between persons (as products of communication) and their psychic systems (as a precondition for communication) becomes obvious.

The same human being can be addressed as a different person in a different setting. For example, somebody's opinion may be considered important when it comes to cars but not gender-sensitive child rearing, so he could be addressed as an expert in the first case and as a non-expert in the second. We are clearly speaking about the same human being, but a different person, contingent on the communicative context. The same human being can be addressed as different persons, for example a Wall Street investment banker whose reckless strategy brought enormous profit to his company at the cost of workers and farmers can be described as a genius, hero, lucky guy, greedy yuppie, or irresponsible servant of capital. He is the same human being, but a different person, contingent on the observing system. We can give another example: a human being who likes to drink a few beers in the pub after work can be addressed as a person with a lust for life, as somebody who likes company, as a consumer, as a sinner, as an alcohol abuser, as somebody who, due to his unhealthy lifestyle, puts strain on the healthcare system and welfare resources, etc.

In a modern, functionally differentiated society, the human being can have a number of different and mutually independent "personae": the corrupt politician, the liberal husband, the involved parent, the exemplary car-driver. Through the "person", the human being enters and is identified in different social contexts, not as the whole human being but only as a section of it. This way of conceptualising human beings in society also cuts a few Gordian knots; somebody's tax fraud does not determine how dutifully she can handle the job of cashier in an association. The understanding parent is not *per se* an understanding middle manager. With the concept of "person", systems theory solves the puzzle of how human beings can be integrated into a theory that considers communication the primary element of social systems. But this is far from an academic wordplay. As we see in the following sections, this is a more accurate and adequate account of the role of human beings in modern society. With this, the wrongful accusation against systems theory that human beings are irrelevant can be rejected.[4] It is the other way round, and in contrast to subject-oriented theories in the humanist, anthropocentric tradition of social thought, systems theory gives an account of the operative difference between social and psychic systems that does justice to the fact that both are distinct, emergent orders, and are mutually opaque environments while at the same time very relevant to each other. The concept of "person" helps us to understand the variation and contingency of how one and the same human being addresses (but also participates) differently in different social contexts.

The human being in modern society: multi-inclusion

With the vocabulary described in the previous section, systems theory can explain an observation shared by many sociologists and social workers: human beings are shaped and socialised through social processes (and hence society). Their social identity is contingent on the way social systems operate. The missing link between human beings as persons, on the one hand, and social systems, on the other hand, is *inclusion* (Schirmer & Michailakis, 2018a). The concept of inclusion refers to the empirically observable phenomenon that people are held relevant in communication (Luhmann,

2005d [1995]), i.e. they are considered as communicative addresses, as persons, as bearers of roles, as accountable actors (Nassehi, 2002).

The way persons are made relevant (and irrelevant) to communication is contingent on the structure of society. Prehistoric segmentary societies, as well as ancient and medieval stratified societies, considered human beings as included in their totality. In segmentary societies, they were full parts of segments (clans, tribes); in stratified societies, they were full parts of their strata (such as nobles, peasants, or slaves). Membership in families and clans more or less completely determined the societal place a person belonged in as well as his/her life opportunities (Braeckman, 2006; Luhmann, 2012). To be included, then, meant to be perceived as part of one, and only one, subsystem (i.e. the clan, tribe, family, or stratum). Inclusion was total because the pre-modern society's subsystems were multi-functional. Being a member in one stratum defined not only the inclusion in production but also one's rights and one's options to found a family.

The transition to a modern, functionally differentiated society has significantly changed the relationship between society and individuals. Nobody in modern society can be included in only one subsystem. Not even in a monastery can one evade inclusion in other systems (as a citizen with the right to vote, as a taxpayer, as a patient in healthcare) beyond religion. Functional differentiation implies that society is the (unity of the) difference between many incommensurable function systems, each fulfilling its own function and pursuing its own rationality that is at odds with the rationalities of other systems. Accordingly, their way of addressing human beings is fundamentally different to those of the subsystems of previous societies.

In contrast to traditional or pre-modern societies, in which affiliation with one stratum by birth largely determined the individual's status for the rest of his/her life, function systems make higher demands of people. Function systems require that human beings actively learn how to successfully participate in them. People have to ensure their "includability" (in the labour market, employability). While there are some systems, such as religion, politics, and law, that usually include people for a lifetime, modern society is characterised rather by systems that regularly include and exclude people for a certain, limited time, for example the education system, work organisations, prisons, or associations.

Another important difference between modern and pre-modern societies is that the modern human being cannot be located in one system only. The modern human being is simultaneously included in a number of systems and is dependent on this multi-inclusion to make a living. Because of the multi-inclusion, it is impossible to define a human being's social standing in an unambiguous fashion. High status in one system is not *per se* correlated with high status in another. A successful painter can be a terrible father to his children and a complete failure in economic affairs. In contrast to stratified societies, there is no hierarchy between the subsystems of modern society. The operative autonomy of function systems ensures that the successful painter cannot prevent the social services from reviewing whether he is suitable for child custody. Neither can he prevent the media from revealing a scandal in his private life or prevent the tax office from uprating the value of his net worth.

Today, individuals do not follow predetermined life courses that provide them with a stable identity and position in society (as Parsons and Erikson still assumed in the America of the 1950s; Erikson, 1950; Parsons, 1951). The modern human being is not only a civil servant or only a single mother or only an ecologically aware consumer or only a supporter of a curling team. Function systems may provide archetypes of professional carrier pathways (to become a judge in the Supreme Court, a high-ranking state officer, or a professor) but this only works within the boundaries of the respective function systems, not in the rest of society. Everyone needs to ensure access to more than just one function system. Today's life courses resemble a patchwork rather than a linear track.

Through the form "person", human beings participate in many different function systems, but only in regard to systems-specific aspects. This means that persons do not participate in function systems as a whole but as carriers of functionally relevant roles. There are two types of roles through which people can be included in function systems: *performance roles* and *layman roles* (Stichweh, 1988).[5]

On the one hand, performance roles are the roles function systems need to fulfil their societal functions and their performance for other systems. Examples of performance roles are priests in religion, entrepreneurs and traders in the economic system, ministers and representatives in politics, researchers in science, doctors in medicine, teachers in education, judges and attorneys in law, researchers in science, social workers in the system of social help, journalists in the media, etc.

On the other hand, there are layman roles, which are associated with performance roles in a complementary way. Laymen are the recipients of systems' performances, carried out by the performance roles. Examples are believers and worshippers in religion, buyers and consumers in the economy, voters, taxpayers, and citizens in politics, patients in medicine, pupils in education, convicts and witnesses in law, clients and users in social help, readers and watchers in the media, etc.

In both cases, the term "role" implies highly scripted behavioural expectation structures. However, there are obviously enough degrees of freedom in the way individuals – as persons – can carry out these role scripts. Some individuals are less successful than others and ultimately can become relevant as clients of social help, as we will demonstrate.

The shift to functional differentiation implies that inclusion in society and its subsystems is no longer determined by family membership, i.e. by class or ethnic background. In modern society, inclusion takes place through a variety of specialised systems, operating according to their specific symbolic codes and rationalities. Whether one is considered relevant as a communicative address now depends on whether one can meet the expectations the various function systems and organisations have of persons (Bommes & Scherr, 2000a). It is obvious that inclusion via performance roles requires more skills, education, and qualities than inclusion via layman roles. For example, becoming a doctor, judge, or scientist requires the successful mastery of many years of study. In contrast, layman roles such as patient, witness, or reader of science publications are, in principle, open to everyone. It is via layman roles that function systems provide a "universalism of inclusion" (Bommes & Scherr, 2000b), according to which everybody who fulfils the function's system-specific requirements is admitted to politics (citizen), law (right holder), the economy (consumer), health (patient), education (pupil), etc.

No inclusion without exclusion

Luhmann notes, "It only makes sense to speak of inclusion if there is exclusion" (Luhmann, 2005d [1995], p. 226). Human beings are excluded from society, both as organic and psychic systems. At the same time, they are included in function systems as *persons* via specific (performance and layman) roles; they receive their specific social addresses in function systems. The concept "person" refers to different aspects of individuals in relation to different social contexts. As a theoretical extreme case, an individual who does not partake in any social context is totally excluded. Homeless people are almost totally excluded from much of society but they participate in a few micro-social contexts (for example when they sell homeless magazines, when they receive food at a soup kitchen, when they are allowed to sleep in a shelter, etc.).

Function systems can only observe their own specialised image of the individual. They observe (and label) human beings in distinct ways in line with function-specific operational modes. Economic systems cannot address (include) the human being as "sinner", "criminal", or "patient". Instead the individual is addressed via an economic rationality, for instance as a utility-maximising agent that must be persuaded as consumer of products or services, and in order to qualify for this, the individual needs to have spending power. However, this economic label of "consumer" differs from the consumers in educational (student), or medical (patient) contexts. Hence, function systems do not address the whole individual but only functionally relevant aspects of the individual (Brunczel, 2010; Wirth, 2009), while disregarding, i.e. excluding, the "rest" of the individual as irrelevant to their operational mode. So students are relevant in the economic system as customers (their need for merchandise and their spending power), not their performance in college.

Inclusion in one function system (being addressed in one specific way by that system through performance or layman roles) means, then, by definition, exclusion of the "rest" of the individual at the same time. The included (addressed) aspect of the individual is relevant while the excluded (non-addressed) parts are irrelevant, as explicated by Bommes and Scherr (2000a):

> By receiving "addresses" in communication, i.e. by being addressed as children, youngsters, parents, experts, scientist, laymen, etc. and thus as persons, their relevance to an ongoing communicative event in education, science or religion is designated – and concurrently their irrelevance to other things, e.g. the children's irrelevance to science or the scientist's irrelevance to matters of creed.
>
> *(p. 77, our translation from German)*

In contrast to pre-modern societies, which include human beings comprehensively and exclusively in one *multi-functional* social system (such as a family, corporation, or monastery), inclusion in modern society takes the form of partial multi-inclusion, i.e. partial inclusion in a number of different *mono-functional* systems (Braeckman, 2006). Individuals are included specifically in social systems, in figurative terms only as "pieces", but as many different pieces in many different social contexts (comparable to Simmel's intersection of social circles; Simmel, 2009). An individual as a whole remains somewhere in the environment of the function systems, i.e. is excluded. In this regard, Luhmann speaks of "exclusion individuality" (Hillebrandt, 1999; Luhmann, 1989c). Among other things, this concept implies that individuals have to integrate a great variety of behavioural expectations (as consumers, bearers of rights, students, believers, citizens) outside society, i.e. in their minds (psychic systems). That is probably why holidays, summer houses, retreats, yoga, and meditation are appreciated by so many people.

Inclusion, exclusion, and the role of organisations

While function systems operate on the basis of universal inclusion (in principle, any individual can be included in either a performance or layman role), organisations operate on the basis of very limited, strictly defined inclusion criteria. As a rule – and in contrast to the universal inclusion of function systems – hardly anybody is included; the great majority of people are excluded from most existing organisations (Jönhill, 2012). To state this as a formula, while function systems are open to everyone, organisations restrict access and are closed to almost everyone (Nassehi, 2005). Organisations include (and exclude) people on the basis of membership (Luhmann, 2000b). They alone define the conditions of membership, which not only cover certain formal entry requirements (such as minimum age, competence, legal track record, and health condition as well as ascriptive criteria such as gender, ethnic and religious affiliation, etc.) but also behavioural expectations (being able to work independently, fulfilling defined tasks, quality of performance, etiquette, etc.). Failure to live up to the latter could jeopardise membership.

It is a matter of course that different organisations require different competences and behaviours than others depending on whether the organisation is a court, school, business, government, church, social care provider, etc. The same is true of different functional and hierarchical roles; a high-ranked manager not only needs more leadership competences than an assembly line worker but also more communicative skills and intercultural competence when representing the organisation in international trade relations.

The distinction between performance roles and layman roles is important for organisations as well. Performance roles almost always require membership (or they are marked as explicit exceptions, for example freelancers or consultants). Layman roles sometimes require membership (such as citizenship, membership in tenant associations, unions, immigrant associations, sports clubs, country clubs, matriculation in universities); if they do not imply membership, they at least require fulfilment of specific conditions (such as financial capabilities, religious confessions, adherence to dress codes).

Often these differences of inclusion levels are symbolised by spatial boundaries, such as counters in banks and public offices, or "personnel only" signs in shops and restaurants. People in performance roles sit behind the counter and have access to the backrooms (representing inside), whereas people in layman roles (customers, clients, citizens) are allowed to enter the front rooms, which represent a limited form of inclusion; excluded people are not even allowed to gain entrance (or they might attract the attention of security personnel).

It should be apparent from the preceding paragraphs that *inclusion is not to be confused with equality*. Despite the semantics of equality (Reich & Michailakis, 2005), universal inclusion does not mean *equal* inclusion (Nassehi, 2002). Especially within organisations, inclusion and inequality do not contradict each other. The difference between performance roles and layman roles already indicates structural but functional inequality. There are different gradations of inclusion via performance roles in organisations that are unequal in terms of salary, status, power, influence, and accumulated knowledge. For instance, nurses, plaintiffs, and research assistants are without a doubt performance roles in their respective systems, but are clearly of lower status than high-ranking professions. As legal sociologist Bora (2002) showed with the example of law, there are also many different gradations of layman roles in that system. Even if everybody (including children and people with severe cognitive impairments) has a basic legal capacity, not everyone is capable of being guilty or able to draw up contracts.

In this regard, inclusion is not only not the same as equality, but inclusion can even be the reason for more inequality (Brunczel, 2010; Nassehi, 2002). This is a co-product of the operational modes of the function systems. The educational system produces good and bad students (with high and low grades), and only those with good grades will be eligible for higher education; the economic system produces rich and poor people, and only those who already have property (and other financial assets) will get better interest rates and larger loans. The legal system produces model citizens and criminals, and those who already have a criminal record are likely to be convicted again. All these examples show effects of inclusion, not of exclusion. Inclusion in modern society can lead to cumulative effects of inequality, which is also indicated by an overlap between the performance role(s) an individual holds and the quality of his/her layman roles (Miller, 2001). Holders of high-ranking performance roles (chief physicians, CEOs, professors, etc.) receive a high income, have high status, and usually have a high level of education, which then enables them to take on layman roles at higher levels in terms of price, status, exclusivity, etc. The reverse is true for holders of low-ranking performance roles (such as cleaners, manual labourers, or janitors), whose inclusion via layman roles in other systems is usually also of lower quality.

Exclusion as a problem

Exclusion individuality is a type of exclusion that is not *per se* a problem; it is rather a structural requirement of modern society. This is so because function systems can only operate properly by including the relevant part (consumer for the market, pupil or student for the educational system), not by including human beings as a whole. Exclusion then refers not only to a structural precondition but to an empirical consequence of functional differentiation (Bommes & Scherr, 2000b). "Individuals" partake in social systems only as long as they are relevant in certain social situations, constructed as "persons." Beyond that, exclusion from organisations is not a problem *per se* simply because of the empirical fact that everyone is excluded from most organisations "by default" and included in only a few. The criteria for inclusion are set by the social systems themselves.

There is, however, another type of exclusion, which is commonly seen to be far more problematic. If inclusion means that people are considered relevant by social systems, exclusion means the opposite. Exclusion designates the situation where people are not considered relevant participants in communication and therefore are not given a communicative address (Luhmann, 2005d [1995]). As a result, this means that such human beings cannot benefit from the performances the function systems offer (such as education, knowledge, wealth, legal protection, medical treatment, etc.) because they are not considered interesting enough for the system (Miller, 2001) according to the selection criteria, which apply equally to everyone regardless of class, ethnicity, gender, etc. Exclusion can imply either that their entry (in performance or layman roles) into a system is not possible or that their remaining within the system is at stake. Apparently, exclusion from some function systems (e.g. the media, arts, religion, or science) is less problematic in its consequences for the individual involved than exclusion from others (e.g. the economy, politics, law, medicine, or education). In order to manage basic life, individuals in modern society need income, the right to vote, the right to defend themselves before a court, access to medical services and education, etc. (Luhmann, 2013). The key to an adequate life in modern society is inclusion not only via layman roles, thereby participating in the performances of function systems, but via (at least one) performance role(s). Assuming that individuals are rewarded via performance roles for their performances, performance roles are the way to ensure survival (Miller, 2001), not just in terms of payment but also in terms of identity, self-esteem, access to romantic partnerships, etc.

With a few exceptions in the labour market, performance roles of function systems are associated with organisations, and as noted, people need to fulfil restrictive requirements in order to be considered relevant by organisations, that is, to be included as members in their performing function. People can find themselves in precarious situations on the way to exclusion if the income from one performance role is not enough to secure economic survival, or if their qualifications or other attributes (such as racial and ethnic identity, gender, age, health, physical impairments) do not fit the official or unofficial requirements of organisations.

In contrast to function systems, organisations do not need to adhere to semantics of equality or universal inclusion. For organisations it is not a problem if an individual is not relevant enough for inclusion as long as there are many other individuals available to carry out the tasks. It is one effect of modernity that – despite the basic universalism of inclusion – not everybody is actually needed. Sociologist Bauman discusses in his book *Wasted lives* (Bauman, 2004) how ongoing modernisation creates an oversupply of people, the "superfluous" population of workless, migrants, and refugees. In the 19th century, the surplus population could emigrate to the newly discovered continents but today, living space in the world is scarce.

While function systems are structurally autonomous and thus separately select whether an individual meets the requirements for inclusion and is given a communicative address, there are so-called *cumulative effects* of exclusion. Failure to meet the requirements of social systems is often empirically interdependent. Exclusion from one system can seriously hamper the chances of inclusion in other systems. Without citizenship documents, be they domestic or foreign (exclusion from politics), someone will have difficulty getting a job in the official labour market, and therefore difficulty getting a loan, a lease for housing, medical care, etc. (Luhmann, 2013). As a result, people in such situations run the risk of becoming increasingly irrelevant and tend to fall off the radar of function systems completely. Terms such as "excluded", "homeless", and "unemployed" refer to the limited relevance of some persons to certain function systems and organisations (Bommes & Scherr, 2000a), which (paradoxically) make them highly relevant to the system of social help, that is, includable via its layman role of "client" or "user".

Social work as exclusion management

The empirical fact that social systems, especially organisations, cannot operate without excluding persons (due to limited available positions, lack of resources, mismatch of skills, etc.) stands in stark contrast to the normative expectation of universal inclusion at the level of function systems. According to its self-description, the modern welfare state is the granter and advocate of inclusion and equality within its territory. Society-wide exclusion tendencies create problems of political legitimacy and, ultimately, of social order. In order to counter this, the welfare state has a wide array of tools at its disposal (including citizenship rights, social insurance, economic compensation, pensions, and compulsory education). As is apparent in a historical and regional comparison, Western welfare policy has reduced economic poverty to a minimum, but it has not been able to eliminate the marginalisation of particular groups in many regards other than poverty. In the long run, the empirically observable tendency of increasing exclusion (long-term unemployed, ethnic minorities in "parallel societies" and "no-go areas") undermines political legitimacy and poses a threat to social order. Historically, the restitution of these groups has been one of the functions of social work.

The crucial difference between the welfare state and social work lies, according to Bommes and Scherr (2000b), in how generalised or tailored the tools of help and support are. Whereas social security programmes apply to everybody in a standardised way (mainly defined by legally determined claims to benefits), social work is a "secondary safeguard" (Scherr, 1999) that becomes active only for individual cases that fall outside the regular security mechanisms. These cases cannot be resolved by standardised measures but require specific, case-sensitive treatment by skilled, competent social workers.

Accordingly, the task of organised help by social work cannot be just "feeding" the poor, as was the case with Christian charity, but is more specifically the "*management of social exclusion*" (Scherr, 1999) in concrete cases. Exclusion management involves working on the social addresses of individuals, with the aim of improving their attractiveness to other social systems, a (re)orientation toward being includable (e.g. teaching an illiterate person to read and write, offering mediating therapies and consultation to clients). In this context, social work researcher Peter Fuchs speaks of social work as an operation to *re-organise addressability* (Fuchs, 2000).

According to Bommes and Scherr, there are three types of *exclusion management*. First, individuals whose inclusion in (some) social systems is problematic or precarious (e.g. ex-convicts on probation, undisciplined pupils, asylum seekers) receive *exclusion prevention* (Bommes & Scherr, 2000a; Miller, 2001). The second type, *inclusion mediation*, focuses on individuals who have (temporarily) lost their social addresses in some social contexts but who want to and, in principle, can be prepared for re-inclusion (e.g. cured long-term sick patients, soon-to-be released prisoners, clean ex-drug addicts). The third type refers to individuals who, for whatever reason, have no prospect of regular inclusion. For these cases, social work offers *exclusion administration* (Bommes & Scherr, 2000a; Miller, 2001), e.g. creating new forms of inclusion beyond regular societal contexts, such as special housing, special schools, psychiatric wards, and retirement homes.

The latter examples indicate that exclusion in modern society differs radically from exclusion in archaic and traditional societies. In such societies, people were included in only one system (as inhabitant of a village, as inborn in a family or clan) in their totality. Exclusion from their subsystem (by banishment after crimes against the social order, heresy, etc.) meant exclusion from society as a whole, and survival outside of society was next to impossible.

In modern society this is different because people are, normally, included in a large number of social systems, and exclusion from one does not automatically mean exclusion from another although there is the risk of cumulative effects, as mentioned previously. However, exclusion *in* modern society hardly ever means exclusion *from* society. Most exclusions are transformed into (other kinds of) inclusions. For instance, criminals are excluded from most parts of society but at the same time included in prisons, corrective educational institutions, or psychiatric wards. Instead of being excluded from society (which means having no address) they receive a very clearly defined address with a very specific role with restricted behavioural expectations.

Generalising from this particular context, we can discuss "*exclusion roles*". As roles are typical forms of inclusion, this term seems paradoxical: exclusion as a specific form of inclusion. However, this form of inclusion is different from "regular" inclusion in function systems and organisations. Alongside those already mentioned, there are other examples of exclusion roles such as those of beggar, homeless, illiterate, illegal immigrant, etc. All of these are excluded from at least one of the vital social spheres (the economy, housing, education, or the political system). In contrast to being excluded completely (as in pre-modern societies or in less developed regions), an exclusion role is not simply the product of exploitation, marginalisation, discrimination, or poverty but should instead be seen as a kind of regulatory mechanism of modern society. In most cases, this mechanism gives the person a special legal and moral status – even if this is a status one would rather avoid having. It is in the nature of the specific normative and semantic stock of social work to regard the carriers of these exclusion roles as candidates for help and support. Social work "transforms problems of inclusion/exclusion into cases of individual neediness" (Bommes & Scherr, 2000a, p. 76), depending on whether they are considered legitimate recipients of help or not (Baecker, 1994; La Cour, 2002; Luhmann, 2005b [1973]). According to Fuchs, the main communicative operation of social work is to *declare cases* (Fuchs, 2000), thereby transforming needy individuals into "clients". "Client" is the exclusion role of an individual included in the context of social work. The role of the client is in fact the layman role of social help (complementary to the performance role "social worker").

This is the very mode by which social work includes persons in its specific way of operation: by declaring cases as clients and treating them by helping. Thus, social work makes excluded individuals (who lack social addresses in other contexts) communicatively relevant by providing them with their own social address.[6] Although inclusion in the context of social work may be the better alternative compared to complete exclusion (with the risk of starvation), it should not be confused with inclusion in other function systems or organisations. Social work can manage and "restore" the addressability of its clients by mediating education, healthcare, therapy, consultation, etc. In this way, it can help its clients regain attractiveness and communicative relevance to function systems and organisations, improving their chance of inclusion. However, social work itself cannot include clients in these other systems (Wirth, 2009); this will be done by the respective systems themselves – or not.

Inclusion in social help via the layman role of "client", then, is a "substitutional inclusion" (Baecker, 1994), substituting for "regular" inclusion in function systems and organisations. Social work is successful at the very moment substitutional inclusion is no longer necessary – that is, when a client regains his/her addressability (and attractiveness) for other social systems. This has the paradoxical consequence that inclusion as a client (which itself is an exclusion role), in the case of successful intervention, is turned into "exclusion work" from social help (Fuchs, 2000). If, however, the inclusion of an individual remains substitutional, Baecker sharply concludes that "inclusion has to be seen as failed" and "the question then is only to what extent and how long society can bear failed inclusion" (Baecker, 1994, p. 103).

In our view, the insights provided by this systems-theoretical approach are highly relevant for social work. One cannot simply assume that exclusion is bad and inclusion good, or that exclusion *per se* is the problem and inclusion the solution. Sometimes inclusion itself can be the source of a client's problems and exclusion might indeed be a (partial) solution. For example, for oppressed female and homosexual members of ethnic cultures of "honour", exclusion could be the solution. Inclusion and exclusion are operations of social systems that treat human beings as relevant addresses for communication.

Systems theory can give a clear and accurate description of what social workers can (and cannot) do with their clients in terms of inclusion and exclusion. To give one example, homelessness can be the result of unsuccessful housing policy, economic recession, an overheated labour market, etc., but social services will not be able to change these social structures.[7] Instead of reforming the housing policy or labour market, social work can help homeless individuals by working on their includability. Social work becomes active when inclusion in function systems that are vital for social existence (for the economy, education, health, etc.) fails. The purpose of social work is "addressability management", i.e. to make individuals whose inclusion in function systems and organisations is at stake relevant as social addresses. Like other systems, social work has its own mode of inclusion: it deems people relevant as clients who are entitled to help and support. Systems theorists in the academic field of social work speak of substitutional inclusion because social work substitutes for clients' inclusion in other systems by temporarily including them in the context of social help. If social work successfully fulfils its tasks, clients should regain their addressability and attractiveness for function systems and organisations. However, social work cannot include human beings in any other system. Social workers need to take into account that the conditions for inclusion are system-specific, i.e. they are different for different social systems, and they may lead to different outcomes. Problematic cases of inclusion and exclusion can be analysed with regard to the involved social systems (function systems and organisations) and their specific conditions for inclusion and exclusion. Accordingly, successful interventions can be tailored to the specific constellation of system requirements and clients' preconditions.

Notes

1 Parts of this chapter are based on our article "The Luhmannian approach to exclusion/inclusion and its relevance to social work" in the *Journal of Social Work* (Schirmer & Michailakis, 2015b).
2 There are many ways to label a human being, such as the labels of employee or trader (economic label), exploited or oppressed (political label), ill (medical label), sinner or infidel (religious label). Note that we do not use the word "label" in a derogatory manner, as in labelling theory and everyday language, where the word is reserved for expressing criticism against giving people negative attributes such as when they are labelled as drug addict, illegal immigrant, criminal, beggar, etc.
3 The question arises as a consequence of society's functional differentiation. In traditional societies, such a question would have not made sense to ask because the human being was a naturally integrated part of an organic community.
4 Certainly, systems theory is non-anthropocentric insofar as the human being as a subject, actor or individual does not inhabit any central position in social systems, but it is not

anti-humanistic because it does not deny the necessity of human beings for social systems to occur in the first place.

5 Sometimes, layman roles are also called "audience roles" or "complimentary roles".

6 This address, however, brings some disadvantages to individuals who carry the label of neediness, since it stigmatises and (perhaps falsely) indicates future or even permanent neediness, dependence, etc., which communicates unattractiveness to organisations.

7 Despite some attempts on the communal level (Hutchinson Strand, 2009; Sjöberg & Turunen, 2007).

5

CONSTRUCTIONISM AND REALISM

Functional differentiation: a short recap

In Chapter 3, we described how modern society – according to sociological systems theory – is differentiated into a number of function systems: economics, politics, law, science, religion, and many more. Each one of them contributes to solving a specific societal problem (for example managing a scarcity of resources [economy]; making collectively binding decisions [politics]; stabilising contradictory expectations [law]; discovery and supply of true and reliable knowledge [science]; provision of meaning and explanations of the unexplainable [religion]; etc.). The function systems follow a unique, function-specific rationality: the rationality of the economy is profit and competition; power is the rationality of politics; legality is the rationality of law; pursuit of objectivity and truth are the rationalities of science. In contrast to stratified societies, a functionally differentiated society has no centre or apex or moral authority that can represent and bind everyone. There is no overarching rationality that transgresses every function system, and there is no common denominator that unites all of them. Instead, there is "only" a set of function systems that operate in their very own system-specific way. As we will see in Chapter 6 this condition gives rise to modern social problems.

In Chapter 4 we demonstrated the consequences that functional differentiation has for the social participation of human beings. When systems theorists speak of a human being's inclusion, they mean that she is held relevant as a social address, as a recipient of communication (mediated through social roles). The historical transition to a functionally differentiated society has also changed the way society includes people. While traditional societies included people as a whole ("total inclusion") into only one multi-functional subsystem (such as archaic tribes or a medieval estate), modern society is characterised by "function-specific multi-inclusion". This means that people today are included in many different systems.

However, each function system includes only those particular aspects ("pieces") of human beings that are relevant for that particular function system. For the economy, their spending power and market value as workforce or service providers are relevant but not their creed, political convictions, or taste in art. The function systems assign specific sets of social roles. We have distinguished performance roles (trader, politician, teacher, priest, journalist, social worker) from complementary layman roles (customer, voter, student, worshipper, reader, client). In functionally differentiated societies one and the same human being can enter different social contexts with different roles (doctor at work, parent at home, customer in the store). Different unique individuals can play the same role.

Toward a constructionism so radical that it is realist at the same time

The purpose of this chapter is to shed light on the stance that systems theory takes in the epic battle in the philosophy of science between constructionism and realism. To begin with, there is no simple answer. Many of the great epistemological issues cannot be determined once and for all because there are always good reasons for one side and as many good reasons for the other. However, those who accept this last statement can develop a much more modest attitude than can radical advocates for either side.

At the risk of incurring the wrath of dogmatic Luhmannian scholars (who regard this strand of systems theory as radically constructionist), we argue in this chapter that systems theory is realistic *and* constructionist at the same time. The point here is not so much to try to overcome the opposition between these epistemologies, like the dialectics of Hegel, Marx, and critical theory going from thesis and antithesis to synthesis. Instead we want to demonstrate that systems theory does not question the existence of the real, observer-independent world (as postmodernists like to do). Systems theory does not consider social systems as inventions of social construction processes or discourses that can be deconstructed. Luhmann explicitly assumes that systems *exist* (Luhmann, 1995). Taking this statement seriously, we can say something about the properties of systems, about their *operations*, how they interact with other systems, and how they relate to each other. In Chapters 3 and 4 we described what function systems *are*, what they *do,* and what properties they *have*. In this regard, systems theory is an ontology with a realistic cognitive interest.

At the same time, systems theory is a constructionist approach insofar as it is interested in how systems, through their factual existence and their factual operations, *are constructors* of social reality: how do systems *create* their own reality through their unique, distinct ways of operating? Every function system has its own means for making sense of the world. As mentioned earlier, function systems pursue their system-specific rationality and use their system-specific criteria for observing relevant phenomena or events in the world. The systems have their own language, a semantic stock for describing and reflecting on the world (Hagen,

2006). According to Luhmann, function systems observe the world with the help of *binary codes* that enable the reduction of the infinite complexity of the world into manageable bits. The expression "binary code" originates from computer science. "Binary" means that the code has two mutually exclusive values (such as yes/no, day/night, or 0/1). Luhmann argues that function systems utilise such binary codes in order to *generate meaning in the world*. The system of law uses the code "lawful/ unlawful": an action can be in line with the law or violate it; the code of science is "true/false": research findings or hypotheses are true or false; within medicine the code is "ill/healthy": a human being (or animal) can either be sick or free from illness and, hence, healthy.

Binary codes are the eyes with which function systems can "see", but they only see what their unique code allows them to see. To everything else, they are blind. The code "lawful/unlawful" does not make it possible to see whether something is true or false. Conversely, equipped with the code "true/false", a system cannot determine whether something is legal or illegal. In other words, in order to determine whether something is a scientific finding, scientific but not legal or political criteria are needed.[1]

Binary codes help in reducing a huge complexity to a small, relevant piece, but they do not allow for nuances. A legal system that only knows the difference between lawful and unlawful does not know when to apply the value "lawful" and when "unlawful"; it has no nuance to punish a murderer differently than someone who criticises the president or someone who forgot to replenish a parking meter. The legal system, thus, requires laws, constitutions, rules, established legal practices, etc. Likewise, the scientific system needs criteria to determine when something is true or false. This is the purpose of theories and methods: the scientific method is to follow rigorous procedures in order to generate data and evaluate hypotheses. Within a systems-theoretical context, we speak of *programmes* (another term the social sciences have imported from computer science). To give an example, the help system operates with the code "help/no help", which it applies to people, groups, or communities that need interventions through helping and supporting efforts. But how would the social services and the individual social work practitioners know who is entitled to help and who is not? Who should receive help? How much? Which interventions should be made? All of this is specified in programmes of the help system, for instance social work theories, social law, approbated intervention methods, and evidence-based manuals (such as those provided by the Cochrane Collaboration and other research institutes).

From our presentation of the concepts "code" and "programme" one might get the impression that the world is full of events, beings, and things from which function systems choose what they want to see.[2] But there is a good reason to take the opposite position. It is the function systems that generate what they see. It is from the economic system that the world appears as a big offer of merchandise, where everything can be expressed in prices. Ideas about profit maximisation or cost reduction only make sense within an economic context. Only with economic concepts and economic programmes can we get the idea of understanding the world as a market. Departing from an economic logic, not only do the exchanges of goods, services, currencies, bonds, and other financial instruments appear as markets, but everything else does as well. Hospitals, schools, care facilities are also interpreted as markets in which investments can be made, costs reduced, and profits made.

Similarly, researchers in search of new, fundable research projects consider more and more phenomena as potential research objects that can be studied, analysed, and reverse-engineered. The use of scientific concepts and theories are a peculiar way of generating meaning (compared to everyday communication); equally peculiar is the use of concepts and theories for "generating" objects that do not "exist" beyond science, such as cells, protons, energy waves, or quarks. The same can be said about concepts from the social sciences: the subconscious, Kondratieff-cycles, class, inclusion, ideal-types, *gemeinschaft*, or society. These are concepts that enable social scientists to "see the society" (Ahrne, 2014).

The boundaries between function systems, therefore, can also be understood as "boundaries of meaning" (Schneider, 2005). Function systems with the differentiated (economic, political, pedagogic, etc.) conceptual apparatuses generate and process information about events in the environment. Events, as such, have no meaning. It is the systems that determine the meaning of an event, but each system may ascribe a different meaning.

We can illustrate this thought with the example of a train accident.[3] This train crash is observed very differently from the perspective of different function systems. Note that it is only a function system's distinct criteria of relevance that appear on its radar:

- For the legal system it is a question of who is liable for the accident: have all the regulations been observed? Has the traffic controller pressed the right button in the control centre? Has the train driver had all necessary training? Was he/she healthy and sober? Would lawsuits against the railway company bear any chances of success?
- For science the accident is framed as a question of causal explanations, particularly regarding technology: was there a technical defect (in the brake system, in the signalling system, with the switch points)? Was there material fatigue?
- From the perspective of economics, the train crash is observed as a question of costs: how big is the financial damage concerning the material? What costs arise for compensation to injured passengers or passengers who missed connections? Furthermore, we may wonder whether rival companies could benefit from the situation; if the railway company is listed on the stock exchange, how will the stockholders react; what is the impact on the company's creditworthiness?
- For the system of media, the accident appears as a potential sensation that promises high newspaper runs, viewing rates, or clicks, and it offers splendid opportunities for dramatic stories about survivors and their suffering.
- The political system treats the accident as a potential question of power distribution between government and opposition. The government may be held

accountable if public authorities failed in their auditing duties, or they may have to promise new resources for making railway traffic safer. The opposition may look for anything that reeks of failure of the government, for instance having pushed privatisation or focus on cost-efficiency too far or having allowed the erosion of standards in the working conditions for train drivers or having invested too little in track maintenance.

- From the system of religion, the train incident could be interpreted as a confirmation of – and even God's punishment for – the human hubris of building bigger, faster, and more advanced technological systems.

We do not expect the reader to identify with all of these possible interpretations, but we believe this overview may persuade her/him that in a functionally differentiated society there is not just one social reality but many, and equally many (function system-specific) perspectives on them. This is what we can call *multi-perspectivity*: the train accident has *effectively and really* happened, to be sure. However, it is socially multiplied by the number of perspectives on it. The term "multiperspectivity" refers to the capacity of a phenomenon to be observed and described from different perspectives. Every observation is selective and leads to partial descriptions. It makes a big difference whether an event, a fact, or a phenomenon is described in terms of prevailing law, in terms of truth, or in terms of payments, profits, and costs. The observed phenomenon receives its specific meaning through the observing (and thereby constructing) systems. Moreover, there is no reasonable way – either in advance or in retrospect – to determine whether a legal, scientific, political, religious, economic, medical, or other systemic perspective is the best one for capturing a certain event, such as the train accident. In other words, a functionally differentiated society lacks a unifying perspective or a perspective that has priority over any other. Moreover, a function system cannot legitimately claim to prescribe or dictate its views and definition of a situation without undermining the autonomy of other function systems, for instance when university departments are evaluated by profits and losses instead of the quality of their research or social help services for women in theocratic cultures are forced to submit their emancipatory programmes to the rule of writings of holy prophets. To be sure, there are situations and contexts in which certain perspectives are more decisive than others. If, for example, the health of a CEO in a meeting is in acute danger, the medical perspective will be more relevant and will receive priority over economic or legal perspectives.

Systems as observers

As mentioned in the introduction chapter, there is a diversity of strands in systems theory all across the social sciences and humanities (within sociology, social work, psychology, political science, literature, etc.) and not all of them agree on their epistemological stance; some of them adhere to realism, others to constructivism. As we also mentioned in the introduction, our aim with this book is not to compare commonalities and differences between various systems theories. Instead, we have chosen to focus on distinct characteristics of systems theory that are relevant to social work and other helping professions and that we can find in the works of the Palo Alto Group in psychotherapy and in sociological systems theory as developed by Luhmann and his disciples.

In this chapter, we argue that these variants of systems theory are simultaneously constructionist and realist.[4] Multiperspectivity is an expression of constructionism insofar as it takes function systems seriously as *observers*. At the same time, however, multiperspectivity is an expression of realism insofar as it assumes that there *are* a multitude of such observers that each create their own reality, as we demonstrated with the example of the train accident. Paraphrasing the words of materialist philosopher Bryant (2011), the train accident happened objectively, as a material fact with material consequences, independent of whether we notice it or have a concept for it or not. In that regard, the function systems observing this accident do not make it up; however, their description of it, their reactions, their sense-making all are *constructions*.

Functional differentiation means multiperspectivity on the level of society. As mentioned in the previous section, there is no single function system perspective that stands above the others, nor is there any overarching perspective outside of function systems that comprises all the others. There is no *gesamtgesellschaftliche* unitary perspective, from which anything and everything could be observed and described, like an Archimedean fulcrum.

This latter statement is both realist and constructionist insofar as it says something about factual conditions (how systems *are*, how society *is*) and about constructions from a certain perspective, namely science.[5] Whether "factual" conditions are really factual or are "just" constructions from an observer's perspective is a question that has been debated in philosophy since its beginnings. Taken separately, constructionism and realism are coherent, consistent systems of thought. That is exactly why the question "Which of these systems of thought is right?" is impossible to answer.

Every perspective, just like every theory (even of the postmodern kind) must assume that its observations and statements have a certain anchoring in an objective reality even if this very reality cannot be accessed directly, only mediated by the mind, by language, through socialisation, by theories and knowledge. Systems theory argues that every system is an observer, and what (and how) it sees depends on the history, structure, and observational code of this system. Conversely, the system cannot see anything that its structure and code do not allow. To give one example from human physiology, we human beings cannot perceive radio-active radiation, ultraviolet or infrared light, or sound with pitch frequencies above 20000 Hz. Equipped with some technical devices we can measure them and translate the signals into something we can perceive with our biophysical setups. For example we can perceive radioactivity translated by a Geiger counter into short clicking sounds; we can perceive high frequency lights or sounds translated into visible wavelengths through an oscilloscope. However, the click noise *is not* the radioactivity, and *neither is* the waveform on the oscilloscope the light or sound. Instead they *are* translations (also on the meaning of Actor-Network-Theory, see Callon, 1986), and they *are* constructions of reality, but such constructions that we can process with our bodily, systemic prerequisites and limitations.

The same principle applies to social systems. A telephone call from the boss, an SMS from a friend, and an advertisement on Facebook are social communications that cannot happen without material infrastructure (telephone line, smartphone, internet), but these technical objects are not the communication itself; in the same way the psychic system is not the brain activity of the neuronal system. Saying that something is constructed does not mean that the construction is arbitrary or random. Certainly, constructions are contingent – remember this term introduced in Chapter 1, which expresses that things, observations, and constructions can assume other ontological states than are actualised (whether the train accident is constructed as an economic, legal, or scientific–technical question). Contingent does not mean arbitrary, insofar as the characteristics of a system (its code and programmes) determine what the system sees. Every perspective from which we, through systems, see the world is partial and conditional (Hayles, 1984).

The descriptions a social system brings about follow the perspective of a certain function system with its distinct rationality, values, and norms that are not shared by other systems. Compare the values and norms of the help system with those of the economic and religious systems. There is no measure of objectivity outside the respective system, which explains why the help system can observe, describe, or construct social relations as negative and in need of repair because this is the way these relations appear from the help system's viewpoint, but not necessarily from another system's viewpoint. An economic crisis such as the Great Recession of 2008 (Mann, 2013) does not immediately lead to problems in the legal, religious, or political systems. What appears as a problem for one system (for example unemployment for politics) can even be a solution for another (the economy).

The constructionism of systems theory comes to the fore in research questions that concern the relation between narrator and narrative, between describer and description, between observer and observation. However, systems theory does not ask questions regarding the relation between observer and reality because this reality is accessible only through observations by a specific observer. And this prevents us from distinguishing sharply between the narrator and the narrative. The narrator is inevitably part of the narrative. Despite all its methods and observational tools, science has no access to reality, but only generates descriptions of reality. These descriptions have been made by someone (some system) and the best way to scrutinise them is by scrutinising how the observer has brought them about: "[a]nything said is said by an observer." According to cyberneticist Heinz von Foerster (Von Foerster, 1995), this statement originates from the Chilean biologist Humberto Maturana (whose work had a big influence on Luhmann).

If everything that is said or written is indeed said or written *by an observer* we have to examine the conditions of how this observer has brought about these particular descriptions: we have to observe how he/she/it observes.[6] More specifically the observation of observers entails a specification of the distinctions an observer has used.[7]

For a naïve realism, upon which much traditional positivist social science is built, the separation between observer and observed (between observing subject and observed object) is not only unproblematic, it is deemed necessary in order gain reliable knowledge. In a positivist philosophy of science, the (subjective) observer is seen as a problem to be eliminated (La Cour & Philippopoulos-Mihalopoulos, 2013; Victor, Scambler, & Bond, 2009) because it stands in the way of an objective description of the world; it is a source of bias in the knowledge process. By contrast, for systems theorists (and constructionists in general) the focus on the observer is crucial and the idea of an objective description of the objective world is a fiction because it takes cognition out of the equation and "the observer is reduced to a copying machine with the notion of responsibility successfully juggled away" (Von Foerster, 1995, p. 7).

To be sure, this book is about social science, but we can point out the interesting fact that the role of the observer has been recognised in the formerly positivist natural sciences by early 20th century quantum physicists such as Niels Bohr and Werner von Heisenberg. Bohr speaks of the "observer-effect", in which particles behave differently when observed. Heisenberg noted that "the observer affects the observed" and "[w]hat we observe is not nature itself but nature exposed to our method of questioning" (Heisenberg, 2000, p. 26). Apparently, there is no way to study a phenomenon without interacting with it, and no way to interact with it without disturbing or affecting its behaviour because it is impossible to free the aim of our description from the description itself, and thereby, the researcher from the observer.

Realism and constructionism: realities of the first and second orders

Despite the strong emphasis on the observer, the strand of systems theory we present in this book is not only constructionist. As the biologists Maturana and Varela (1987) have demonstrated, systems theory requires living systems and physical conditions with the right amount of oxygen in the air, adequate temperatures, sufficient nutriments, etc. Furthermore, systems theory (as communication) requires that the grey matter of the brain, with synapses, blood circulation, or metabolism operate according to biological laws and that the psychic systems process thoughts and perceptions in a way that does not require psychiatric treatment. Without nature, in which the human being with her biological body is part of everything that is organic or inorganic, there would not *be* any communication, hence no economic, political, or scientific systems, and no society, and we would not have to talk about observations and constructions at all. We would not *be* there either. And the denial of all this could not even be understood as the foolishness it is.[8]

How do we know that all these systems on lower levels of emergence exist? We know this thanks to communication (society) and our psychic systems, and all of these are "only" observers and thereby constructors of reality bound by their perspectives and cognitive constraints. Unfortunately (or fortunately?) there is no way out.

Philosophies of science do not differ in their answers to the question of what the foundation of cognition and thought is. The answer cannot be proven objectively because the selected answer is contingent on the epistemological frame, which in return will deliver a set of concepts that will determine the answer and its justification. Philosophies of science cannot deliver a foundation for our epistemological pre-assumptions (axioms) – we are caught in a self-referential loop! What we can do in the best case is evaluate the consequences certain axioms entail, i.e. how far do we get with this or that axiom, which questions can we answer, and which questions will remain unanswered? Once we, consciously or not, assume a certain axiomatic position, we have laid the foundation of our system of thought, which determines our answer, but also the questions we can ask in the first place.

There is one formative distinction that we consider very helpful because it makes sense in several epistemological systems of thought. It was introduced by Paul Watzlawick, the psychiatrist from the Palo Alto Group we encountered in Chapter 1. He proposes distinguishing between realities of the first and second orders (Watzlawick, 1984). Somewhat simplified, we can call the first order the world of facts, and the second order the world of meanings. The first-order reality refers to the physical characteristics and qualities of a thing, event, or situation that can be measured or calculated without interpretation. Examples are temperatures, sound, the number of people in a given social situation, the number of people infected by a virus, the percentage of votes a political party gained in an election, or the result of a football game. Second-order realities are created whenever we *attribute meaning to first-order reality*. Objectively measurable temperatures can be comfortable or uncomfortable, just right or too warm or too cold; objectively measurable sound can appear musical or noisy; objectively countable people in a given social situation can be relevant conversation partners or physically co-present but socially irrelevant bystanders; the objectively measurable and countable number of infected people can be interpreted as a neglectable hygienic problem or as an epidemic; the percentage of votes a political party gained can be interpreted as the voters' expression of discontent or as an expression of a vivid democracy; the victory of the winning football team can be interpreted as undeserved and lucky.

All of these are examples of second-order realities that occur on top of the first-order reality. The same is true of the train example earlier in this chapter. Factually, the train has derailed and crashed, and all of this can be noted without interpretation. The interpretation, the attribution of meaning – "the social construction of the train accident" – begins when the first-order reality comes into contact with economic, legal, political, medical, and other rationalities and criteria of relevance. To call the train accident a "catastrophe" or a "tragedy" is already an interpretation, and, thus, a second-order reality. In social reality, we mostly move in the world of meanings. Observations are frequently connected to values, rationalities, social norms, overarching patterns of interpretation, ideologies, or *Weltanschauungen* (world views).

A systems-theoretical approach that gives space for both constructionism and realism does not claim that the world is a product of our own imagination. It does not deny but presupposes an objective reality. However, to explain how an observer observes, how he/she/it creates the second-order reality on the basis of first-order realities, systems theory does not need an image of the objective, outer world of first-order reality. While things happen (first-order reality), their meanings are not immanent to the objective world. What we need to explain, thus, is how these meanings are constructed, while we need to avoid explaining away first-order realities. What also needs to be explained is how and why different observers describe first-order realities differently, as in the train example.

In analogy to particles in quantum physics that behave differently when observed, the observations made by social systems affect the factual first-order reality. There is, for example, no necessity for a society to have an economic system of the phenotype "capitalist market economy". The market economy is a historically new (only a few centuries old) type of economic system, but as Weber (2009 [1904]) has shown, it imposes on its agents (from individuals to small businesses to multinational corporations) certain, rather unnatural, behavioural forms such as the exploitation of natural, human, and financial resources. Capitalism is contingent, not cast in stone; it is a system built upon a certain ideology (Achterhuis, 2010) but it has real consequences in first-order reality, outside society, beyond any social construction, by causing environmental pollution, human attrition, work-related illnesses such as stress, burnout, etc. A radical (and fussy) constructionist may object that all of these are social constructions (for example by the medical system). We agree: they are. However, they are *simultaneously* biological and physiological effects, beyond society, that *really* happen. Remember the example from Chapter 1: if I feel bad and tell you about it you will not feel my pain; you can only imagine how I feel, while the medical system has a number of routines for sorting symptoms and making diagnoses (Michailakis & Schirmer, 2010) in order to establish an objective basis for my pains.

Whatever we say about reality, we cannot communicate about it from a position outside society. This is not a mere artefact of a framework defining society as the unity of any communication. It goes deeper than this. We always have to use language (verbal or non-verbal) in order to communicate about something, and some ways of observing are already ingrained into the syntax and grammar of the language. Thus, every observation that is communicated, for instance the description of an event, refers back to society. The observer always participates in what he/she/it observes, and any utterance refers back to the observer. When human beings with their senses and their minds observe events in society, this happens, technically speaking, outside society and, thus, is an outside observation because psychic and social systems are operationally closed, distinct types of systems. The psychic system can observe its social environment, society, from outside: we can think many things about society and the persons in it. But when our thoughts (observations in the psychic system) are communicated they enter the realm of social relations and society (with all its pitfalls; remember the two coffee examples from Chapter 1). Thus, their observations become part of society and subject to the rationalities of social systems.

Causality from a systems-theoretical perspective I: circularity

We believe that the helping professions can benefit from a theory that incorporates the observer (for instance the therapist, social worker, researcher, etc.). Properties of social relations that welfare officers, social secretaries, or field assistants "detect" are properties that an observer attributes to the observed, not properties immanent and to be detected within the described. This becomes obvious when professionals give explanations for social relations. The causes they claim to have detected are actually their own causal attributions, and, hence, relative to the observer. This means that the causes behind social issues are what an observer (for instance, the social worker) in a particular situation *regards as* causes according to her/his perspective, underlying assumptions, and theories, her/his selections of which aspects of a multifaceted and ambiguous phenomenon are deemed important to highlight.

The claim that causes are relative to an observer's perspective is not immediately combinable with the folk concept of causality. Everything has a cause, for example the cause of the light turning on is that somebody pressed the switch (or entered the room, if a motion sensor is connected to the lighting). How could this cause be relative to an observer? It is the same with effects: the room is lit because somebody pushed the light switch. Again, we can ask: how could this insight be observer-dependent? Isn't the causal relation (cause-effect) obvious?

Much of traditional science builds upon the Cartesian assumption that truth and cognition use the same approach to causality: if we want to explain a certain phenomenon we have to examine its causes. A science that works with this approach to causality admits that there is frequently a combination of causes (for instance when somebody who has been diagnosed with lung cancer is a smoker; however, he may also have lived in a street with a high concentration of fine dust, worked in a chemical plant, etc.). Moreover, different factors interact with each other, and in that way generate or amplify some effects (for instance a person who feels discriminated against in a threefold way because he is an immigrant, homosexual, and short) or they neutralise each other (for example the mediocre school performance of a pupil who comes from an upper-middle class family but has attention deficit hyperactivity disorder [ADHD], which increases the complexity insofar as the linear cause-effect chain has to be amended with more advanced methods of data analysis [multivariate regression, multilevel analysis, and others]). However, advocates of this approach agree – in accordance with a realistic understanding of science – that we only have to "find", "detect", "uncover" the real causal relations and then the puzzle is solved, and if we are not there yet, this is because our methods or our data were not good enough yet.

Aristotle was the first to formulate a rigorous concept of causality. He called the type of causality just described *causa efficiens*,[9] which aims at catching the effect that something has on something else (like the light switch on the light). If we use the expression "because of", we apply the efficient cause. The cause precedes the effect. This concept of causality has had the most impact on classic physics, and much later on the folk concept and social sciences. According to this model, the communicative behaviour of one person (cause: a friendly greeting), causes a behaviour of the other person (effect: return the greeting). In another of Aristotle's four types of causality, the *causa finalis*, the causal relation is equally linear but works in the other direction, from the end. My present behaviour is the effect of an expected goal in the future: because I want to become rich in the future, I need to work hard now. I read a book about social work methods (cause) because I want to pass the exam for my social work licence (goal). The logic of preventive social work follows this "final" causality.

According to this pattern, every behaviour has a cause, be it in the past or future, and it can be mapped in a chain of events. Explaining a phenomenon, hence, means to identify a causal relation among the parts that are involved in the chain of events or in the behaviour to be explained. In the field of psychology, we can recognise this line of thought in the theory of behaviourism, which explains behaviour as response to a stimulus. Other examples of this type of explanation can be found in medicine, where bacterial infections are treated by fighting the cause of the infection (bacteria) with the help of antibiotics.

Linear causality rests on the assumption that we can isolate the causes from the effects, whether the causes are situated in the past or future. Without assuming the possibility of unequivocally isolating causes from their effects, and thereby ascertaining which causes lead to which specific effects, the whole model of linear causal explanations collapses. In the trivial examples of the light switch, cause and effect can be isolated without getting observers involved. This is not the case for the behaviour of non-trivial complex systems.

Cyberneticists, who had a big influence on the systemic perspectives in psychology and social sciences, questioned the appropriateness of linear causal models for explaining the behaviour of complex systems. In their study of systems they have found that causality sometimes works in a circular manner, for example when A causes B, which causes C, which causes D, which, in turn, causes A. We dealt with circular causality in Chapter 1, when we discussed some pathological situations that can arise within communication systems even if none of the participants wanted them to happen.

Circular causality is a reciprocal causal relation in which the behaviour of one person in a social system triggers and stimulates the behaviour of other persons, which results in specific, unique dynamics in the system. Circularity, thus, is one of the central concepts in systemic therapy. The relations between family members or between teachers and pupils in the classroom form a system in which the behaviour of every participant is both cause and effect at the same time. The interacting individuals form a circular relation. To give an example, a pupil comes late to a lecture – like many times before – which irritates the teacher because the latecomer disturbs the lesson. The teacher's irritation provokes the pupil, who already dislikes the teacher. Therefore, the pupil starts talking to his classmate and plays with his mobile, to which the teacher responds by raising her voice. Another example is the relationship between a social worker and his client, who both observe each other and who are both aware that they are observed by the other. This forces them to watch what they say and how it comes across: they affect each other through the mere fact that they observe each other.

More generally, we can observe a circular relation in any system between actions and reactions of the involved individuals. One action causes a reaction which in turn causes another action. Family therapy was one of the first areas within the social sciences to highlight and therapeutically use circular causality in dysfunctional family relations. In particular, the so-called Milano school of family therapy, around Mara Selvini-Palazzoli (for instance, Selvini-Palazzoli, Boscolo, Cecchin, & Prata, 1994), which was influenced strongly by the Palo Alto Group and cybernetics, has proposed non-traditional ways to change dysfunctional patterns. When trying to understand a certain pattern in the communicative structure of a family, their focus is not on *why* the behaviour of a family member has led to a certain effect (the counter-reaction of another member) but on *how* the family members cooperate with each other and thereby generate a pattern in which cause and effect intermingle. The behaviour of the members of a system functions like a feedback loop with potentially destructive escalation effects (Blom & Van Dijk, 1999).

When a model of linear causality searches for the cause of the pathological behaviour of one family member (the symptom) in the latter's (potentially disturbed) personality, preferences, and interests, a systemic approach would search for circular causalities in which the pathological behaviour is the expression of a pathological interaction with other members on a system level. In order to understand a relation, we cannot study individual behaviour separated from the system and the other members, but the cycle of interactions between the members – think of the example between a teacher and a pupil in this chapter, or the examples of the married couple and the mother of a schizophrenic child in Chapter 1. By focusing on circular causality a systemic perspective allows for the insight that individuals should be studied as parts of a whole (system), and researchers, practitioners, and therapists should focus on the (circular) relations between the individual behaviours that, together, form the system.

Causality from a systems-theoretical perspective II: causality as construction

What we have described in the preceding section – linear and circular causality – are both situated on the realist level. So far, we have not brought the observer into the equation. The overarching topic of this chapter is to show the extent to which systems theory is a realist and constructionist theory at the same time. Systems theory embraces the notion of causal relations existing "out there", in the world as such, and this notion can be summarised with the formula "systems operate according to circular causality" (remember the difference between trivial and non-trivial machines).

At the same time, systems theory reserves a special role for the observer when it is about causality. Systems theory cannot *determine* whether causality is a condition in the world because systems theory is also (just) an observer. We can assume that it is, but we have, as mentioned earlier, no direct access to reality, to the world, and this is independent from methods and theory. This applies to positivism, too, although positivism is less reflective about it. With reference to Watzlawick's distinction between first- and second-order realities, we assume that there are objective causal relations "out there" – otherwise there would not be any life; we noted that in the previous section. In the social world, however, we are almost always on the level of second-order reality, on the level of observations through language-based understanding, understanding through images, music, or gestures, descriptions, and interpretations within a certain culture, with a certain ideology or system of thought and belief.[10]

Once we accept that causality (also) takes place on the level of second-order realities, it follows that causality is a scheme of meaning, and thus the construction of an observer. If we treat something that happened as an effect, the obvious step is to search for possible causes: the train accident is the effect, but what caused it? By contrast, if we identify an event as a cause, the obvious step is to look for potential effects. According to the constructionists Bateson (1972), von Foerster (1984), and Watzlawick (1984), causality is a scheme whose function is to generate coherence between events or actions. Without a scheme of causality at our disposal to achieve order in our observations, we could not execute most of what we do in everyday life. Toddlers learn to understand how things, events, and actions relate to each other (grab a thing and throw it, so it falls and makes a noise; cry and wait until someone comes to help; play around with chalk and see how a drawing emerges).

The construction of causal links is a way to create order in a complex world. Assuming that causal links represent or mirror the real world can lead to simplified explanations, and as a result, mislead intervention measures. Imagine the following, not-too-quixotic example of a political party that claims that uncontrolled immigration is to blame for economic and cultural decline (the causal construction behind such an ideology is something like this: if there were less immigration, there would be less unemployment, more social order, less crime, etc.) or that leaving the European Union would increase the welfare and well-being of the country. Parties of a different *couleur* may claim that equality is one of society's normative pillars and therefore the search for biological causes behind gender differences, ethnicity, and physical abilities should not be supported. Then there are research studies that confirm or question the validity of such causal claims and replace them with their own. What we get from all of this is a large amount of more or less contradictory causal constructions and we do not know who is right and who is wrong. We only know that, logically, not everybody can be right at the same time. And ultimately a diversity of social criteria determines the outcome of the contest between which observers and descriptions within and outside the system of science we rely on, like, or are forced to believe in order not to be declared crazy or evil. Once again, we have to deal with second-order realities instead of first-order realities. Can we, for example, question man-made climate change without facing social sanctions? Could someone a few centuries ago question whether the earth was flat and the sun was hanging somewhere on the firmament without facing social sanctions? Could we less than a hundred years ago question that non-white people were inferior and of less worth than whites without facing social sanctions? Could we less than 50 years ago question that homosexuality was an illness and/or morally condemnable without facing social sanctions?

Most of these examples relied on contemporary facts from "exact" natural sciences that, certainly, have since been revised totally. However, we think this justifies asking for the observer behind causal descriptions. Von Foerster claims that causal links are constructed by observers, and thus the link refers back to the observer. The observed causal link mirrors the observer's interests, goals, underlying assumptions, and theories, regardless of whether these are conscious or not (Von Foerster, 1995).

From the theory of society of functional differentiation (Chapters 3–5) we know that different systems (and thus observers) observe differently, and there is no reason to assume that this is not the case regarding the issue of causality. Not surprisingly, this pattern also occurs within psychic systems. The social-psychological attribution research (Försterling, 2001) has shown that different observers describe the causes and effects of a certain phenomenon in opposite causalities contingent on their own position. The classic example is the attribution of performance at school (Weiner, 1974). If pupils in an exam perform better than average, the teachers tend to attribute this to their own pedagogical skills while the pupils attribute it instead to their tenacious study efforts. If, by contrast, the result is weaker than average, the teachers tend to attribute this to the lack of learning abilities and poor efforts of pupils while the latter tend to blame the teacher's sub-par teaching skills.

From these findings of attribution research we can generalise that causal explanations reduce complexity by selecting from all possible causes and all possible effects those that appear most appropriate or most convenient (Michailakis & Schirmer, 2015). In the context of circular causality, in Chapter 1 we presented Watzlawick's example of the married couple, in which the husband withdraws while the wife frequently nags. The cause of these actions on the level of first-order reality is circular: the wife does something (nag) *because* the husband does something (withdraw) *because* the wife does something (nag), etc. Each of their behaviour *is* an effect of the other's preceding behaviour. However, this example can also be interpreted from a constructionist perspective on causality. In accordance with attribution theory, we can regard wife and husband as observers who each construct their own version of the causal relation between them. For the wife the situation appears as if the husband acts by choosing to withdraw and not engage in conversation with her. Her nagging is an action, but for her this action appears as necessary, induced, and, hence, is not a free choice: if he did not withdraw she would not have to complain. If he in turn withdraws even further, she does not experience this as his behaviour being induced by hers but as his (more or less conscious) choice, which in turn forces her to complain. From his perspective, the situation is similar but inverse. He feels forced to withdraw because she chooses to complain. Our description of the example looks similar to that in Chapter 1, albeit with a small but important difference. Here we focus on the *attribution of agency*, i.e. the question of who is the agent and who the patient in a certain situation. In both examples, the school and the married couple, the protagonists attribute agency (and thereby causality) in diametrically opposed ways.

Agency has become a very important concept in social science for explaining social phenomena. This is particularly true for approaches that draw on methodological individualism and that take the individual as a point of departure for their causal explanations. For instance, micro-economy (Udéhn, 2001) and rational choice theory (Coleman, 1994; Hechter, 1986) assume that individuals aim at maximising their own utility. Individuals are said to have a personal hierarchy of preferences from which they prioritise possible actions over others by estimating benefits and costs. Since everyone does that, certain social structures emerge, which in turn create positive or negative incentives for selecting future actions. Such radically agent-based approaches form one end of a continuum of opposed standpoints. At the other end are the structuralists (Lévi-Strauss, 1963; Piaget, 1971), who regard the individual as a result of social, psychological, and biological structures of all kinds (classes, culture, sex, genes, mental state).[11] Expressed more clearly, the action of an individual is the result of the structural situation in which she finds herself. It is society that assigns her a certain position and status, from which it is (more or less) determined what she is able to perform, what she regards as a worthy goal to strive for, which career paths she could appropriately pursue, etc.

The traditional political worldviews of right-wing/conservative and left-wing/liberal are divided by this line, too (Haidt, 2012): do people have their own agency or are they victims of social circumstances? Do people forge their own destiny (as the libertarian and the American dream promise) and can we achieve anything if only we work hard enough for it? Or are there social conditions and power structures that block our progress every time we put extra effort into our work and keep on fighting until we bump our heads against the glass ceiling, while certain privileged people get everything (and even more) for free? The question of agency has been pursued in philosophy, religion, and almost every theory in social sciences without being resolved – just as in the question of realism vs constructionism.

Here we want to state that we deal with causal attribution, not incontestable facts, in both camps. Having agency or being a victim are prime examples of causal attribution in the social world. In an influential article, the sociologist Stephan Fuchs (2001b) suggested abolishing "agency" as a category for sociology altogether, but not because we are not agents – which we are to a certain degree, and which not even hard-core structuralists would doubt.[12] Fuchs' point is another one. For him as a constructionist the more interesting question is when, under what conditions, any event or phenomenon is the result of agency, and when not. Phenomena such as motivation and attitude are constructions aimed at explaining behaviour (Reich & Michailakis, 2005). People who interpret the behaviour of other people tend to assume the latter's agency to be an objective fact, but it actually is a contingent attribution.

We claim that a constructionist approach has its merits for resolving the questions of causality and agency. Causal attribution and the attribution of agency become relevant when we are confronted with something unexpected, strange, or unknown. Causal schemes presuppose that every cause, in turn, has its own cause (more precisely, an infinite number of causes and side causes); likewise, every effect creates new effects and an infinite chain of side effects. It is the decision of an observer to break this infinite network and select (a limited number of) causes that create (a limited number of) effects: observers punctuate (like the couple in Watzlawick's example).

Attribution of agency is a recurring problem that helping professions have to struggle with. For example, in order to evaluate which measure to take a social secretary needs to assess the extent to which the client himself is responsible for his own problems. Was it alcoholism that made him beat his children? Was it unemployment that made become alcoholic? Was it the economic recession that made him lose his job? Was it his low formal education that allowed him only to apply for jobs that are easily automated or moved to low-wage countries? Was it the educational policy that did not support people in striving for better education? We could continue this chain of questions that touch possible causes of causes *ad infinitum*. We can wonder what "agency" the client had at certain moments before he ended up in the current situation, i.e. would the client have chosen to finish his degree, put more effort into his work, refrained from drinking before he became addicted, and sought social help before the family situation escalated?

We do not know, but we believe that neither those who have to evaluate the client nor he himself or his relatives can know. Like any observer, the social secretary is forced to cut the causal chain at some point and introduce the agency of the client at some point. Otherwise, she would never come to a decision. As we argued in Chapter 2, organisations (for which social secretaries work) need to make decisions. Every observation of causality, hence, involves a selection of certain causes and effects from a principally infinite number of possibilities. The very selection is an action executed by an observer, and we can assume that, dependent on the observer's affiliation to a certain system (function system and/or organisation system), the selections vary. We return to this issue in Chapter 6, when we discuss the constructionist approach to social problems.

Another example of contingent attribution of agency is from a field in which we have conducted our own research, namely responsibility in healthcare (Michailakis & Schirmer, 2010, 2012; Schirmer & Michailakis, 2011, 2012, 2014). The question here is about whether people should be held responsible for their illness and injuries when healthcare resources are scarce. The responsibility principle holds that under the condition of a restricted budget doctors should set priorities among patients: those who can be held responsible for their illness should end up further down on the waiting list than those who cannot be held responsible. Obviously, the focus is not on hereditary diseases but on so-called self-inflicted illnesses and injuries that can be associated with certain lifestyles.

Let us assume that science has proven a watertight causal link between smoking and increased risk of lung cancer, or that studies show overwhelming evidence for an increased risk of cardiovascular diseases due to regular intake of meals with high fat and sugar concentrations. Now if a patient suffers from lung cancer that needs treatment, and it turns out she is chain-smoker, the responsibility principle could be relevant. The same is true when somebody with bad eating habits (bad from a medical perspective, that is), who likes to sit at home on the couch, and who takes the car for any errand gets serious heart problems.

Advocates of the responsibility principle refer to appropriateness and fairness: those who do not "take care of themselves" should receive lower priority compared to those who take good care of themselves but get the same illness.[13] Moral philosophers and health ethicists have come up with a number of suggestions for how to solve this problem. One of those philosophical schools is *luck egalitarianism* (Cappelen & Norheim, 2005), which states that people should be treated equally as long as they are "victims" of their illness without being at fault, for instance when they get lung cancer despite having never smoked. It is, therefore, a question of good luck or bad luck if one gets ill. If, however, the illness is caused by the patient's own actions (in contrast to misfortune), for instance by smoking, she is no more treated as an equal (among other lung cancer patients). This stance has been criticised from many directions (Crawford, 1977; Wikler, 1987, 2002) because of the impossibility of ascertaining responsibility (and agency) in the first place.

The attribution of responsibility presupposes the attribution of agency, i.e. choice. As was the case in our example with the alcohol abuser, we may wonder when smoking is a choice in the first place. Maybe the patient grew up in an environment in which everybody smoked all the time and non-smokers were treated as outsiders. Is smoking an act of choice or compulsion by peer pressure? What if the patient became addicted to nicotine before unequivocal research findings and anti-smoking campaigns started informing about the health risks? It is easy to say that lifestyle is a choice, and therefore one should be held accountable for one's lifestyle-related health issues (like bungee jumpers and extreme skiers who have to take responsibility for their increased risks of injury through paying higher insurance premiums). There are good reasons to argue that the freedom of choice is not as expansive as we may intuitively think it is (Minkler, 1999). The advantage of a constructionist approach to causality, and agency in particular, is that we get an understanding of when, under which conditions, by whom, and by which system an individual, group, organisation, or other social system is attributed agency and with what consequences. In contrast to conventional approaches to causality and agency, constructionist approaches are sensitive to the variability of causality and agency in social processes.

Application case: teachers in a "blackboard jungle"

In the remainder of this chapter, we present an example of burnout among teachers working at schools in problematic urban settings. Named after a novel by Evan Hunter that was filmed in 1955, the expression "blackboard jungle" refers to problems at inter-racial schools in inner cities. This example was published in one of our previous articles in a Swedish journal (Michailakis & Schirmer, 2015).

Many teachers have been diagnosed with burnout. Interdisciplinary research has suggested many different causal explanations for teachers' burnout on many levels, such as the individual level, the level of social interaction, or the organisation or society level. Such explanations can be based on anything from cultural to religious differences between pupils and teachers, pupils' socio-economic background (unemployed parents, negative attitudes in the family toward the dominant white or Western culture), pupils' psychological state (ADHD, traumatic experiences, domestic violence), managerial problems in the school, benchmarking pressure on formerly merited and respected teachers, constantly changing curricula with short implementation plans, limited career opportunities for teachers, excessively large classes, failed integration policies, too much income inequality, racism, etc.

In line with what we argued in the preceding sections, causal explanations are attributions made upon certain assumptions that need to be made clear. Moreover, different explanations entail different measures for solving the problem, each contingent on their particular definition of the problem. In the following paragraphs, we discuss some possible explanations of the teachers' poor psychosocial condition and the measures based on these explanations.

A common view is that burnout among teachers is the result of lack of *competence*: their excessive stress could be the result of their being ill-suited for handling a teaching job in multi-ethnic classrooms. In that case, the competence of teachers needs to be improved to better prepare them for teaching assignments. A possible measure in line with this problem diagnosis would be to send teachers to training programmes about managing crises and conflicts in classrooms. Another, complementary, measure would be to require them to get acquainted with pupils' cultural backgrounds and value systems in order to make them more capable of understanding how pupils brought up by immigrant parents behave.

If the definition of the problem, by contrast (or complementarily), departs from the broad xenophobia and racism prevalent among the population despite the establishment's calls for diversity and multiculturalism, it is more likely that the explanations focus less on the teacher's poor competence or immigrants' outdated cultural traditions and their unwillingness to integrate but rather on the xenophobic and racist power structure in the country. Pupils with migrant or racial minority backgrounds, then, appear as *direct* victims, and, as a consequence (due to the pupils' protesting attitude and non-adaptive behaviour), the teachers appear as *indirect* victims of failed integration policies and failed efforts to fight xenophobia and racism.

The teachers may keep on believing in their pupils and continue with a strong ambition to teach them, help them, and sometimes reach them, and they experience on a daily basis frustration that many of the pupils neither can nor want to put any effort into school work. This goes on until the teachers cannot take it anymore. A related causal explanation assumes that racism, racial segregation, and discrimination against children from a racial minority background leads to an atmosphere in which the pupils do not find any meaning to studying because they will end up excluded from or on the low end of tomorrow's labour market. Even in that case, the work environment for teachers is very conducive to burnout.

Yet another causal explanation for teachers getting burnout relies on the assumption that education only works properly if the teaching profession is recognised and respected. If everyone is entitled to mutual respect, not only should the pupils with a minority background be respected, but so should the teachers and their work. In line with such a diagnosis, the problem could be tackled by re-installing teachers' lost authority in the classroom: more autonomy for teachers to determine pedagogical means and content and what marks to give, less negotiation with pupils and their parents about how teaching should be conducted, etc.

The latter explanation goes hand in hand with the causal explanation that the family has failed in its role of raising the children before they enter school. To resolve the issue, more talks with parents and more support from school welfare officers and social authorities for pupils growing up in problem families are needed. The foundation of these measures is the assumption that the political system (read: the welfare state) has to live up to its responsibility of realising a functioning society. These duties cannot be pushed upon the teachers. It is the task of families, and if families do not accept their responsibility (or are unable) to make sure their children do not miss chances to integrate, it is the welfare state that needs to help out. According to this diagnosis the measures have to focus more on family and social policy than on integration and education policy.

The last possible causal explanation we want to discuss here departs from the assumption that boys who live beyond the influence of family and society receive their socialisation and their worldviews through gangs on the street (Anderson, 1999). Obviously, the values of the gang clash with those of school and public life. Instead of embracing widely accepted values, they adopt values about strong displays of masculinity (Willis, 1993), unconditional loyalty to the group, readiness to use violence, regarding women as sex objects and trophies, etc. Those who would actually like to behave in line with school rules and participate in teaching for the prospect of a better future risk harassment for "acting white" (Fordham & Ogbu, 1986).

What our illustrative examples show is that burnout among teachers is a problem caused by people – pupils and others – who are symptom-bearers of complex social problems on the macro level. The social problem "unemployment and lack of prospects among minorities" enters the classroom and reaches teachers who work with the children of this underprivileged group. But where should we cut the causal chain, and according to which criteria? Which causes should be taken into account in such a fuzzy, multi-causal complex? Is the burnout of teachers ultimately due to an impossible situation at school, where an increasingly competitive social environment in a globalised world clashes with frictions typical of societies in transition, such as gang-mentality and outdated displays of masculinity that do not fit in a modern, liberal, enlightened society? Or should we search for causes of teachers' burnout in political decisions on communalisation, decentralisation, a new mix of pupils, or in the (lack of) specific skills and competences of the teachers (and thus search the causes in their psychic systems)?

Common to all of these explanations and affiliated solutions is that they imply an enormous reduction of the vast complexity in the described phenomenon. Taking the full complexity into account is no solution either because it would paralyse policy attempts: the welfare state cannot steer other social systems that operate with their own rationalities and logics (Luhmann, 1997b; Schirmer & Hadamek, 2007). Chapter 7 deals more extensively with social steering.

Defining causes means actively attributing causes, selecting between the causes that, for instance, best fit certain purposes. Depending on how we define the causes of a problem, we can propose different solutions. In the case of a rising number of teachers diagnosed with burnout one solution can be to medicalise the problem, another to blame poor pedagogical skills, a third to problematise parents' lack of will to integrate, a fourth could be to emphasise the xenophobia to be tackled, a fifth to point out television programmes and video games with violent content, and a sixth to tackle ghettoisation with new policies against segregation. The proposed measures are contingent on the underlying definitions of the problem and the political interests behind the definitions of the problem. This will be the topic of the next chapter.

Notes

1 In the one-party system of the Soviet Union, of course, the situation was different: the central committee decided by decree that Marxism–Leninism was science, while neo-classical economics was not acknowledged as science, and professors had to accept this if they wanted to keep their positions.
2 Later in this chapter we return to the questions of how far the world and its content exist objectively and how far we have access to the world.
3 We borrow this example from an article by the German sociologist Uwe Schimank (1999).
4 More orthodox representatives of sociological systems theory may perhaps reject objectivism and argue that systems theory is purely constructionist. However, we argue that such a narrow interpretation misses important insights and runs the risk of ending up in theory-immanent contradictions, as was brilliantly pointed out by Volker Schmidt (2005).
5 Systems theory is a part of the scientific system, and within the scientific system it competes with rival theories and philosophies of science that more or less acknowledge their own limitations.
6 Heinz von Foerster, and after him Luhmann, speaks of *second-order observations*: the observations of observations. "First-order observation" refers to observations of things. For example the economy observes the breakdown of a market (first-order observation by the economy), and we observe how the economy observes this market crash with the help of economic rationalities (second-order observation by us). The concept pair "first-/second-order observation" should not be confused with the concept pair "first-/second-order reality", of which we speak in the next section.
7 More specifically on the relevance of analysing distinctions used by observers for research methods, see Andersen (2003a).
8 Of course, in real life nobody would deny these things but sometimes, we get such an impression when reading constructionist or postmodern texts that say, like a mantra, that everything is a construction.
9 Aristotle actually distinguishes four types of causality. In addition to the efficient cause there are the *causa finalis, causa materialis*, and *causa formalis*. See http://plato.stanford.edu/entries/aristotle-causality/ Retrieved on 15 July 2018.

10 Science is also a social system (Luhmann, 1990a) and within social systems, social rules prevail that are determined by power relations within and between organisations (rival universities, departments, chairs), by reciprocity (of citation cartels), by money, and not least, by emotions (such as admiration and respect but also, and more prevalent, envy and jealousy), all of which never appear in science research textbooks and which young researchers have to learn "the hard way".

11 We summarise a very heterogeneous group ranging from anthropological structuralism, traditional critical theory, and sociobiology under the label "structuralism". The reason is that all of them, despite their differences, share a certain view on the limitations of individual agency through biological, psychological and/or social structures.

12 At least in their private life outside of academia, as Homans has noted with some irony (Homans, 1958, p. 606).

13 Note that low priority is not the same as no treatment. It only means that the treatment happens later, may be of lower quality, cheaper, or the patients have to pay higher premiums or their own contributions.

6

SYSTEMS THEORY AND SOCIAL PROBLEMS

The academic discipline of social work builds its identity around social problems (Michailakis & Schirmer, 2014a): their causes, consequences, and potential solutions. Mostly, researchers in the discipline take the problems for granted as an objective condition. For empirical social work research on topics such as poverty, discrimination, social exclusion, homelessness, juvenile delinquency, domestic violence, and human trafficking, it is usually taken for granted what "the" social problem is.

Modern societies are characterised by high levels of pluralisation and differentiation of classes, milieus, subcultures and minority cultures, and other groups. For this reason, one cannot simply assume that all agents involved in a certain social problem have the same understanding of it in terms of definition, conditions, remedies, and so forth. There is even a disagreement on what actually counts as a social problem in the first place. Even if there is agreement that, say, too much social inequality is a social problem, there is no consensus on what exactly determines the problem and even less on its causes and solutions. Is it an unfair distribution of wealth and access to resources? Is it the result of a lack of incentives or individual initiative? Are those in powerful positions responsible, or does blame lie with those who experience the distribution as unfair and fail to do anything about it? Depending on who observes the problem, their moralities, interests, and many other factors, the answers to what the problem "too much social inequality" is look different.

Practitioners in the field are very aware that social movements, public authorities, and service users or clients frequently have very different ideas about the essence and characteristics of a particular social problem, and even more so, how it should be solved. Quite often it is not the most accurate scientific description of the problem that wins the struggle over definition but the description that has the most persuasive arguments or that has mobilised the most support (Loseke, 2003).

There is not even much agreement between social work researchers on what makes a social condition a social problem. For empirical research it is often enough to know whether the "field" is regarded as a social problem. In social work text-books and programmatic articles, the agreement goes only so far as acknowledging that social work deals with social problems (Healy & Link, 2012; Payne, 2005; Smale, Tuson, & Statham, 2000; Staub-Bernasconi, 2010; Wodarski & Thyer, 1998). Something similar can be said about sociological research on social pro-blems, albeit with the difference that sociologists more or less explicitly ask for the definition of social problems. The classic sociological theory of social problems has been dominated by functionalist approaches (Merton & Nisbet, 1971), conflict theories (Fuller & Myers, 1941), and labelling theory (Becker, 1966; Lemert, 1972). Despite a number of conceptual differences, there is a consensus in sociol-ogy that social problems (1) generate difficulties for a large number of people, (2) have social causes and/or social effects, and (3) require social solutions. Merton and Nisbet (1971) argued that the observation of social problems establishes a difference between what is (a problematic, unwanted condition) and what should be (a world free from such a condition). Many contemporary theories share this view (Abbas, 2007; Glynn, Hohm, & Stewart, 1996; Horton, Leslie, Lawson, & Horton, 1997).

There is, however, a considerable body of constructionist research literature on social problems, which began with the book *Constructing social problems* by Malcolm Spector and John Kitsuse (1987 [1977]). These authors criticised the mainstream lit-erature for lacking theoretical or methodological coherence, despite its attempts to define social problems objectively. Instead of trying to capture the gist of the objective conditions behind social problems, Spector and Kitsuse suggest conceptualising social problems as constructions by so-called *claims-makers*. Later in this chapter, we will return to the constructionist approach and deal with it more extensively because there are some interesting overlaps with a systems-theoretical view on social problems.

At the same time, and here we reconnect with the epistemological discussion from Chapter 5, we will demonstrate that the systems-theoretical approach we advocate in this book has a realist and a constructionist stance toward social pro-blems (Nissen, 2014). This is, in accordance with our argument in Chapter 5, neither a contradiction nor an incoherence. Both components are prerequisites for each other, and this has to do with functional differentiation. Systems theory is a realist theory insofar as it takes the systemic nature of social phenomena seriously. It rejects simplified ideas about causality, planning, steering, and intervention (see Chapter 7), which often are inherent to traditional approaches to social problems. At the same time, systems theory is constructionist insofar as it takes social systems seriously as observers that each construct their own image of reality, and this entails unique and varying definitions of social problems. With the help of a number of examples from our own research we will describe the constructionist component, but first we deal with the realist component.

Systems theory and social problems: realism[1]

Functional differentiation has led to a radical rise in complexity, knowledge, options of choice, mobility, equality, and welfare. However, Luhmann was well aware in many of his writings (Luhmann, 1989a, 1990c, 1998, 2012, 2013) that functional differentiation does not entail a unidirectional improvement of society. Like Ulrich Beck in his work on reflexive modernisation (Beck, 1992) and Zygmunt Bauman on the ambivalence of modernity (Bauman, 1990), Luhmann noted that the structure of society and the operations of its primary subsystems can potentially destabilise or destroy society itself.

Functional differentiation as the primary structure of society does not guarantee that subsystems remain compatible and do not develop in diverse ways from each other. The question is how "develop in diverse ways from each other" turns into "against each other". In this context, systems theory speaks of "subsequent problems" (*Folgeprobleme*) of functional differentiation. This term refers to problems that occur in society that, at the same time, create problems for society because they pose direct or indirect threats to the survival of society in its current form. In his more recent writings, Luhmann (2012, 2013) gave a number of casual examples of subsequent problems, such as the expansion of education, that prolong adolescence and delay family reproduction (compare the high average age for getting married in the West with that in other parts of the world). Another casual example that he gave of subsequent problems is the economisation of non-economic social spheres, which leads to an increasingly unequal distribution of welfare on a global level. A third example is the unprecedented expansion of the welfare state, which makes political parties promise ever more non-financeable and unfulfillable measures before elections.

There are three greater subsequent problems of functional differentiation that received more attention within Luhmannian systems theory. We discuss two of them: mass exclusion (Luhmann, 2005d [1995]) and ecological self-endangering of society (Luhmann, 1989a). The third one, which we cannot address here, is risk (Luhmann, 1993).

In Chapter 4 we dealt with the question of how people who do not fulfil the requirements for inclusion in organisations and function systems are socially excluded. In contrast to pre-modern societies, modern society includes not the whole person but only a "piece", a role that is normally related to a task, and this only in accordance with very specific criteria. In modern society it is common for people to be included and excluded at the same time (for instance included as a pupil but excluded as a friend; included as a member of a housing cooperation because of one's spending power to buy an apartment but excluded from the neighbour community; included in an association but excluded from the labour market due to lack of marketable skills). Inclusion and exclusion of the modern kind are, therefore, immediate consequences of the societal form of differentiation. If a society is organised politically through a welfare state system (as is the case in the West) there are even ways to include socially excluded people through exclusion roles such as those of homeless person or undocumented immigrants. Paradoxically, exclusion roles are a form of inclusion in the welfare state and in the help system (through social work). This means, among other things, that no homeless person or illegal immigrant needs to fear dying of hunger or being denied medical care and basic human rights.

However, there is an increasing number of so-called "exclusion areas" in Western countries that are populated by people who do not have access to functionally differentiated society. TV series such as the American *The Wire* show societal conditions similar to those in the *banlieux* of France, slums of Great Britain, and *invandrartäta förorter* of Sweden, which are brought into the living rooms of the well-integrated middle class audience. Such exclusion areas are largely no-go zones from which the police have withdrawn, where regular legislation and other codes of civil behaviour are suspended, where ambulances get vandalised, buses are attacked with stones, women are afraid to leave the house without company, and social life is ruled by family clans. During a journey to Brazil, Luhmann observed life in urban slums (*favelas*) and concluded that exclusion cannot be explained simply as an expression of social inequality, oppression, or exploitation – there is nothing left to exploit from people who do not even appear on the radar of function systems. Luhmann wondered whether inclusion and exclusion (as a subsequent problem) could replace functional differentiation as a new, overarching differentiation form. Functional differentiation would still prevail in the inclusion areas, while the exclusion areas, decoupled from world society, would be governed by other, retro-traditional codes (such as the code of the street; see Anderson, 1999).

From the perspective of social problems, exclusion and exclusion areas are results of the way function systems operate, while at the same time there is no function system that can take on the responsibility to steer other systems toward more inclusion. Mass exclusion is a problem on the societal level because it threatens the structural foundations of society.

The same is true for the other big and subsequent problem of functional differentiation that Luhmann was concerned about: the self-inflicted ecological endangerment from environmental pollution and exploitation of natural resources. Society as an entity is only an entity of differences. There is neither an apex nor a centre from which environmental pollution can be stopped and nature protected. Protest movements (such as the Green Party's grass roots activists) and protest organisations (such as Greenpeace) point out the detrimental effects of industrial exhaust fumes, mining, car traffic, etc., and protest against society, but society cannot do anything other than approach the ecological problems through its function systems. However, the potential solutions through function systems are also the causes of the problems, comparable to the problem of mass exclusion. As shown in earlier chapters, function systems divide the world into spheres of relevance. They operate with their function-specific rationalities and consider certain norms while they ignore others. This limits the scope of how the social problem "environmental pollution" can appear on the radar of function systems. The situation is structural, just like in the example with the train accident in Chapter 5.

For the *economic system*, environmental pollution appears as a market with financial opportunities and dangers: new corporations can be established to produce environmentally friendly products such as energy-saving fridges, cars with low CO_2 emissions, better filter systems, phosphate-free laundry agents, renewable energy sources, etc. Non-sustainable products, such as leaded fuel, diesel cars, or sprays with chlorofluorocarbons, can turn into shelf warmers and sooner or later will be discarded. Insurance companies can adjust to environmental problems by increasing their premiums for insurance against damage caused by environmental disasters such as climate change, toxic waste, or increased radiation. From the economic viewpoint, environmental pollution is rendered into a question of profits and losses.

The *system of science* finds pollution to be a giant research field for studying causes and consequences (climatology, environmental sociology) as well as searching for sustainable and environmentally friendly materials for production within chemistry, biology, or engineering – all of this improves prospects for research funding, careers, and reputations.

Political parties have to develop programmes that address environmental problems to ensure the sympathy of voters. As parts of governments, they can change the law against poisonous products and exhaust, increase or lower thresholds of fine dust, define five-year plans for reducing energy through fossil fuels, support research, and subsidise certain technologies, such as electrical cars. But everything they do, they do in order to gain or maintain governmental power.

The *legal system* can, on the basis of new laws, sanction "sinners" and reward "angels". Savvy lawyers can organise class action lawsuits against foreign car companies that have used fraudulent software in order to circumvent environmental laws.

Because *the media* operate through publishing news that aims to achieve high audience rates and newspaper runs, they prefer catastrophes (such as oil spills in the ocean) or scandals about environmental crimes committed by respectable firms. Positive news, such as reduced mortality in former industrial centres or slow improvements due to technological progress, hardly makes it to the top pages.

All these examples give a taster of how function systems can handle environmental issues, but – just as in the train example – each in their unique way. There is nothing on the horizon that looks like an overarching or transcendental rationality. Moreover, there is no collectively binding ethic of the type "thou shalt not destroy your environment" – regardless of what religious communities claim. There is no inhibitory mechanism within function systems (Luhmann, 1990c), e.g. there is no economic reason for behaving less economically rationally (for example to strive for less profit), no legal reason for less law (less bureaucracy, less regulation), no political reason for less power (and more power for the opposition or the "common people"), no scientific reason for less knowledge (more innocence, more romanticism, more enchantment, more esotericism, more emotions, and more alternative facts). In sum, there is no genuine interest within function systems in less environmental pollution – only as long as it is in line with the rationalities of the systems and only if it appears on their function-specific radar in the first place. With a systems-theoretical diagnosis of environmental self-endangerment of society, it is hardly convincing to attribute environmental pollution to the behaviour of reckless or evil individuals – not even greedy capitalists who enjoy making profits by destroying the environment (such as Montgomery Burns in the cartoon series *The Simpsons*). Against the systems-theoretical analysis, occasional calls for more responsibility and environmental ethics are rather pointless, fears Luhmann (1989a).

Systems theory and social problems: constructionism

If we regard systems and their operational modes as causes of social problems, in particular those that are a direct consequence of the interplay between function systems, we assume a realist standpoint toward social problems. In this way, the observation and analysis of mass exclusion and environmental pollution are realist. However, this is only half of the story. Systems theory, particularly as represented by Luhmann and Watzlawick, is recognised instead as a constructionist theory. The idea of non-trivial machines helps to bridge the gap between realism and constructionism, particularly when we want to study social problems.

We have seen that social systems operate in specific, non-trivial, non-linear ways. By way of their operations, these systems observe their environment. Observation is one of the most important things a system can do. Through observations, a system generates its own reality. Even this last statement is, basically, a constructionist statement, an observation by the system science. What a system can see, how it interprets what it sees, how it selects and what it ignores, all of this is the result of the operational mode and the history of a system. As mentioned earlier, the economic system constructs the world as a market full of commodities with a price tag; the system of politics constructs the world as a jungle full of power struggles; the system of science constructs the world as a giant collection of research objects; etc.

A scientific theory, such as systems theory, that studies how social systems observe, how they construct their realities, is therefore genuinely constructionist. Constructionist theories do not take the descriptions made by systems as a sort of objective reality. The world *is not* a market; it is the economy that constructs the world as a market. The world *is not* a jungle of power struggles; it is the political system that constructs the world as a jungle. The world *is not* a collection of research objects; it is the system of science that constructs the world as a collection of research objects. With this, we have not said that any of these constructions are untrue, but that they are constructions from specific perspectives, in a certain historical period, following certain rationalities, values, and norms that are not necessarily shared from other standpoints.

The attentive reader may recognise the idea of multiperspectivity (presented in Chapter 5) that we apply to the field of social problems. A system can observe, construct, or portray a social condition as adverse and in need of a remedy because from the perspective of this system, this condition appears as such. However, this does not mean that it necessarily looks that way seen from the viewpoint of another system. An economic crisis cannot automatically be translated into a legal, religious, or political problem. On the contrary, a problem in one system can be beneficial for another system (to give but one example, reduced trust in how a government handles economic aid to developing countries can lead to more economic and social support for NGOs). What appears as a problem for one system can even turn out to be a solution for another system (as we will demonstrate in Chapter 8 with the case of priority-setting in healthcare).

There is an essential affinity between systems theory and the constructionist approach to social problems in the tradition of sociologists Malcom Spector and John Kitsuse (1987 [1977]). In their criticism of objectivist approaches to social problems, they question the foundation of how we can study social problems as measurable deviations from undesirable conditions. According to Spector's and Kitsuse's constructionism, social conditions that are adverse for some groups may exist, but they do not pose a social problem before someone categorises them as problematic, unfair, and in need of countermeasures. Obviously, there are a large number of adverse conditions in society but only a limited number of them are established and recognised in society as social problems while others are not. Additionally, there is huge variation across different cultures regarding what is recognised as a social problem. Within the same culture there is also variation over time. Social problems are, hence, what we earlier called "second-order realities" in Watzlawick's sense: they are not free of interpretation, but neither are they free from power relations, interests, and ideologies.

The constructionist questions, then, concern which social conditions have a higher chance of being established as social problems and why (Holstein & Miller, 1993; Loseke, 2003; Loseke & Best, 2011; Spector & Kitsuse, 1987 [1977]). In order to answer these questions, constructionism focuses on how images of social issues arise, are articulated, and are institutionalised. It is the very process that is analysed, from drawing attention to something to recognising that something as a social problem. Constructionism claims that objective social conditions do not suffice to be quailified as a social problem. Additionally, a group with social influence that identifies and points out that this condition is problematic is required.

One of the main representatives of the constructionist approach to social problems, Donileen Loseke, draws on Spector's and Kitsuse's idea that social problems are the result of ongoing activity by *claims-makers*, for instance social movements, interest groups, or politicians. Such claims-makers highlight some adverse social condition and fight for acknowledgement of this condition as a social problem, i.e. a recognised, undesirable but existing condition that violates standards of fairness (or other values), that affects certain groups negatively, and that demands a remedy. The constructions of a given social problem can vary within the following four parameters (Loseke, 2003):

- *Conditions and causal relations*: What is wrong (and needs to be corrected)? What are the causes and consequences?
- *Cultural themes*: Why is a certain condition morally unacceptable and why does it provoke indignation? Which (culturally- and historically-specific) values does it violate?

- *People*: On the one hand, successful claims-making needs victims who suffer from the condition, who themselves are not responsible and therefore deserve sympathy. On the other hand, there are villains who actively or passively contribute to the problem and might even gain something from the status quo and therefore are (morally) responsible. The villains can be individuals, groups, or systems, but also social forces or social structures.
- *Solutions*: Claims-makers construct a general line of action (what ought to be done) in order to solve the problem and attribute responsibility to those who should solve it (this need not be the villains). Depending on the other three parameters, some solutions are deemed legitimate and others excluded.

Whether or not the claims-making process is successful depends largely on the prevailing social climate, the choice of audience, and the arenas the claims-makers have access to for promoting their claims, as well as access to power and resources. Weaker groups face more difficulties getting their claims noticed. In this context, social media are new, more democratic arenas (at least they were in the beginning; see Van Dijck, 2013). Gaining the attention of the general public and convincing them is an important part of the claims-making process. Exaggeration of figures and consequences that sometimes inflate the problem images is one way of increasing attention.

If we combine the constructionist approach to social problems (social problems as results of successful claims-making, hence, second-order reality) with the systems-theoretical idea of multiperspectivity in a functionally differentiated society, we can formulate the hypothesis that function systems and their key performance roles construct not only their own unique social problems that other systems do not have (economy: scarcity; politics: binding of collectivities; science: knowledge; religion: transcendence; etc.) but also *their own unique versions of the same social problem*, such as poverty or widespread substance abuse. The "problem" does not have to be "real" in the realist sense – it is sufficient if it is preceded by successful claims-making activities through which the issue has entered the public arena, and other agents (corporations, governments, interest groups, researchers, journalists, etc.) attempt to contribute to the discussion of solutions that inevitably follows. In such discussions, different agents try to promote their own definition of the problem in line with their systemic perspectives and rationalities.

If we assume a differentiated society that contains a large number of systems (which contain a large number of performance roles and rationalities), it is easy to grasp that there is a potential multitude of perspectives on the "same problem". The empirical question is over what range and in which dimensions the problem images divert. By combining constructionism and the systems-theoretical idea of multiperspectivity, we have a framework that is relevant for research and practice alike.

The overarching question is, how do different claims-makers and social systems construct (the same) social problems differently? For researchers, this question is very interesting because it opens up new horizons for comparison between descriptions that vary in the four parameters, which, among other things, help to unveil hidden interest constellations. By asking this question, we can analyse how successful claims-makers proceed, and from there we can draw conclusions on how such claims-making activities can be translated to other systems.

Even for practitioners in the care sector, a constructionist approach combined with multiperspectivity is of high relevance in the daily work. A social secretary involved in handling a difficult social problem, for instance apprehension of children from multi-problem families, has to be aware that the legal definition of the problem perhaps does not coincide with the problem image seen from the viewpoint of the client, doctor, school, or neighbour, which requires the social secretary to take a mediator's per-spective in order to understand and translate different perspectives on the same pro-blem. Furthermore, it is very important for practitioners to be able to understand whether they are really helping the client or whether they are only pursuing some (party-) political or economic interest underlying a certain claims-making activity. Thus, it is important to get the insight across that no help is given without a counter-claim, whatever entitlement the client may have. Help in most cases is only a tem-porary solution, as a transition toward a life free from violence, abuse, or misery.

In what follows, we will illustrate the presented framework with two cases from our own research: suicide among people with mental illness and loneliness among older people.

Illustration: suicide among people with mental illness as a social problem

Since Émile Durkheim's well-known study from the late 19th century (Durkheim, 1979 [1897]), suicide has been established as a research object of the social sciences. Durkheim's distinct contribution was to treat suicide as a *social fact*, not an individual matter. It was thanks to Durkheim that suicide was interpreted as *social problem* and not (simply) as the result of mental illness, because he pointed out a number of social causes that required social solutions and preventive efforts by many different agents and institutions, such as the welfare state, social workers, therapists, etc. Suicide among people with mental illness is therefore a good application case for illustrating a theoretical framework that combines constructionism with multiperspectivity.

We will present three excerpts from texts that can be seen as manifestations of claims-making activities, and they all originate from different social systems. The first one is from an editorial in the member's magazine of the Swedish National Association of Social and Mental Health (RSMH), a protest organisation that is part of the Swedish disability movement. The second excerpt is from a public investigation commissioned by the government, thus a political communication, and the third excerpt is taken from a text by a psychiatrist, published in the journal of the Swedish Medical Association (*Läkartidningen*), which we consider as a com-munication in the function system of medicine. In what follows we will see a variation in the four parameters that we distinguished based on the works of Loseke (conditions and causes, cultural themes, people, solutions).

Excerpt 1: "Scary statistics" from the chairman of the RSMH[2]

> Over the past few years, suicide in healthcare has been continuously on the rise . . .
> an increase of almost 30 per cent within the last four years. It is not news to us at the
> RSMH, and our youth organisation RUS, that many children, teens and young
> adults are feeling worse than ever. There are also many reasons for this. As for the
> youngest, we know that there are major problems at school; classes are getting bigger
> and bigger while the staff are getting smaller and smaller. The school health services
> are cutting their activities and in many places there are neither school welfare officers
> nor school psychologists available in the first place . . . Suicide is a problem that
> requires extremely powerful measures. We at the RSMH find that the government
> must begin to work immediately and pro-actively toward a "vision zero" of suicide
> which they in fact announced in 2008 . . .
>
> *(Trevett, 2011)*

The RSMH, an interest organisation, is part of the disability movement (and the
faction representing disability due to mental illness). Social movements are social
systems (though not function systems) that communicate "protest" (Luhmann,
2013), i.e. communication that criticises social conditions in a blueprint type of
claims-making activity. Protest communication divides the world into two camps:
those who protest and are affected by adverse social conditions and those who
represent, profit from, or refuse change to overcome the conditions – the addres-
sees of the protest. The divide is legitimised by reference to ethical principles
deemed morally superior to the ethics of the opponents. In this excerpt, we can see
how suicide (especially among younger people) is constructed as a social problem
violating core values and in need of instant remedy. The author of the text notes a
rise in suicide rates among young people over the past few years despite the government's promise to take action to reduce the prevalent rates. Typical of protest
communication, there is an almost complete identification with the victims: people
represented by the organisation. Similarly, protest communication works with
simplified causality in terms of causes and solutions. The increased occurrence of
suicide is attributed to factors external to the movement and the victims, for
instance changes in the school management, budget cuts, less psychological and
medical care. Furthermore, the moral responsibility is attributed to the government
because of its past failure to keep the promise of implementing an efficient policy
to reduce suicide rates; there is also a demand that the proposed solution be
delivered by the government, but the claim of "forceful measures" remains rather
vague. However, it is not the function of protest movements to solve the problem
but to point out the adverse social conditions in the first place.

Excerpt 2: "Swedish Government Official Report 2010:45: event analyses of suicides in healthcare and social service"

> [T]he government notes that the vast number of suicides and attempted suicides as
> well as the enormous socio-economic costs and the mental suffering these cause
> implies that suicide ideation, attempted suicide and suicide in general constitute a

major social problem. Suicide is seen as the final step in a long or short process in which biological, social, psychological and existential factors interact. Furthermore, the government notes that effective suicide prevention is based on the insight that suicide can be prevented. Suicide prevention requires broad cooperation and coordination that transcend sectors between local, regional and national agents. The need for systems thinking is emphasised and advised – as in other fields of injury prevention; the chain of events preceding a suicide should be examined through event analysis. Lessons can be learned from such analyses that can reduce the risk that a lack of availability or procedures, negligence or a lack of knowledge will be contributing factors to suicide.

(SOU, 2010, p. 26)

There is consensus between Excerpts 1 and 2 that the victims of the social problem are suicidal people. However, in contrast to protest communication, the focus of this example of political communication is on complex causal relations regarding both the causes of suicide and the solutions to counter the problem. Another important difference between political communication and protest communication is the role of agency. While claims-makers from protest movements describe themselves as non-agents who identify with the victims, political claims-makers affiliated with the government emphasise their own agency (but note that claims-making by the opposition often resembles protest communication). This is even true for cases where the causes of the social problem are beyond the scope of action for politics, for instance biological or psychological factors. Suicide can be prevented, the excerpt says, thus the government can take preventive measures. Despite the complex causalities the government (actually) knows what to do. Accordingly, the proposed solutions imply more bureaucracy (increased cooperation, coordination, more and better action plans, more investigations, redistribution of responsibilities, etc.).

Excerpt 3: "Suicide has become less common", by a chief physician at a psychiatric clinic

It is of the utmost importance to emphasise that treatment with antidepressant drugs is likely to be a powerful intervention to prevent suicide. The treatment of mental illness with drugs has been regularly criticised, without the enormous benefits with respect to human suffering and human life being taken into consideration. This is particularly the case with antidepressant drugs, which are attacked from every possible vantage point. The most foolish arguments come, of course, from ideological organisations. Antidepressant drugs are also attacked from a narrow economic perspective even though the costs for medication constitute a very small percentage of the total healthcare budget . . . One does not need any scientific training to understand that a decrease in suicide rates of almost one third along with a five-fold increase in the prescription of antidepressants since the 1990s indicates that medication reduces rather than increases the risk of suicide.

(Isacsson, 2006)

In Excerpt 3 we see an exemplary case of how doctors construct suicide as a medical problem that can be treated by medical means. Because suicide is observed as a symptom of a diagnosed mental illness (psychiatric illness) it is appropriate that suicidal patients and their illness be treated. The system of medicine not only has the exclusive competence to determine whether the prescription of antidepressants is a successful method of preventing suicidal patients from taking their own lives, but medicine also claims to have clinical evidence on its side. In Excerpt 3 this is used as a communicative device to reject objections from protest movements. In accordance with scientific communication, it is important for medical claims-making to cut the causal chain in such a way that the causes and consequences of the problem can be defined in purely medical terms.

Illustration: loneliness among older people as a social problem

The second example from our own studies is claims-making on loneliness among older people (Schirmer & Michailakis, 2016). Within popular literature, the media, and scientific research, loneliness is portrayed as a growing social problem. While it concerns many groups, older people are particularly prone to experiencing loneliness because, after retirement, they lose much of their social network. Declining physical abilities, illnesses, and the deaths of partners and friends also increase the risk. There is a vast body of research literature that has found covariation of loneliness with ill health, limited finances, and small personal network size (Coyle & Dugan, 2012; Dahlberg, Andersson, McKee, & Lennartsson, 2015; Dahlberg & McKee, 2014; O'Luanaigh & Lawlor, 2008). We present two examples of how loneliness among older people is portrayed as a social problem from the perspectives of two function systems that, at first sight, are not typical candidates for claims-making: religion and economy.

Excerpt 4: "Battling the siege of loneliness"

> Yet for others longing to be with brethren, the lack of handshakes and fellowship can take its toll, sowing the seeds of loneliness. When allowed to germinate, these seeds can sprout into feelings of discouragement, and will eventually mature into a state of despondency. . .This becomes a fertile field for Satan to sow seeds of doubt and a perfect climate for his negative influence. Satan preys on the lonely, who are perhaps his easiest victims. You can be sure he will take every opportunity to heap on more negative thoughts until he has the person so "down in the dumps" that he or she will want to quit altogether. This is at least a part of the reason God intended we all have Christian fellowship . . . We must realize that although human fellowship is important in combating loneliness, it is not the most important.
>
> The apostle John wrote, "That which we have seen and heard we declare to you, that you also may have fellowship with us" (I John 1:3). John wanted the brethren to have fellowship with one another, but notice the primary stress: "And truly our fellowship is with the Father and with His Son Jesus Christ." Without contact with God, you might have friendships, but not true Christian fellowship. Our spiritual closeness with God guarantees that our contact with each other will be profitable and edifying. No human or group of humans can substitute for contact with God.

> Many of us might like to see our needs met by other humans from what is termed "the human connection." But the human connection is not enough. Simply stated, we cannot and will not be close to each other as members of the Body of Christ unless we are first close to God! As we draw closer to Him, we will inevitably draw closer to each other. Conversely, when we drift away from God we will find ourselves forsaking each other. Recognize that our first line of defense against loneliness and every other negative emotion is our personal contact with our Creator. Fellowship with God is the best kind there is.
>
> (Echelbarger, 2007)

This excerpt is taken from a publication by a religious community called "The Restored Church of God." In a section preceding the excerpt, the text mentions a number of social causes of loneliness, such as changes in family structures and values and lack of intergenerational contact, as well as medical, biological, and psychological causes. While the text acknowledges mainstream descriptions of loneliness as a social problem, it is interesting for our purposes insofar as it addresses loneliness in a genuinely religious way.

According to the text, loneliness is dangerous because it opens a person up to influence by the Devil, the supernatural villain in this problem construction. The Devil is said to push "dark thoughts", epitomised by depression and suicide, onto the lonely person. As for causality, the solution to loneliness and its consequent increased exposure to the Devil's influence is communion with God, expressed in Christian fellowship, which protects lonely people. Communion with God eliminates loneliness both on an individual and a collective level, and thereby tackles loneliness as a social problem: if people are willing to find a way to God, they will find a way to each other, and thus will no longer be lonely. While loneliness can be triggered by different social, medical, and other factors, its ultimate cause is insufficient contact with God. More contact with God is the solution to loneliness because it enables contact with other human beings as a consequence. Important for our argument, such a perspective on loneliness only makes sense from a religious point of view, i.e. a function system that puts the focus on the distinction between immanent (earthly) and transcendent realms. In the latter, entities such as God and the Devil exert forces beyond human control and understanding, and one of them – the evil one – can only be countered by submitting to the other, i.e. the good one. Communion with God (no loneliness with God) is portrayed as superior to this worldly human fellowship.

Excerpt 5: "Inheritance tax reform"

> Perhaps it's time to review our obsession with keeping older people "independent" and our fetish about "keeping people in their own homes". Now don't get me wrong, I am not recommending a return to the era of asylums for people who can't cope on their own. Nor should anyone who wishes to remain independent and on their own be prevented from doing exactly that, if it suits them . . . What I am saying is that, as a society, we have insisted that everyone should have a little box to call their own, be they a young single mother, a professional so-called "first-time buyer", and even vulnerable or elderly members of our society whose needs are met by "care in the community". We ensure that these people have a roof over their

head and their physical needs are met, but we seem to be missing out on the better quality of life that having a shared living space can bring for those who want or need it . . . A start would be a reform of the taxes . . . that affect families when two generations live together. At present, if an older person sells their home and gives the money to a younger family member so that the two generations can buy a home together, there may be either inheritance tax implications under the "gift with reservation of benefit" rules or an income tax liability under pre-owned assets rules or both, depending on the arrangement. The reason is that the older person who makes the gift is treated as if they haven't given the money away, because they are still enjoying the proceeds of a purchase made with it. Similarly, an older person cannot give away their home tax-free to a son or daughter who moves in with them to care for them, because in this case they continue to live in the house alongside them, benefiting from the asset that they have intended to give away. This must be a huge disincentive to the generations living together. Why would you want to give up your own home to move in with Granny, only to find yourself hit with a bill for inheritance tax when Granny passes away, potentially leaving you homeless if you now need to sell the house you live in to pay the bill?

(Shaw, 2013)

Excerpt 5 is taken from a British journal article that starts with a criticism of contemporary society. The latter is said to put people under pressure to live alone and to ignore the lost quality of life that comes with it. Loneliness among older people has to be seen in this context. In this example of claims-making, it is clearly considered a social problem and an undesired outcome of the wrong incentives created by flawed tax rules in the United Kingdom. Because the tax system financially punishes families when older parents sell their house and give the proceeds to their children, it seems more rational to let older people keep their own home and live separately. The result is lonely older people. In other words, loneliness is a consequence of families saving money; it can be combated with a revised tax system that promises a higher payoff when people live together. Loneliness among older people is framed in terms of economic causes and economic solutions and as an outcome of people living in economically rational ways. The claim, however, is addressed to the government, which is institutionally responsible for changes in tax laws.

Both examples, suicide and loneliness among older people, demonstrate that different social systems construct the same social problem in different ways. As a complement to the constructionist approach to social problems, systems theory is a relevant and adequate tool that helps to account for how and why different claims-makers – on the basis of their system-specific rationalities – construct social problems differently.

Notes

1 Parts of this chapter are based on our contribution to the *Cambridge Handbook of Social Problems* (Schirmer & Michailakis, 2018b) and on the article "Loneliness among older people as a social problem: the perspectives of medicine, religion and economy", published in *Ageing and Society* (Schirmer & Michailakis, 2016).
2 All of the three translations of the excerpts from Swedish are our own.

7

INTERVENTION AND STEERING

One reason why social workers, therapists, and social policy-makers should benefit from basic knowledge in systems theory is that to a large extent their profession is about intervention, guidance, and support. Almost everywhere, the targets of interventions are *systems*. Things such as the consciousness, the family, the economy, politics, science, religion, the church, social media, the classroom, and small-talk at the coffee break are all examples of systems. Social and psychic systems are emergent orders that behave according to self-referential, unpredictable and non-linear logics. In contrast to automats and simple mechanic systems, social and psychic systems are non-trivial machines. Trivial machines are deterministic, which means that they can be defined analytically. Once we know the input and output, we can reconstruct the mechanism in the machine and predict its activities, and this is a prerequisite for *linear steering*.

Let us take the example of a radio that is playing bad music far too loudly. Because we want to listen to better music at a more pleasant level, we have to *steer* the system. Since the radio is a trivial machine, we can control everything we need through two parameters: the channel and the volume. Normally we can change them through sliders, knobs, or buttons. We can increase or lower the volume by dialling or pressing the buttons; changing channels works the same way. By operating the controls, we can achieve the desired result directly and reliably.

A common mistake made within social work and psychotherapeutic contexts is confusing social and psychic systems with trivial machines that work the same way as a radio. In Chapter 1 we showed why this is not the case. Already simple interaction systems, such as a conversation at the dinner table, show that the course of communication is affected by its own history (what happened right before the conversation). Whatever is said receives its meaning through the context of what has been said before, and vice versa (put to the extreme in improvisation theatre).

A similar mistake underlies the transmission model of communication. There, communication is treated as a medium through which the speaker can steer the behaviour of the receiver. I say something to the other, and the communication is deemed successful if the other behaves in the desired way.[1] But the communication and the receiver (her psychic system) are emergent, non-trivial systems. From our own experience in everyday life, and from Chapter 1, we know that the receiver sometimes reacts in expected ways, sometimes surprising ways, and sometimes not at all. This is so because the system changes its state every time the system operates (Von Foerster, 1984). Since communication is such an unreliable medium through which to steer other people there is no reason to stick to the transmission model as a basis for the steering of complex, non-trivial systems. Despite these circumstances, the transmission model is as common as the steering optimism within policy-making and helping professions.

Expectations structure systems

In the following paragraphs we discuss how social and psychic systems can be steered after all, granted that the intervening system understands its mode of operation. The key to understanding systems is understanding their structure. Within systems theories that treat systems as temporal entities (entities that reproduce through time, such as the consciousness through thoughts, or social systems through communication), the concept of "structure" aims at *expectations* (Luhmann, 1995). Social systems reduce the complexity and unpredictability of the environment by building up their own complexity through expectation structures. With the help of expectations, the system can orient in a complex, dynamic environment filled with a large number of other systems, which each have their own expectation structures.

Psychic and social systems are compelled to interpret the behaviour of systems in their environment, including the expectations directed at the system from outside. We all have experienced situations in which we orient our own behaviour to how we interpret other systems' expectations on all levels: psychic systems, interactions, organisations, function systems (such as at a job interview or in a therapy session). The system can create and reproduce an internal expectation structure through which repeating situations can be recognised and interpreted. Repeated observations of the environment are transposed into internal cognitive routines. Gained knowledge and experience can be mobilised in comparable situations in the future. Ideal types of this procedure are the conditional programmes of organisations: they are built to deal with environmental dynamics in ways that remain predictable for the system. When new, unknown situations occur, the systems can, as a proxy, use established expectations and potentially revise them or re-structure by introducing new expectations. However, there are risks that expectations in the environment may be misinterpreted or that the system may foster unrealistic expectations about its own role. Think about a situation in which a family member behaves in a way that is not in line with the expectation structure in the family. After finishing her degree in economics at a well-respected business school, the daughter of a European entrepreneurial family chooses to work for an NGO in a developing country instead of beginning her predetermined career in the family business. When things like this happen, the expectation structure of the family system is challenged by the new, unexpected situation. The structure either needs to be adapted by new expectations (accepting the daughter's choice as an appreciable expression of individuality and respecting her engagement in the idealistic organisation as a token of tolerance and openness) or maintain the prevailing expectations (and obstruct the daughter's new career). Whether the family would succeed in their attempt to steer their daughter is an open question.

Systems theory distinguishes between *normative* and *cognitive expectations* (Luhmann, 1995). Cognitive expectations are expectations that are adapted after being repeatedly violated. The repeated frustration of unfulfilled expectations gives rise to a cognitive learning process. What can the system do to protect against future disappointments and failures? In our example, the family could allow younger generations to choose their first jobs as they wish (for instance working for an NGO in a developing country).

Of course, the family could also stick to their original plan and command the daughter to take on the position in the family business and threaten her with dis-inheritance or other family-typical sanctions. This is when expectation structures are normative. "Normative expectations" refers to expectations that are maintained even when violated repeatedly. While a system built upon cognitive expectations learns from its incongruence with the environment and adapts, systems characterised by normative expectations maintain their structure even if the expectations go against experience and facts. A good example of this is the policy of the Catholic Church during the last few decades.

In most social systems, there are cognitive and normative expectation structures, although the balance tilts toward one or the other. The system of science is largely characterised by cognitive expectations: the system is ready to be surprised by and learn from its environment. Thorough researchers adapt their hypotheses when they appear incompatible with the latest evidence. They reformulate and adjust their hypotheses and theories in line with what facts, experiments, and experience suggest. Without this openness the system could no longer produce a reliable, controllable form of knowledge.

By contrast, the key characteristic of the legal system is to keep up the pursuit of laws and norms even if they become counterfactual over the course of time (such as laws that prohibit homosexuality or withhold from women the right to drive). The law operates with normative expectations when actions occur that are illegal according to current law. As mentioned in Chapter 3, the function of the legal system is to stabilise expectations between different agents. Hence, the function of the legal system can only be fulfilled by a set of normative expectations that determine with authority what should happen in situations where contradictory expectations create conflicts (King & Thornhill, 2003).

Political steering

Steering describes a peculiar relation between two systems, one of which attempts to change the "behaviour" of the other. In line with the previous section, "steering" and "intervention" can be described as the aspiration to affect another system's set of expectations and, thereby, change the "behaviour" of that system. In this section, we are particularly interested in one type of steering: political steering. With "political steering" we mean the process when the political system (and its organisations, such as the welfare state, the government, etc.) aims to steer other social systems in order to counter or prevent the rise of social problems. More specifically, the political system aims to influence the operations of other social systems toward a certain political goal – a goal outside the target systems. On the macro level, typical goals are inducing economic growth, reducing unemployment, reducing pollution, or preventing uncontrolled mass migration; on the micro level, a frequent goal is to improve the inclusion opportunities for people facing difficulties in the labour market, the housing market, or the education system.

In Chapter 6 we explained how function systems deal with social problems, problems that modern society generates and the political system is expected to tackle. Such social problems bring the need for societal steering and intervention. Steering of social systems is difficult and the effects are not predictable, and unintended consequences are rather likely. In his analysis of environmental pollution, Luhmann (1989a) emphasised the lack of a central agency in modern society that could formulate programmes that all other systems have to follow. Functional differentiation means a heterarchy of autonomous systems that operate on the basis of their distinct rationalities, semantics, codes, and programmes. The logic and semantics of the political system differ from those of the economic system, the scientific system, etc. Nor can expectation structures that have consolidated through long socio-cultural evolutions be disrupted or dictated from the outside. The fact that one system cannot impose its own logic on another system is a central hindrance to societal steering. Because there is no vertical order among function systems, no system can simply elevate itself and claim society's apex, as was the case in pre-modern stratified societies that were dominated by religious or politico-monarchical expectation structures.

Even if the welfare state has assumed the role as the governing centre and has generated a *self-description as the problem-solving agency in society*, this self-description does not coincide with its factual position in a functionally differentiated society (Schirmer & Hadamek, 2007). This ambitious self-description has been fostered over a long time and has prompted claims-makers of all kinds to look to the welfare state for interventions, subsidies, and solutions to social problems. If the political system were able to steer society, this would mean that the political system and its institutions represented society within society. However, no system – politics is no exception – can represent the whole society or speak in the name of society – and certainly not in democracies of the Western type.

Now, if a system's expectations can only be changed by the system itself, what can other systems, such as the welfare state, do? According to systems theory, every system can observe how and with what result other systems handle and control their own expectations. For instance, the system of science (sociology, history, etc.) can observe how the economy generates and reformulates its own expectation structures about how a market should react to new, disruptive products or interest rate reductions. Likewise, the economy can observe how the legal system handles its expectation structures when a new law comes into force.

Interventions and attempts at steering always evoke reactions, either positive or negative. Evoking reactions can be an intentional goal with a certain plan in mind – think of symptom prescriptions in psychotherapy. Reactions can be anticipated by the targeted system, reckoning with having its expectation structure used in a creative way. It is the latter anticipation that gives the political system the possibility to induce self-steering of the target system. In order to succeed, this type of intervention requires knowledge of the expectation structures in the target system.

Against the background of everything we have said so far, the steering of other systems cannot be anything other than steering of the context of a system, which systems theorist Helmut Willke called *contextual steering* (Willke, 2001). The system that aims to steer another system tries to evoke reactions in the other system by changing variables in the *context* of the target system. Successful steering requires that these variables be relevant to the target system in such a way that the expectation structure of the target system makes particular desired reactions likely. Contextual steering then triggers a reaction in the target system. Reactions are, however, self-referential operations of a non-trivial machine. Hence, steering is neither a linear chain of events, nor a direct linear causal link between systems. The target system remains a black box for the steering system, and despite the possibility of contextual steering there are no guarantees that an intervention can achieve the expected results. Remember the problem of environmental pollution from Chapter 6. If the state wants environmentally unfriendly products off the market, it can forbid them or put a higher tax on these products. This way, it does not steer the economy (and its organisations) directly but steers its context; the economy (as the target system) reacts in its own way: if the products are still profitable despite tax, factories will continue to produce them, but once customer demand drops, they will disappear from the market. Note that the economic system reacts with economic operations.

Despite the assets of contextual steering, we have to consider another constraint to the political system's ability to steer other function systems: much governing happens by legislation (at least in a constitutional state). The widespread expectation that the welfare state will find solutions to social problems is outsourced to the legal system because it is the legal system's function to handle contradictory expectations by applying law. The political system can steer society indirectly, through contextual steering, by making new laws that allow, prohibit, define, or limit actions, social practices, behaviours, products, etc. These new laws are processed by the administration (a sub-system of the political system; see Luhmann, 1981) and the legal system. Therefore, policy-makers need to consider that the legal system is also an autonomous system, operating within its own boundaries, with its own criteria, interpretations, and expectations. Accordingly, political interventions need to be "translated" and integrated into the "logic" of the legal system – into new laws that do not contradict old laws, into clear criteria about how and when the new laws apply, etc. In analogy to the issue of "translating" thoughts into communication (Chapter 1), the "translation" of political intentions through new laws into the logic of the legal system limits the *political* effects of the intervention. Political steering through legislation requires that both the political and the legal system develop their perceptiveness (through more fine-grained programmes and better feedback mechanisms) of expectations in and reactions by the other systems in their environment.

Steering optimism or steering pessimism?

Is the systems-theoretical account of steering pessimistic? Not necessarily. Evaluations over the years demonstrate that interventions in the operational mode of other systems can lead to unexpected reactions by the target system. From the viewpoint of the steering systems these reactions appear as unintended side effects or subsequent problems. For example, the government, in another attempt to introduce sustainable policies, wants to reduce the number of non-returnable aluminium cans for beverages, so it introduces a deposit fee. As a reaction of the target system (the economy), parts of the beverage industry switch from non-returnable cans to non-returnable PET bottles, which puts a number of tinplate producers out of business and thousands of workers out of their jobs.

Luhmann's approach to the limits of steering (Luhmann, 1997b) can be regarded as a sort of social criticism against outdated dogmas on the plannability of social life. Other theories of society develop their criticism on the explicit or implicit premise that political decisions are the instruments with which the welfare state (as a quasi-centre) can control, steer, and plan the development of society. Their criticism, then, is directed at the means and programmes that inform the decisions, the goals, and, not least, the way they are executed. Luhmann's criticism goes deeper, arguing that the notion of political steering is problematic in the first place (Schirmer & Hadamek, 2007), both in extreme cases, such as that of the Soviet communist party, which ran its country as if it were a factory (Derlugian, 2013), and in "lighter" versions, such as the Scandinavian model of the welfare state.

Driven by the welfare state's ambition to include everyone, ongoing political intervention in other social spheres leads to a spiral of increasing expectations (Luhmann, 1990c), accompanied by the demands of voters who fall for political promises about social support, benefits, and better conditions (such as free education, free day-care, free public transport, retirement at age 60, support for housing). The welfare state "feels" responsible for operating beyond its own boundaries and overestimates its abilities, but it generates and spreads *unrealistic expectations* that lead to ever-new disappointments and protests that are followed by new promises, followed by new disappointments and protests from election to election. This is one of the reasons why some welfare states (particularly in southern Europe) are struggling hard to keep their finances together, and also why populist parties on the left and right are so successful in the short term: they can pinpoint all the welfare states' failures, and – because they are only a small faction within the opposition – can promise heaven on earth without having to fear accountability.

Systems theory does not spread new hopes, new promises, or new utopias but it is not afraid to abandon hopes that cannot be fulfilled in the first place, promises that are never kept, and myths about a golden future (Moeller, 2012). In general, systems theory takes a neutral, analytic, and cognitive stance toward societal development: better to learn from society than teach it, better to study than embellish. Probably as a result of this neutral stance, most of the literature on steering within this paradigm appears "pessimistic" because it questions the capabilities that states have to steer other social systems without perturbations or counterproductive (from the viewpoint of the steering system) consequences.

Steering of organisation systems

With the theoretical tools of systems theory, we can distinguish between the steering of organisations and the steering of function systems. While function systems are assemblages of logics, rationalities, codes, and semantics, organisations have communicative addresses; they have conditional and goal programmes and a structure of decision premises, each of which can be the target of intervention. All of this makes it easier to steer organisations. Organisations such as hospitals or universities (in contrast to the function systems of medicine and education) can be addressed by political decisions because they operate with financial resources and within (or beyond) the law, require educated personnel, are dependent on legitimacy (Meyer & Rowan, 1977), etc. To give an example from the context of social help, the political system cannot steer the rationality and expectation structures in the help system (what is good help? what is "best practice"?) but it can steer social services via social law, or by distributing resources according to benchmarks within a "new public management" programme.[2] Organisations need to find ways to adapt, or their whole operation is at stake.

However, steering an organisation is not the same as making decisions for the organisation – this would, again, violate the operative autonomy of the organisation system. While the political system has the capability to reduce weekly worktime to 30 hours nationwide, this should not be confused with the authority to determine what happens after this collectively binding decision has been made, for instance increased labour costs, less productivity, decreased competitiveness on the global market, an increased number of leisure-related accidents, etc.

The operative difference between function systems and organisations enables us to understand how the Swedish Social Insurance Agency or other public authorities can decline a refund for medical treatment to certain individuals or groups who, according to the criteria of the medical system, are ill. Being ill and receiving a refund for medical treatment are events that take place on two different system levels. Therefore, the Swedish Social Insurance Agency cannot determine which diagnoses are medically valid, nor which methods are the best to use for making diagnoses. Diagnoses and methods of diagnosis are matters exclusive to the *function system* of medicine, not of an *organisation* mandated by the welfare state. There are many examples of shifting responsibilities between organisations that handle compensation for people on sick leave or on long-term welfare support. By differentiating between the definition of a diagnosis in medical programmes (function system) and its application in healthcare, the Swedish Social Insurance Agency (organisation), we can see that the political system does not steer the programmes of the medical system but does steer the programmes of some organisations. For instance, the Swedish Social Insurance Agency determines how doctors are supposed to write legitimate sick-notes (Michailakis, 2008).

Political steering connects the decision processes of organisations with certain conditions. The state can outlaw certain treatments but interdiction is not steering because it does not fix the future development of the function system (Luhmann, 1997b). Maybe certain medical treatments that violate national law are offered in other countries or on the black market, so sooner or later the political system needs to adapt by switching from normative to cognitive expectations. The political system can affect the decisions of organisations within their respective realms, and this is *de facto* what happens.

By distinguishing the levels of function system and organisation, we can also understand conflicts about compensations of several kinds (for instance for people with impairment). There is a discrepancy between programmes in a function system and the decision premises an organisation works with. This discrepancy, however is subject to constant contestation due to changing conditions. The discrepancy between the principal right to inclusion (universalism of inclusion) and factually occurring exclusion (through administrative rules, organisational practices, etc.) explains many social conflicts.

Case study

In the remainder of this chapter, we want to illustrate the difficulties of political steering with a case study. We draw on our own research on the attempts of the Swedish welfare state to foster the inclusion of functionally impaired people in the labour market (Michailakis, 2000, 2002). One of the goals of Swedish labour policy was to make the labour market accessible to everybody. People with functional impairments should get the same opportunities to work as non-disabled people. The difficulties functionally impaired people face on the labour market increase along with harder demands on the unemployed and increasing competition, even in skilled jobs.

For decades, the government tried to fight discrimination through labour policy programmes and anti-discrimination laws in order to open pathways for people with functional impairments to attain attractive jobs. Given the central role work plays in people's lives, the political system formulated a principle of the right to work (similar to that in the former communist German Democratic Republic), which emphasised work as an end in itself and as a human need (in order to make a living, to be independent from welfare, to actualise goals and dreams such as having a privately owned home). Across party affiliations, politicians have fought for the inclusion of functionally impaired people.

Technological changes in the labour market (computerisation, automatisation, robotisation) and structural economic changes (deregulation, restructuring, globalisation) require a more flexible labour market. These developments have perturbed the political system insofar as welfare state policy requires and aims at almost full employment. When these changes in the environment of the political system drastically reduced the need for a workforce, they led to perturbations in the labour market and shook up the programmes of political parties that depend on the support of the masses.

Over the years, a number of programmes have been introduced to increase the inclusion of functionally impaired people (wage subsidies, adjustments in the workplace, IT-based assistive technology, job protection). However, the results have not been encouraging. One example of the lack of success is the largely unaffected low employment level of impaired people even in times when the employment of non-disabled people booms. The theoretically most potent instrument to affect the expectations of employers is the financial subsidy. In the case of Sweden, the national health insurance (the Swedish Social Insurance Agency) takes over the wages of functionally impaired employees for a certain period. The intended purpose of these subsidies is to enable a transition to regular employment (paid by the employer, not the state). This is a political, not an economic, programme (thus an external attempt at steering – not inherent to the labour market), which can be noticed in a number of ways, including that the contracts for subsidised work differ from regular labour contracts. The latter are characterised by agreements between individuals and employing organisations: the workers sell their labour to the employer for a certain price in relation to a defined work effort and time. By contrast, subsidised employment is an agreement between the employer and the Swedish Social Insurance Agency, which is a governmental authority. Another difference between regular wage labour and subsidised employment is that the employer regulates the selection of the workforce in line with the employee's *capability* to do the job; the subsidised programme selects "workforce" according to the employee's *lack of capabilities*. The qualification criteria in one system (economy), thus, are diametrically different to those of the other (politics). This is one of the reasons why trade unions did not wish to represent subsidised employees: the latter's employment undermines the interests of union members. From a systems-theoretical perspective, indignation about failing to achieve the proclaimed political goals is misguided. If subsidised employees have faced worse contractual conditions in recent years, this is because the government has cut the funding for the subsidies programmes; it is not an effect of worsened conditions on the labour market, because these conditions had worsened long before.

With this example we aimed to illustrate the extent to which labour policy programmes fail to steer the labour market, partly because the range of the programme depends largely on the government's capability and willingness to pay for it. Labour market policy measures (subsidised employment, entry jobs, job protection, etc.) are built on the faulty assumption that the employer voluntarily transforms these politically supported jobs into regular (business-financed) jobs. However, employers (in line with their organisational goal programmes) do not increase wage costs for less work value unless they are compensated by the government – the programme is a political, not a market-based, measure. So, from a systems perspective it is not surprising that employers replace functionally impaired individuals whose subsidised period is over with new subsidised employees, or with non-disabled individuals. Organisations active on the labour market implement political steering only to the extent that it is beneficial to them.

Notes

1 Compare Weber's ideal type of bureaucracy: the most successful bureaucratic organisation is the one in which people act like trivial machines. Another example is military drill that also tries to trivialise non-trivial machines.
2 Although such attempts at steering are often rejected by the help system as illegitimate "managerialism" (Roose, Roets, & Bouverne-De Bie, 2012).

8

FUNCTIONS AND LATENT PROBLEMS, SYSTEMIC CRITICISM, AND SOCIAL WORK AS A REFLECTION THEORY

The purpose of this chapter is to bring together constructionism, causality, social problems, and steering, which we discussed in Chapters 5–7. We present a systems-theoretical variant of the functionalist method (equivalence functionalism), which rids itself from traditional versions such as structural functionalism and anthropological functionalism (Malinowski, 1944; Parsons, 1951). In this context, we will also discuss some thoughts about systems theory as a means of social criticism. Equipped with concepts such as multiperspectivity, contingency, and equivalence functionalism, Luhmannian systems theory is tolerant of other theoretical perspectives and viewpoints, which also prevents it from claiming the role of a be-all and end-all. We will conclude the chapter with a systems-theoretical view on social work research, which argues that academic social work operates through the logics of two function systems: as an academic discipline within the system of science and as a reflection theory within the social help system.

When we discussed social problems in Chapter 6, we argued in line with the notion of multiperspectivity that a given social problem looks different depending on which social system defines the problem image. In line with the constructionist paradigm we have also noted that different agents and social systems actively *construct* social problems differently on the basis of variation within some parameters. The given social problems vary in their meanings (second-order realities) because different images of them are grounded in different constructions of causal relations. Different agents highlight different, sometimes contradictory, causes of the same problem, for instance the problem of mass unemployment as a crisis of capitalism vs mass unemployment as a result of too-high wages and social costs vs unemployment as a bad match between the demanded and supplied competences (too few engineers and doctors, too many lawyers and business administrators). It is obvious that some agents emphasise one causal explanation and tend to downplay or ignore the other explanations.

Another aspect of causality construction touches upon the question of where, i.e. which link in, the causal chain is "cut". By "causal chain" we mean a basically infinite chain of causes to causes to causes to causes. The same can be turned around as a chain of effect of an effect of an effect of an effect. For example, if we want to explain why there is life on earth, we can cut the causal chain at God, which is what the larger monotheist religions do: God created the earth with all its properties, then God created plants, animals, and finally the human being. Or, if we base our argument on interdisciplinary research, we can cut the causal chain elsewhere: life is a consequence of processes within organic chemistry, which is a consequence of a certain constellation of processes within the inorganic chemistry in an environment that, combined, enable organic processes. However, inorganic chemical processes and a "life-enabling" environment are the results of physical forces, properties of material matter, and their relations, thus also physics, and so on, so we come back to the beginning of everything: the big bang (or again, God?).

For our topic it is especially interesting if we scrutinise how human action is explained by different theories that each have their own distinct points of departure in the chain. Explaining human action is very central in social work, sociology, behavioural sciences, law, education, politics, markets, and a number of other social spheres. Action theories such as that of rational choice (Coleman, 1994; Hechter, 1986) assume that the causes of social actions are rooted in the preference hierarchy of utility-maximising actors. "Preference hierarchy" means that there is a vertical order of goals an agent would like to attain, in particular when scarce resources and time constraints enforce prioritisation. Psychoanalytical and psychodynamic theories (Freud, 2003; Guntrip, 1995) go a step further down the chain by looking at unconscious currents that cause an individual's specific preference hierarchy (for instance what happened during childhood that makes her have such desires?). Marxists tend to regard actions as motivated by affiliation with social classes and material conditions, and thus, explain the preference hierarchies through class interests (because she is from the working class she has such and such interests). A very similar, albeit more sophisticated, argument has been made by Bourdieu (2013 [1979]), according to whom people, depending on the social milieu they grow up in, develop a certain habitus that drives actions, tastes, and preferences. Sociobiologists, evolutionary psychologists, and evolutionary sociologists (Pinker, 2002, 2007; Sanderson, 2001; Van den Berghe, 1990) go yet further down the causal chain when they depart from innate drives and genetic predispositions in order to explain human action. The purpose of this short overview was to pinpoint variation in causality constructions within the social sciences.

Systems theory and the functional method

Systems theory, in particular through its constructionist component, is less interested in causal explanations for social action. Rather, it is interested in how different agents make their own causal constructions by selecting from a wide range of possible causes and then attributing these to events in the system or environment. This is also true for strategically operating agents who want to push through their economic or political interests by promoting a particular definition of a certain social problem and suppressing others (Loseke, 2003). In strategic action, problem definitions build on a principle similar to that of causal explanations. Problem definitions are contingent selections in a potentially infinite chain. A problem and its solution are part of this chain; they form a complementary relation insofar as the problem requires a solution, and the solution is only a solution in regard to the problem. Depending on preference and viewpoint, the problem can appear as the solution and the solution itself can appear as a problem. Like causality, they also form infinite chains. A problem is a solution to a problem that precedes it in time, which creates new problems in the future, which, in turn, require new solutions. Seen from other perspectives or in regard to side effects, these new solutions create yet new problems that require yet new solutions, etc.

Regardless of how we divide the world in relation to problems and solutions or relations of causes and effects, we always deal with chains that need to be cut off somewhere. While the *distinction of cause/effect* is the most common within the world of science and in everyday life, the *distinction of problem/solution* has practical relevance in the art of engineering, on the one hand, and a strong tradition within social anthropology, on the other.

We can call the first tradition *mechanismic* because it looks for mechanisms (Hedström & Swedberg, 1998) and the other *functionalist* because it looks for functions. While the first tradition has been the foundation of modern scientific thinking since Galileo and Newton, the functionalist tradition has a much shorter history and a much more contested role. Following Durkheim, functionalism is mostly associated with the classic works of anthropology by Malinowski (1944) and Radcliffe-Brown (1940). During the 1940s and 1950s Parsons' structural-functionalist theory was the leading paradigm in the social sciences, but its dominance has provoked massive criticism from advocates of causal explanations such as Dore (1961) and Hempel (1959).[1]

In order to understand the objections brought forward by these critics we have to look at how mechanismic and functionalist approaches differ in their definition of research problems. Mechanismic explanations are interested in mechanisms from cause to effect expressed through questions such as, "What is the cause of X?" and, "What is the effect of X?" Functionalism is interested in problems and solutions; hence, the corresponding functionalist question is, "What is the function of X?" The function is defined as the solution to a problem. X can be anything, for example inequality. If inequality fulfils a function, it must be (by definition) a solution to something else. The task of functional analysis is to find out what the underlying problem in need of solution is in the first place. Here we speak of the "reference problem" (*Bezugsproblem*) of X – the problem that "X as solution" refers to. Phenomenon X, inequality in our example, is a solution that refers to an underlying problem. In order to understand X, we therefore have to uncover its reference problem.

But what is so different about a functionalist method in contrast to the mechanismic method? One could object that both paradigms want to know "*why* there is inequality". And yes, the traditional functionalism, or what Luhmann called "causal functionalism", actually also wants to give explanations, but such a procedure equates the distinctions of cause/effect and problem/solution.

The main objection against the functionalist method is that the latter is built on a logical fallacy, namely the confusion of a functional question with a causal question. This is exactly what happened in the classic and simultaneously falsified functionalist study of inequality by Davis and Moore (1945). By regarding a given phenomenon as a solution to some underlying or preceding phenomenon (reference problem) they wanted to *explain* the phenomenon's existence. At the same time, they claimed, something exists, *ergo* it must fulfil a function (otherwise it would not exist). That way, classic functionalism presupposes something as pre-requisite for an explanation (the prevalence of inequality) that it wants to explain in the first place (the prevalence of inequality). Functionalism tried to replace or make obsolete the mechanismic causal explanation but is actually built on a circular logic, a tautology that explains nothing (Hempel, 1959).

So can we *explain* anything at all with a functionalist method? The critics say no, and we agree with them. Within the framework of a modern systems theory, however, we can use the functionalist method to great benefit; the method has high value to offer if used properly – and proper use entails that the functionalist method is *not a substitute for causal explanations*. Luhmann (1995) proposed getting rid of the problematic parts of classic functionalism, such as its claims of explanations and its equation of functions with causes. His version of functional analysis does not have much in common with the traditional (justifiably criticised) variant (Lee & Brosziewski, 2009). For Luhmann, functional analysis works well as a heuristic method to describe phenomena as relations of (reference-) problem and solution, not as a "hypothetico-deductive system" (Luhmann, 1979). As a heuristic device this method is not suited to the search for causal explanations; it is best used to provide a horizon for comparisons (*Vergleichshorizont*) between alternative, "functionally equivalent" solutions to the same reference problem (Luhmann, 2005c [1964]). As previously described, the reference problem is not always visible and must be unearthed through the analysis.

If we observe the phenomenon "hierarchy in a group", we can ask for the function of hierarchy and search for the reference problem. In egalitarian groups it can be difficult to make fast and efficient decisions that bind group members collectively. Hierarchy is one possible solution to this problem – and conversely, decision-making is a possible reference problem to hierarchy. When we look at the relation between decision-making in a group and hierarchy as a relation between problem (decision-making in a group) and solution (hierarchy) we see the contingency in the solution. As mentioned in earlier chapters, "contingency" means that something is neither impossible nor necessary: it could be different. Hierarchy, from this perspective, is a contingent solution to the decision-making problem. The function could be fulfilled through other solutions, so-called "functional equivalents".

One such functional equivalent is the right to vote, combined with the rule of the majority. Another alternative is a rotation system, a third one is a lottery or throwing dice. Note that the equivalence between hierarchy, rule of the majority, rotation system, lottery, or dice only holds in regard to their function: they all (potentially) fulfil the same function (decision-making in groups), hence have functional equivalence. However, this does not mean equivalence in regard to other aspects, such as fairness or effectiveness, for which the five solutions may be anything but equivalent.

Remember that we always have to deal with *chains* of problem–solution relations. Every one of the solutions creates or fosters new (subsequent) problems, which, in turn, require a solution. For instance, hierarchy means inequality, and this may be problematic in a society that celebrates equality as a key value. Moreover, hierarchy could foster the abuse of power. A lottery and throwing dice would avoid (or solve) the problems of inequality and power abuse but they entail unpredictability and dependence on coincidence. The right to vote with majority rule may avoid random results and inequality but opens new cans of worms such as coalition-building, bargaining for votes, populism, and empty promises – in short, everything we know from parliamentary elections.

From this brief example, it should have become clear that every functionally equivalent solution to a reference problem leads to (its own) subsequent problems. What we want to show in this chapter is that the functionalist method in the Luhmannian (not the classic) understanding offers added value. However, we also want to stress that such a method is not a substitute for causal, mechanismic explanations but a complement that allows for different, but equally illuminating, scientific questions. Equivalence functionalism is highly compatible with constructionism, multiperspectivity, and systems theory because it helps to reveal the contingency behind any social phenomenon, and thereby contribute to its deconstruction, which is something usually appreciated by critical, emancipatory social theory. However, in contrast to many of today's poststructuralist and deconstructionist works, for equivalence functionalism *decon*struction does not *per se* entail *de*struction.

Moreover, equivalence functionalism is a suitable method for research inspired by systems theory because of the latter's interest in *latent* problem–solution relations. The sociologist Merton (1968) introduced the distinction between latent and manifest functions as a reaction to criticisms against Parsons' structural functionalism. Despite the partly justified objections against the distinction of latent and manifest functions (for instance, Helm, 1971), this distinction helps us to understand two things: first, problem–solution relations are not always openly visible but hidden in latency (why else should we need a functional analysis in the first place?) and second, what we see on the surface is possibly something other than what (actually) happens or has to happen for a social system to function properly.

Merton's famous example was the rain dance of the Hopi people. The manifest function of the dance was to make the gods provide the rain the Hopi so greatly depended on for agriculture. The logic was simple: if they danced, there would be a chance of rain. Although they were no experts in meteorology, anthropologists found that the causal link between dance and rain was less robust than the Hopi believed. The dance was very important anyway, and that was because of an underlying, actual, "latent" – hence unconscious – function, which was to maintain and increase group cohesion and ensure solidarity and integration in an environment of fading resources.

Within systems theory, we can use the latent/manifest distinction in order to distinguish between functions and their reference problems. A reference problem can be manifest, i.e. known to everyone. However, there can be an underlying, latent reference problem that is neither obvious nor known (sometimes nobody knows about it, sometimes it is well-hidden so that economic or power-political interests do not become public). It is the task of the functionalist researcher to unearth latent problems and their solutions.

Psychotherapists, family therapists, and social workers should apply this method, too, when they want to understand and remedy their clients' pathological symptoms and problem images. In the helping professions it can be of enormous help to regard a client's pathological behaviour as a solution to an underlying problem that is invisible on the surface. The pathological symptom and problem images fulfil a function for the client, and savvy, creative psychotherapists, family therapists, and social workers discover the latent reference problem.

Here, we can even reconnect the idea of systemic steering with the functional method. Linear attempts at steering, such the command directed at the client to stop behaving in this "strange way" or to threaten punishment, have miniscule chances of success. If the client were able to, he would have stopped on his own long ago. Approaches of linear steering (such as old-fashioned drill at schools) miss the fact that the clients' psychic systems are non-trivial, self-referential, operationally closed systems. We want to keep in mind that attempts at steering have to pass the needle's eye of "communication", i.e. a social order emerging between the therapist's and the client's psychic systems.

As the Palo Alto Group has shown, pathological behaviour is not *per se* a consequence of some wrong wiring in the brain but is frequently an expression of something that went wrong in the communicative patterns the client is or was part of. The pathological symptom is a way for the client to handle the tensions that arise through distorted communication patterns (such as the double-bind); hence the "real" pathology is to be found in communication patterns, and the client's "strange" behaviour is a function of this. In order to successfully treat a client and achieve the goal that he no longer needs the pathological behaviour (which is what therapists regard as a successful *systemic* steering), the therapist has to find the latent function of the behaviour. The pathological behaviour is a functional necessity in order to cope with a conflicting and unbearable situation. What the therapist – just like an anthropologist – needs to do, then, is to look for the reference problem of the behaviour, which is usually not known to the client, hence, is latent. After the latent problem has been laid open, the therapist can look for, or develop together with the client, a new behaviour that is functionally equivalent insofar as it fulfils the same function of solving the latent problem. Preferably, this new behaviour has neither pathological nor unhealthy side effects, nor is it regarded in a given culture as an indicator of mental illness. Of course, the ideal treatment would be one that solves the latent problem altogether, such as finding and eliminating the root of destructive communicative patterns (Chapter 1). Unfortunately, this is not always possible because the therapist does not always have access to the entire family, gang, bully, boss, or colleagues, etc. The discovery of functional equivalents to pathological behaviour is an enormous help because it shows clients that the current image of illness or mental disorder is contingent: it can be changed, deconstructed, and replaced by something better.

Illustration: the latent function of the Ethical Platform in healthcare priority-setting[2]

In the following paragraphs, we illustrate the relation between latent problems and functions with an example from our own research on priority-setting in healthcare (Michailakis & Schirmer, 2010, 2012; Schirmer & Michailakis, 2011, 2012, 2014). Like those in many other countries in the West, the Swedish healthcare system is troubled by budgetary problems. New medical and pharmaceutical advances are generating new possibilities for diagnosing and treating illness but, correspondingly, are leading to new demands for treatment, and in consequence, increased healthcare costs. Demographic ageing and decreasing tax income have put extra strain on finances. Since the 1990s, the Swedish state has begun to consider whether priority-setting may be inevitable (Calltorp, 1999; Riksrevisionen, 2004; Swedish Government, 1996, 2008).

A public investigation from 1993 (SOU, 1993), and slightly modified in 1995 (SOU, 1995), proposed what was called an "Ethical Platform" built upon three principles for priority-setting. The first principle is the *human dignity principle*, which states that everyone has an "equal worth and the same rights, regardless of personal properties and functions in society" (Socialstyrelsen, 2006). It is accompanied by the *need and solidarity principle*, which ensures that resources are distributed according to medical need and urgency. The third principle is called the *cost-effectiveness principle* and notes that an "appropriate relation between costs and effects" should be aspired to (Socialstyrelsen, 2006). The principles are intended to be followed in a hierarchical order, due to which cost aspects only play a subordinate role compared to aspects of dignity and need.

The Ethical Platform was presented in a government proposition (Swedish Government, 1996) and was adapted by the parliament as an official guideline to priority-setting in 1997. A few years later, however, the National Audit Office found that the Ethical Platform in its current form had failed in its aims both to provide decision-makers with guidance and to save significant amounts of money (Riksrevisionen, 2004). As a consequence, the National Centre for Priority Setting (*Prioriteringscentrum*) was commissioned by the government to propose revisions and improvements to the Ethical Platform. *Prioriteringscentrum* published its report in 2007 (Prioriteringscentrum, 2008)[3] and suggested major changes, including, amongst others, that the platform should be expanded with a principle of individual responsibility for one's health, according to which people can be given lower priority if their lifestyle threatens their health or the effectiveness of the provided medical treatment.

By distinguishing between manifest and latent functions as well as manifest and latent problems, we demonstrate how the Ethical Platform, according to our functionalist analysis, fulfils a latent function. The manifest function of the problem is twofold: it partly helps in resolving the problem of lack of resources, and it partly provides guidance for how doctors and other decision-makers should set priorities – which illnesses, treatments, and groups of patients should be prioritised.

In contrast to its official (i.e. manifest) function of saving money and providing guidance, we argue that the Ethical Platform fulfils a function for a latent problem of the welfare state. Regardless of how we look at it, priority-setting in healthcare always means *selection* and thus exclusion of certain patients from treatment (temporarily, if they end up further down the queue, or definitively, if the government decides that the public health insurance will not compensate the costs for a certain treatment).

This fundamental exclusion contradicts both the Swedish welfare state's self-description as an agency that includes everyone and the preamble of the Swedish healthcare law: "The goal of healthcare is good health and care on equal terms for the whole population" (Health and Medical Service Act, 1982). In its modern form as a welfare state, the political system is held accountable for the well-being of its citizens and for the provision of collective goods such as security, technical infrastructure, education, and not least, healthcare (Willke, 1992). But the inclusion of the interests and basic needs of the population as a whole not only includes ensuring the minimum requirements of social welfare and security for everyone but also a constant optimisation of the "good life" for everyone.

The preamble is the legal foundation for a publicly financed healthcare system that builds on solidarity, i.e. an individual citizen's spending power (big or small) should not affect the access, degree, and quality of the care she is offered. Ideally, everyone should get the same care, of the same quality and equally fast – something that clearly is not the case, as repeated studies have shown (for instance, Socialstyrelsen, 2011). In practice, the preamble is the basic clause for a collectively financed healthcare system, and the conditions and exceptions come second.[4]

The latent problem for the welfare state is the question of how to combine the idea of the human dignity principle (i.e. ensuring equal value for everyone) with legitimising exclusion/selection by setting priorities in healthcare. A *de facto* consequence of priority-setting is that some patients (or groups of patients) do not get the treatment they should have, according to their medical evaluation, fast enough or at all. Naturally, this contradicts the healthcare system's projected goal of giving everyone the care they need. This conflict can only be solved in the unlikely case of abundant resources over a longer period (as is the case in some oil-producing and exporting countries). The alternative is to reduce the range of inclusion and offer less access to healthcare, which would require an adjustment of the self-description as an all-inclusive welfare state.

We argue that the latent function of the Ethical Platform is to protect the self-description of the welfare state as the provider of good healthcare to everyone. This protection is achieved by *making invisible the structural contradiction* between unconditional access to healthcare for everyone (inclusion) and priority-setting, the effects of which are the opposite (exclusion).

How did the Ethical Platform of 1993/1995 solve this latent problem? According to our analysis, the platform text utilises a communicative trick:

The human dignity principle is placed in the first position of a hierarchical order of principles, followed by the needs and solidarity principle, and only in the third position comes the cost-effectiveness principle. Furthermore, human dignity is declared unconditional while the selection effect of "prioritisation" is relegated to the second and third ranks.

The label "ethical" simulates a fictional unified perspective across structural societal differentiation that does not coincide with the conditions the platform attempts to solve, i.e. competing perspectives between economy, medical capabilities to heal, and a population with increasing needs and demands. Expressed in systems-theoretical terms, the reference to ethics points beyond the structural differentiation of society (in particular between medicine, economy, and politics) while disguising the role of the welfare state (politics).

Let us first look at the human dignity principle. The first public investigation from 1993, which provided the vastly unchanged basis for the platform, describes the human dignity principle as follows:

> According to the human dignity principle, the individual human being has a unique worth and every human being has the same worth. Human dignity is not linked to individuals' personal characteristics or functions in society such as capabilities, social status, income, state of health etc. but to their very existence.
>
> *(SOU, 1993, p. 95)*

Drawing on the same value system as the UN Declaration of Human Rights, this idea of "equal worth" refers to something intrinsic, not something determined by society and culture. In the same paragraph (not contained in the excerpt), the report adds that "nobody is more prominent than anybody else". Human dignity is seen as unconditional and absolute as it implies "that one always and under all circumstances considers and treats the human being in terms of what she is and not in terms of what she has or does" (Swedish Government, 1996, p. 9).

When, however, equal worth is ascribed to everyone due to their human nature (born as equals), rankings and exclusions on this basis become difficult. Whereas the reference problem of prioritisation is *how to exclude some people*, the human dignity principle's contribution is to support the claim of *including everybody*. Selecting some at the cost of others *does not take place because of, but only despite* equal human worth. The human dignity principle basically contradicts the very idea of prioritisation.

Therefore, the human dignity principle cannot give guidelines for how decision-makers should set priorities, but only for how *not* to. The idea of equal human value, then, can only serve as a barrier to any type of illegitimate (unethical) discrimination. In terms of decision-making, the human dignity principle obviously does not seem to be a great help. Yet, it plays a decisive role in the Ethical Platform because the emphasis on equal human value and anti-discrimination strongly supports the self-description of the inclusive welfare state. We argue that the human dignity principle is a key to the latent function of the Ethical Platform. Because the human dignity principle is placed in the first and most important position of the platform, any legitimate prioritisation decision can be framed as meeting the criteria of "human dignity" and "equal human value".

At the same time, the Ethical Platform and its accompanying documents protect the self-description of the welfare state by blurring the human dignity principle's capacity to serve as a criterion for prioritisation. The public investigation that preceded the Ethical Platform also minimises the semantics of prioritisation as a means to rank, select, and, in certain cases, even exclude people of equal value, as the following passage from the 1993 investigation can illustrate. The excerpt is taken from the section where the three principles are presented:

> The *human dignity principle is a necessary but not sufficient ground for prioritisations in healthcare*. If everyone has the same worth and the same rights but resources are not unlimited, not everyone can get what they actually have the right to. The *dilemma is then* to choose those who should get what they have a right to without getting into conflict with the human dignity principle. Therefore, the report wants to suggest the need or solidarity principle as *additional* principle for priority-setting.
>
> *(SOU, 1993, p. 95, our emphasis)*

On the one hand, the excerpt admits the insufficiency of the human dignity principle to direct priorities *if resources are scarce*. While scarcity is introduced as a merely conditional constraint for the practicality of the human dignity principle, the text obscures the fact that prioritisation is necessary just *because there is scarcity* in the first place. The underlying logic applied here seems to be as follows: if resources are not scarce, the human dignity principle is an important criterion for prioritisation. If, by contrast, resources *are* scarce, the human dignity principle, with its claim that all have equal value and equal rights, needs to be complemented by another (set of) principle(s). But why, we may wonder, would one need to postulate that priority-setting is necessary independent from resources? What is here presented as the dilemma of whom to select corresponds to the very idea of prioritisation and exists independently from the human dignity principle and its implications. We believe that this argumentation actually aims at something else.

Inclusion of everyone is a political aspiration, while exclusion of certain (groups of) people under certain circumstances because of a lack of resources does not contradict the overarching principle because the overarching principle – human dignity – is presented as a means (albeit insufficient) of priority-setting. The principles that are meant to accompany the human dignity principle, the needs and solidarity principles and the cost-effectiveness principle, are hierarchically inferior to the human dignity principle. The communicative trick applied in the excerpt allows keeping the general impracticality of the human dignity principle under the surface. Even more important is the fact that the very meaning of prioritisation is hollowed out by being based on an overarching principle that makes selections actually impossible. The 2004 investigation's finding that the Ethical Platform is difficult to apply in decision-making should not be a surprise to anyone. Cost-effectiveness, the only principle that deals with economy and scarce resources, is only on the last and lowest rank.

However, in line with the latent function of the Ethical Platform, the self-description of the welfare state can remain intact because prioritisation and the right of everyone to healthcare (operationalised via the human dignity principle), no longer appears as a contradiction to cost-effectiveness and medical needs but as something that has been taken care of after the overarching principle is considered.

The Ethical Platform fulfils its latent function of protecting the self-description of the welfare state in another way. Despite its claim to be of general relevance for all actors involved in prioritisation in healthcare (doctors, hospital managers, patients, and relatives) the platform is essentially a *political* document. Typical of political documents, it uses a description of society that assumes a collective of human beings who share values, norms, culture, or anything else that makes them form a community. At the top of this community are normally the political system and its governmental organisations (such as government, parliament, authorities, and municipalities). In this case, however, the Ethical Platform puts *ethics* at the top, while at the same time disguising the special role of politics (the latent problem). By labelling the platform itself and its principles "ethical", the report simulates a fictional unified perspective across structural differentiation.

A practical consequence of a functionally differentiated society is that priorities are set on many organisational levels (national, regional, communal, hospital, care centres, etc.) and by different professional roles (politicians, administrators, economists, hospital managers, doctors, etc.). Not only do they deal with different aspects, they also follow their own rationalities as required in the functional and/or institutional contexts within which they operate: the economical rationality of reducing costs, the political rationality of steering and surveying resource administration, the medical rationality of providing the best and most suitable treatment for the patients in relation to their prospects to be cured.

Structurally, "ethics" cannot bridge the gaps of differentiation. Ethics provide (only) one vantage point among many, which is neither better nor more legitimate nor more insightful than the ones from the function systems. If something is observed from a perspective of ethics, it appears as "ethical" or "unethical", but nothing is said about values that only play a role within certain function systems. As Luhmann states, the function systems operate "on a level of higher amorality" (Luhmann, 1989b, 1990b), shielded from ethical restrictions. For example, court decisions have to be based on laws and evidence, not on moral reasoning. Important for scientific research is the truthfulness of hypotheses, not the moral discomforts they create. The economic value of an investment is measured by the profit (or loss) it generates, not by its potential ethical dubiousness. Political interests can (and sometimes have to) be pursued without caring about morality.

The Ethical Platform should not be expected to remove the differentiation of perspectives and rationalities; that would be structurally impossible. Instead, the achievement of the Ethical Platform lies just in the communicative *obscuration* of these social-structural differences. Even the cores of the principles of the Ethical Platform refer to political (solidarity), medical (needs), and economic logics (cost-effectiveness), but by framing them as "ethical", the platform can be presented *as if* it addresses a higher goal that transcends the incompatibilities of system rationalities.

According to the Ethical Platform, priority-setting then becomes a matter of ethics (and not primarily of economy) when avoiding expensive treatments if cheaper ones are available. It becomes a matter of ethics (and not primarily medicine) if patients with higher urgency are prioritised. Finally, it becomes a matter of ethics (and not of politics) when people have to accept that they are competing with others for the scarce resources (Why him and not me? Why you and not the other?). In this regard, the ethical perspective claims *semantic primacy* over the perspectives of function systems. The label "ethical" simulates a common moral denominator between the involved parties that diverts attention away from the political inducement behind the shape of the Ethical Platform as a means of protecting the self-description of the welfare state. As prioritisation becomes an ethical issue, accountabilities are shared, and politicians appear no more responsible for successful prioritisation than administrators or doctors.[5]

Social criticism with systems theory

As we will argue in this section, the study of latent problems and latent functions is essentially social criticism. There is a long tradition within social work, sociology, and philosophy of studying society with the purpose of criticising social conditions. This is true for Karl Marx and Friedrich Engels and their criticism of capitalism (Marx & Engels, 2014 [1847]); Ferdinand Tönnies and his criticism of the loss of community in a society that is dominated by market and contract relations (Tönnies & Loomis, 1964 [1887]). Even Max Weber's works on rationalisation and bureaucratisation (Weber, 1968) and Emile Durkheim's works on suicide and anomy are well known for their very distanced attitude toward their contemporary society (Durkheim, 1979 [1897], 2012 [1893]), and interestingly, all of them are still highly relevant to our society.

When we think of social criticism, we mainly think about the *Frankfurt School* and philosophers such as Max Horkheimer and Theodor W. Adorno (2002 [1947]) as well as their successors Jürgen Habermas (1991, 1992b) and Axel Honneth (2007). Despite personal differences, all of them agreed that capitalism and administration had led to alienation and injustice. One of the aims of this strand of criticism is to foster the emancipation of humankind from these oppressive logics. Much of today's critical research and theory within social work refers to the Frankfurt School in one way or another (see, for instance, Fook, 2002).

Beyond the Frankfurt School there are many theories and movements that can be summarised under the labels *identity politics* (Bernstein, 2005) and *cultural studies*. These theories and movements want to replace the old Marxist observation of superordination and subordination according to social class (ownership or non-ownership of capital and means of production) with other hierarchical distinctions. Since the decline of classical Marxism, critics claim that inequality and oppression are no longer questions of unfair distribution of resources (*politics of redistribution*) but questions of respect and recognition of minorities as being different (*politics of recognition*).[6] Examples of these theories and movements are feminist studies, gay and lesbian studies, several strands of ethnic and racial studies such as African American studies or Native American studies, several strands of postcolonial studies, and disability studies, which all have the goal of highlighting the identity of a certain minority as an alternative perspective to prevailing mainstream descriptions of society, which are dominated by white, male, heterosexual, non-disabled, neurotypical norms.

There are also combinations of minority perspectives, for instance "black feminism" (Crenshaw, 1991), which reject traditional feminism as "racially blind" because it is said to ignore the privilege of white women over black women. The same is true when functionally impaired women experience worse conditions than their male counterparts (Krahn, Walker, & Correa-De-Araujo, 2015; Söder & Hugemark, 2016). Multi-minority experiences and identities are usually summarised under the label "intersectionality" (Hill-Collins, 1998) to highlight the intersection of several lines of categorisation and discrimination.

As with many of the cultural studies, there is an internal dividing line between two groups. On the one hand, there are those who emphasise the identity and essence of minorities (in contrast to majority identities and norms), which means they emphasise the categories and associate them with pride, with positive difference. On the other hand, there are those who want to get rid of the categorisations altogether. Examples of the first group are traditional feminism, which emphasises how women *are different* from men, or gay & lesbian studies, which emphasise how homosexual people *are different* from heterosexuals. Examples of the second group are those who believe that differences between men and women (gender) are not biologically essential in any regard but are socially constructed means of power and domination, and, henceforth, should be abolished (deconstructed) completely so that no gender category is necessary any longer (Butler, 2002). Within intersectionality research there is also a tension between highlighting the special identities and alternative views of people on the intersections, on the one hand, and the aim of deconstructing the very categorisations they have just built, on the other.

"Deconstruction" is a term that originates from the postmodernist and post-structuralist movement that has its roots in French philosophy, literature, and history. Among the most important names are Jean-François Lyotard, Jacques Derrida, and Michel Foucault. The latter in particular had a great influence on critical deconstructionist research in social work (Høgsbro, 2012; Mik-Meyer & Villadsen, 2013). Postmodernist research is popular among social work researchers because it questions categorisations and power orders, which give rise to discrimination and injustice. As was mentioned previously, for postmodernists, sex, ethnicity, physical ability, age, and sexual predisposition, but also medical and psychiatric diagnoses, are not naturally given essences, but social categories manifested in a discursive order. Accordingly, researchers (and activists) subscribed to this paradigm see their task as unveiling the power structures behind categorisations, or as we would describe it, discovering and pointing out contingencies.

The latter is an apparent point of overlap with systems theory, to which we will return in a while. Systems theory has no particular reputation for criticising social conditions. This is particularly true for Parsons' structural–functionalist systems theory, which dominated much of the social sciences during the 1940s and 1950s, and which has been accused of conservativism (one of the worst labels a social theory could receive) because the theory focuses too much on stability, integration, and equilibrium between society's parts, while it had hardly anything to say about social change and social inequality (Homans, 1967; Mills, 1959). Parsons' theory has also raised objections because of its emphasis on functional properties that maintain the social structure, which, according to critics, means a justification of existing unfair social conditions.

Parsons' successor, Merton (whom we mentioned in the context of the functionalist method), tried to liberate structural functionalism from its conservative label by researching typical "leftist" topics such as stratification, status, and social problems (for instance, Merton & Nisbet, 1971). Merton gave up the positive attitude that classic structural functionalism had toward the concept "function" – that functions are good for society – and he studied dysfunctions, i.e. adverse and detrimental effects on society (Merton, 1968). During the 1960s and 1970s the dominating Parsonian position within sociology gave way to a more pluralist theoretical landscape in the United States. By this time, systems-theoretical thinking had won some territory in Europe. One milestone was the 1971 book *Theorie der Gesellschaft oder Sozialtechnologie: Was leistet die Systemforschung?* (*Theory of society or social technology: What is the contribution of systems research?*), which was edited by Habermas and Luhmann together (Habermas & Luhmann, 1971) and which triggered the so-called Habermas–Luhmann debate in West Germany. Among other things, this debate was about whether systems theory should be critical and normative. Because Habermas, as heir of the Frankfurt School, had already assumed the critical position in their joint book, Luhmann automatically appeared as the one who wanted to preserve social systems, as the designated successor to the "conservative" Parsons, a role Luhmann did not identify with at all. To be sure, Luhmann was not interested in criticism as a prime goal of social theory. Furthermore, he made several statements that marked a certain distance from progressive movements (such as the environmental movement, Luhmann, 1989a) but we believe that none of this justifies calling his systems theory conservative.[7]

Regardless of what the person Luhmann (who was not the only contributor to the systems theory we advocate in this book) believed and said, what counts is the theoretical tools and concepts we can use for scientific analysis and social practice. If we look at the theoretical framework, we find a number of points of contact for social criticism. We only need to be careful about what we mean by "criticism" and "critical theory": do we mean that contemporary society is not ideal according to our own political or moral preferences? Can we, from a scientific perspective (which is about truth and valid and reliable methods), say and defend *with scientific arguments* what is ideal? Or is it rather that our political and moral preferences determine what we consider as ideal (Haidt, 2012)? There is good reason to assume that a social democrat has different ideas than a libertarian or a conservative on what a good society is. Do we really want our political worldview to decide what is scientifically true?

We argue that in much of the so-called critical research on social work and sociology it is already determined before the study what are good or bad, desirable or undesirable results. The systems theory we have presented so far cannot give political or ethical guidance. It cannot (how could it?) give guidance about what we should believe to be good or bad, desirable or undesirable. Systems theory is about fact statements, and it is impossible to derive value judgments from statements about facts, as Campbell (2014) rightfully pointed out. It is exactly for these reasons that we have political, aesthetic, and ethical pluralism (see again, Haidt, 2012). What a scientific theory can do – and here we believe that systems theory has a great potential for social criticism – is provide tools to question what is taken for granted, to point out alternative perspectives and alternative solutions.

If we remove the link between social criticism and politically motivated criticism, we can claim that everything we have presented in this book is actually criticism – criticism not in the sense that we are against the phenomena we describe, that we dislike them or would like them to change (against communication, against systems, against functional differentiation, etc.). We may or may not like them, but this is not relevant when describing a scientific theory. When we speak of "criticism" we mean something that shows the contingency behind everything, something that shows the emergence when things behave differently than steering agencies would prefer. Instead of prescribing how society and social systems *should* look according to an allegedly morally superior perspective, we want to be humble and learn from society, and study how social systems operate. Only in that way we can bring about better interventions in practice – exactly what the Palo Alto Group has shown in the field of psychiatry. For them, the contingency within communication was central, not predefined biological deviations in the brain.

By understanding society as a collection of an infinitely large number of operationally closed, emergent, autonomous social systems that pursue their own rationalities, each with their unique history and observational perspective, one acquires insight and a feeling of tolerance.[8] This is the core of multiperspectivity, and multi-perspectivity has its foundation in functionally differentiated society. With this, we do not claim that functional differentiation, as such, is something desirable or good. As shown in Chapter 6, it has its own subsequent problems and some of them can be quite destructive. What we do say, however, is that functional differentiation needs to be taken seriously, and this means that researchers in their analyses and practitioners in their interventions should keep different systems apart and respect their different logics. Moreover, they should address the right systems and not direct their expectations at something that cannot be addressed; society is not an organisation. Likewise, the individual is not an interaction system and, therefore, should not be held responsible for something that is the result of the dynamics of the interaction.

By asking for the latent functions behind something, we are already questioning the dominating discourse because it implies that things are not as they seem, or at least that they do not have to be the way they are. In today's democracies we will not be punished for questioning the dominant social order, but within dictatorships and theocracies and pre-modern monarchies doing so is/was one of the biggest crimes to commit. How could someone be so impertinent as to question the divine vertical stratification and claim that everybody, noblemen and peasants alike, is equal?[9] The search for latencies, uncovering latent problems that some would like to keep in the dark, and the search for functional equivalent solutions are potentially threatening to those who have to lose some of their power, resources, or reputation. Hence, functional analysis is also criticism *per se*.

Social work research as a reflection theory of the help system[10]

In the remainder of this chapter, we take a look at social work research observed from the viewpoint of systems theory. In Chapter 3 we argued that social help, i.e. the activities of the social services, is subject to a societal function system, just like the economy, politics, science, religion, education, etc. To the extent that social help is an autonomous function system and not simply an auxiliary agent for the welfare state or the legal system, the help system itself – that is, its code and programmes – determines what/who is a case for social help and what/who is not.

This section presents an argument mainly developed by Luhmann scholar André Kieserling (Kieserling, 2004a), namely that most (though not all) function systems have their own academic disciplines,[11] which in systems theory are called *reflection theories*. Economic theory is the reflection theory of the economy, political theory is the reflection theory of the political system, pedagogy is the reflection theory of the education system, theology is the reflection theory of the system of religion. In this section, we will argue that the academic discipline of social work is the reflection theory of the help system. Before moving on, we need to explain the concept of reflection theory in more detail.

On the one hand, reflection theories usually consider themselves to be *scientific disciplines*. Reflection theories are, like any other academic discipline, represented by professorships and university departments; they guide and carry out research with the help of scientific methods of data collection and data analysis. Further-more, they have publication outlets with peer review and impact factors.

On the other hand, reflection theories have a specific relation toward their function systems; more precisely, they are what systems theorists call *self-descriptions* of the function systems. In contrast to outside descriptions (*Fremdbeschreibungen*), which can afford to formulate more or less critical views of the system – think of a Marxist criticism of the market economy – self-descriptions are compelled to be more loyal to their system (Kieserling, 2004a, pp. 49, 88). As Kieserling (2004a, p. 58) argues, the *raison d'être* of reflection theories is to reflect on and positively evaluate the code and societal function of their function system. In other words, reflection theories have an *affirmative* nature regarding their function system: legal theories appraise the law, economic theories endorse markets and rationality; poli-tical theories usually esteem the state or equivalent forms of governance. Negative evaluations of (and even indifference toward) the function would cause irritation rather than appreciation within the function system. Imagine a theology that chal-lenges the existence of divine, transcendent beings, a philosophy of science that denies interest in knowledge or truth, a pedagogical theory that questions the possibility of changing individuals by means of teaching.

While theories in purely scientific disciplines submit to the code of true/untrue (Luhmann, 1990a), reflection theories also align with the code of their function systems (Kieserling, 2004b). This means that they are more restricted in terms of choice of and attitudes toward research topics than, say, a sociological description. Research informed by reflection theories must satisfy claims of usefulness for the respective function systems. In order to be intelligible by the practitioners of the respective system (judges, priests, pedagogues, social workers, etc.), reflection the-ories strive for a semantic unity of plausibility and evidence (2004b, p. 59). They cannot simply convey research findings that contradict the plausibilities and values within their function systems. Kieserling argues straightforwardly that this makes reflection theories part of their function systems, rather than part of the function system of science. From a systems-theoretical perspective, reflection theories, then, appear as internal subsystems of function systems. Whereas a function system dif-ferentiates itself from its societal environment (politics and society, education and society, religion and society, help system and society – with society always being the environment, but a different one for each function system), a reflection theory differentiates itself from the practice of its own function system (political theory and political practice, pedagogic theory and pedagogic practice, theology and reli-gious practice, social work theory and social work practice).

Reflection theories observe and reflect on the practices of their function systems (help, teaching, preaching), while *reflection theories as practices themselves* take on the practice forms of science, that is conducting and publishing research, finding and producing knowledge. From the viewpoint of the reflection theory, this internal differentiation appears as tension between theory and practice or between knowledge production and knowledge application (Kieserling, 2004a, p. 72). By associating themselves with science, reflection theories legitimise their own status within their function systems. Associating themselves with their function systems, they might assert their usefulness in solving societal reference problems and develop self-descriptions based on both scientific truth and community benefit. Both associations are necessary, especially because reflection theories are important for educating, training, and socialising future practitioners in their professional fields: lawyers and judges require training in law, priests in theology, physicians in medicine, and social workers in social work.

One last note on reflection theories is necessary. As Luhmann (2014 [1972]) noted, function systems do not just host one reflection theory but several of them. Economic theory, political theory, the theory of law, for instance, all consist of many different schools (or sub-theories), each competing with the others for the status of the best descriptions of their field. So, while Keynesianism and neo-classic economic theory have differing views on how economic policy should look, they are both part of "the" reflection theory of the system of economy. The same is valid for realist and idealist theories of international politics, which strongly disagree on how to achieve security from potential enemies but share the view that security is a key goal of political theorising, which makes them reflection theories of the system of politics. Similar examples can be found for the reflection theories of other function systems.

In line with what has already been discussed about reflection theories, we argue that the discipline of social work serves as a reflection theory of the help system. We will provide some arguments to support this claim. Reflection theories convey positive attitudes toward the function of their host system in society, which makes them basically (though not always explicitly) *normative*. As is true of the help system itself, help is also considered to be something good in the discipline of social work. Accordingly, good help (in line with professional ethics) is better than less good help. The omission of help where help is possible is worse − except in the para-doxical case when social workers cease their help efforts as a means of fostering the client's self-help, which in turn could be a particular method of providing help.

This strong focus on good help has become very obvious in the debates for and against *evidence-based practice* (Gambrill, 1999, 2001; Nevo & Slonim-Nevo, 2011; Otto, Polutta, & Ziegler, 2009; Soydan, 2008; Webb, 2001). Whatever side the debaters are on, they always argue for improving the quality of help. Depending on the side, "good practice" can be achieved either by usage of the "best evidence available" (Sackett, Rosenberg, Gray, Haynes, & Richardson, 1996) or by protecting professional discretion against manualisation and bureaucratisation (Harris, 1998; Webb, 2001). What the debaters all have in common is that each claims to represent the "better practice", thus the better help. By contrast, a sociological analysis might be interested in how different ways of defining what "good" practice is vary across eras, across countries, across observers and stakeholders, across scholarly paradigms, etc. It is important to note that a sociological analysis is neither constrained by the imperatives and normativity claims of the help system, nor forced to take sides.

Since a reflection theory is a subsystem of its hosting function system, it tends to submit to the host system's code rather than to that of science. Sometimes there can be an outright contradiction between what is scientifically true and what is in line with the semantics of "help", and in such situations, reflection theories support what is plausible in their function system. For example, one finds hardly any academic social work texts that make use of evolutionary psychology to explain gender or power differences, or that use neuroscience to explain deviant behaviour, despite the fact that there is an abundance of scientific evidence (Pinker, 2002; Turner, 2002), sometimes even acquired with the "gold standard" of randomised controlled trials. Similarly, statements that question the benefits of social equality would hardly be welcome in social work journals, not even when tying them to the facilitation of decision-making (which is relevant for any social work organisation consisting of more than one member) or to the sociological fact that even the most democratic societies require stratification in order to function properly (who is going to do the low status jobs? see also Etzioni, 2000). The implications of such findings would be unacceptable to academic social work because they would contradict professional values and be irreconcilable with human justice. A very controversial example is prostitution. In social work, it is widely treated as a social problem that requires remedies, particularly because it is regarded as an engine for human trafficking, slavery, gender oppression, etc. Non-normative and non-obvious[12] research could examine the stabilising functions of prostitution for marriage (Davis, 1937). We do not aim to defend such research in the slightest but consider it instructive evidence for the argument that there are some things that could be studied in the social sciences that one simply cannot consider in social work and still expect to remain a respected member of the discipline's community.

The key to understanding all of this is that – in contrast to science, where truth and verifiable knowledge are the chief reference problems – social work takes sides with the marginalised, the poor, the deprived, the victims of oppressive structures, etc. and aims to promote social change for their benefit. Scholarly social work conducts research and writes for their benefit (Ife, 2012), either directly by advocating for their interests or indirectly by informing and educating those who work to help them. As a result, social work follows the imperatives that prevail within the help system, not within the system of science.

There is substantial overlap between science-oriented communication and social work communication (what is "good" help can also be true, and vice versa), but in potential cases of conflict, the help code is superior to the scientific code in social work. As shown in the previous section, this is neither a peculiarity of social work nor is it a weakness – it is simply a structural characteristic of any reflection theory.

While most of the scholarly practice takes place in the context of academic social work (conducting research, publishing, grant applications, PhD supervision, etc.), there is always the – sometimes latent, often manifest – link between academic practice and professional practice (Parton, 2000). Whatever academics write is almost always expected to have relevance to practice in some way. This is important for the legitimacy of the reflection theory in its function system; likewise, this legitimacy is underpinned by attempts to connect the methodologies of the reflection theory more closely to the scientific canon, as can be seen in recent debates about whether social work is or should be a science (Brekke, 2012, 2014; Merten, Sommerfeld, & Koditek, 1996; Staub-Bernasconi, 2007). On the other hand, however, the functional divide between reflection theory and professional activity is an explanation of what is often criticised as a suboptimal relation between theory and practice (Michailakis & Schirmer, 2014b).

Reflection theories tend to overstate the impact they have (or ought to have) on society and other function systems. For example, in textbooks one often reads that social work has the mandate to solve social problems and promote social change (Healy, 2001). Certainly, there is no doubt that social workers in their daily work deal with social problems and their consequences, and the more they consider themselves as social pedagogues (particularly in continental Europe), the more they engage in social change by educating and helping to empower their clients.

However, it would be easy to argue that social problems are solved and social change is achieved by other systems than the help system. Economists might claim that capitalism and the liberalisation of markets have reduced global poverty and raised global living standards; scientists might claim that their innovations and advances have facilitated more comfortable lifestyle, survival, longevity, mobility, and communication; politicians (as well as administrators and planners) might claim that their political programmes have provided inclusion, equality, employment, etc. We should particularly mention social mass movements such as the bourgeois movement (French Revolution), the labour movement (welfare state), the suffragettes (women's political inclusion), and various minority movements that, at least on the macro level, forced dominant classes, power structures, or discourses to give way, thereby enabling social change.

From this *ad hoc* comparative perspective, one might wonder why, of all movements, social work should be the engine of social problem-solving and social change. Our position is not to question the efforts and successes of social work on behalf of this – quite the contrary. Our argument is rather that reflection theories typically overestimate the function and its positive effects on society as a whole, and social work (being the reflection theory of the help system) does not differ in this respect from other reflection theories of other function systems. Put roughly, while liberal economists think that a greater market is good for society and that social problems are the result of too small a market, political theorists, by contrast, believe that more governance is good for society, while social problems are the effect of too little governance, that is, too much *laissez-faire* toward other systems. In a similar vein, social work scholars assume that because there is too much injustice in the world, more help (understood as motivation, activation, empowerment, illumination, solidarity, equality) is needed to solve the problems. What all these views have in common is that the source of the problems is considered to be outside the function system, while the solution is to be found inside it.

Considering the discipline social work as a reflection theory has at least three implications with added value for social work research and practice. This view provides new answers to three old questions concerning self-reflection of the help system: (1) the identity question, (2) the question of academisation/scientification and (3) the question of the relation between theory and practice.

1) The identity question is as old as the professional practice itself: what is social work about? What is its unity (what is common to all social workers) and its difference (what is genuine about social workers in comparison with psychologists, psychiatrists, nurses, pedagogues, sociologists)? Similarly, the academic discipline is torn by its uncertain identity: whether it ought to be a science-based action theory to guide practitioners (Brekke, 2014; Obrecht, 1996), a critical social science of social problems and social change (Dominelli, 2002; Fook, 2002), or even a "discipline without qualities" as Kleve (2007) suggests in allusion to Robert Musil's famous novel *The man without qualities*. The sociological answer to the identity question, based on Luhmannian systems theory, is twofold: first, there is the help system, which as a function system of society fulfils an exclusive function (exclusion management) in an autonomous way. With its focus on help, this system offers a perspective on society and social problems that is distinct from that of other professions and other function systems. Second, if we locate the discipline of social work as a subsystem within the help system, the identity problem looks less severe because, as a reflection theory, its tasks and its exclusivity (in contrast to neighbouring disciplines) are given by the functional logic of the help system. Obviously, being classified as a reflection theory, this does not entail any kind of degradation – that is, that social work was not (yet) good enough to meet the requirements of a fully-fledged and fully respected science (whatever that might be). On the contrary, reflection theories are crucial to their function systems for boundary management. They are important gatekeepers for fending off intrusions by other function systems (not least those of the economy, politics, and positivist science) that tend to impose their own codes on the logic of the help system. The latter has become an issue, particularly in the context of outsourcing formerly public social services to the private sector. Private social care organisations (unless they are non-profit organisations) strive for economic profit. The "good help" then becomes relegated to an interchangeable means of profit, not an end in itself as the professional ethics of the help system would require (Gethin-Jones, 2012). A reflection theory needs to formulate principles and programmes to safeguard the fulfilment of the societal function of its system. Similarly, the recent rise of New Public Management, which has gained in popularity among welfare administrators who are looking for ways to reduce costs and maintain a belief in the efficiency increases that New Public Management keeps promising, could be interpreted as a failure of social work by focusing too much on the competition with other research disciplines and too little on defending the integrity of the function system itself. This leads us to the second point.

2) Similar to the identity question, the aspiration toward academisation and scientisation is also almost as old as the profession itself. While academisation, i.e. the establishment of a discipline at universities, is useful in terms of legitimising the systems-internal differentiation between practice and reflection theory, the aspiration of scientisation runs contrary to the *raison d'être* of the discipline. We certainly do not question the necessity of an interdisciplinary scientific foundation for the knowledge base of social work professionals. However, we argue that attempts to

completely transform social work into an empirical science – be it bio-psycho-social natural science-style positivism or a sociology of inequality and social problems – would imply abandoning the reflective function it has for the help system. The more social work is turned into a positivist natural science, the more it will find evidence and contribute to its own knowledge base but the less it will be able to interpret and normatively evaluate the meaning of all this evidence for practitioners, who not only need to follow programmes but, at least equally important, must attach meaning to these programs. This meaning can only come from the help system itself. If, on the other hand, social work tried to turn into an empirical science of social inequality and social problems, it would be more difficult for it to remain distinct from sociology. The latter situation has led some commentators to reject the necessity of social work in the first place (for a Swedish case, see Börjeson, cited in Brante, 1987, p. 41), arguing that the discipline should be abolished because it cannot keep up with sociology. We find that such statements miss the point completely because sociology cannot replace social work for the simple but nonetheless compelling reason that social work as reflection theory has a different function than a (purely) scientific discipline. While both sociology and social work make statements about inequality and social problems, the associated meanings are completely different (a matter of truth or a matter of help and assistance).

3) Finally, regarding academic social work as a reflection theory of the help system gives a new interpretation of the enduring conflict between theory and practice. In our view, the often observed dysfunctional or problematic "transfer" from theory and research to practice is based on misleading expectations. As a reflection theory, the usefulness of practice does not lie in empirical findings and their translation into concrete guidelines for practitioners. Quite the contrary – most practitioners do not want to sacrifice their professional discretion; they consider social work as an art rather than as assembly line work in the best Taylorist–Fordist sense. The usefulness of the "theory" comes to the fore especially in the education of future social work practitioners. In their training, they learn more than just a lot of facts and practical methods. A key function of training is socialisation in the core values, creation of meaning, and provision of a normative compass for what "good practice" is. Similarly, with its academic practice (papers, books, lectures, etc.) as reflection theory, the discipline of social work can prevent hardened professional practitioners from turning into cynics over their long careers, when they constantly have to deal with inter-professional, political, or client-related obstacles.

One last thought on the relation between theory and practice: as academic practice, a reflection theory entails the conduct of research, both empirical and theoretical. While this kind of research aligns itself with the code of the scientific system (true/false), it is subject to the code of its function system (help/not help), which means that both topics and approaches are restricted. To maintain its internal differentiation from professional practice, a reflection theory as an academic discipline requires a certain amount of relative autonomy from professional practice. The discipline itself does not practice help; it researches, publishes, debates.

On the other hand, the relative autonomy needs to be mutual. Subordination of one to the other (when the discipline prescribes how practitioners should do their work, or vice versa, when practice defines what research the discipline needs to conduct) is dysfunctional for the system itself (Michailakis & Schirmer, 2014b). Relative autonomy should not be confused with autarchy, as both are parts within and oriented toward the same function system. In this regard, they share the same identity.

Notes

1 For a more recent and well-argued criticism of classic functionalism, see Sanderson (2001). The classic criticism against structural functionalism and Parsons' work – most prominently, Homans (1967) and Mills (1959) – was directed against much more than the functionalist method, namely the theory of society itself. It presented a harmonistic or teleological image of society and too much focus on societal needs, equilibrium, and maintenance of the normative order while more pressing issues, in the eyes of many, such as social change, and inequality hardly received any attention or space within this framework.

2 Parts of the following paragraphs are based on the article "The latent function of 'responsibility for one's health' in Swedish healthcare priority-setting", published in *Health Sociology Review* (Schirmer & Michailakis, 2012).

3 References are taken from the English version, which was published in 2008.

4 It is interesting to note that the particularly Scandinavian view understands healthcare as privilege provided by the generous welfare state – differences to Anglo-Saxon healthcare systems are striking.

5 The 2004 report by the Swedish National Audit Office (Riksrevisionen, 2004) showed that the Ethical Platform of 1993/1995 has not fulfilled its manifest function to guide priority-setting and save money. The 2007 report by the National Centre for Priority Setting has, therefore, proposed an improved Ethical Platform, which, according to our functional analysis, achieves a solution to the manifest function without threatening the latent function. The key to achieving this is a redefinition of the human dignity principle from unconditional inclusion to conditional inclusion (based on agency) and the introduction of a responsibility principle, according to which inclusion (and full access to healthcare) requires a responsible lifestyle. Therefore, exclusion can be justified in the name of ethics. In this way, the new Ethical Platform (which, by the way, was never adopted) serves as a functional equivalent to the old one. We do not have the space to go deeper into this matter here but we invite interested readers to take a look at our other publications (Michailakis & Schirmer, 2010, 2012; Schirmer & Michailakis, 2011, 2012, 2014).

6 A very interesting read in this context is Nancy Fraser's work on paradoxes and contradictions between the politics of redistribution and the politics of recognition (as developed in Fraser & Honneth, 2003).

7 A closer analysis by King and Thornhill (2003) has demonstrated that the political ideas of the "radical liberals" Habermas and Rawls are actually not very different from Luhmann's.

8 Tolerance does not mean that we have to like something but that we accept alternative viewpoints. So tolerance means that we do not fight something because we do not like it, and in this regard it is an achievement – that currently is under threat by the so-called "culture wars". In contrast to respect, however, tolerance has rather a negative connotation but it is sometimes as good as it gets (Schirmer, Weidenstedt, & Reich, 2012).

9 It was not until Rousseau, who in 1755 formulated the idea that human beings are born as equals and that all inequality was a product of society. Instead of demanding equality

among non-equals, Rousseau criticised the inequality among equals. That way, he turned upside down one of the most central foundations of social justice (Reich & Michailakis, 2005).

10 Parts of this section are based on our article "The help system and its reflection theory: A sociological observation of social work", published in *Nordic Social Work Research* (Schirmer & Michailakis, 2015a).

11 "Academic discipline" refers to a system of concepts and methodological rules employed in the endeavour to interpret and explain phenomena that result in a specific body of knowledge. Disciplinary knowledge is hosted in academic departments.

12 In the sense of Randall Collins' non-obvious sociology (Collins, 1982).

CONCLUSION

The aim of this book was to present some insights from sociological systems theory for an audience in social work and the helping professions. It is not primarily a social work textbook but rather a book about an interdisciplinary theory that social work and other helping professions – both in academia and practice – can benefit from. Like other complex theoretical frameworks, this sociological systems theory offers in-depth, condensed insights through some key concepts based on certain presuppositions. The framework has its origin in natural sciences and provides, to some extent, a common vocabulary for natural sciences, social sciences, and the humanities. Hence, the framework is abstract and difficult to access but its openness to influences from other disciplines and theories makes it suitable for describing a large number of phenomena as systems. The framework can be applied equally to cells, neuronal systems, minds, and several types of social systems, including societal function systems (politics, law, economy), but also small interaction systems (such as a counselling session between a social worker and a client) or medium-sized organisations (such as a care facility).

In line with the Palo Alto Group from the field of psychiatry and Luhmannian sociological systems theory, we have argued that social phenomena can be understood as parts of communication systems. Communication is that which is genuinely social, while everything that is not communication (including human beings) is part of the environment.

Within mainstream sociology, social work, and even therapy and pedagogy, it is common to study social phenomena in an essentialist manner, departing from individual characteristics and actions. We wanted to show how individual actions can be interpreted as parts of systems. According to systemic thinking, social systems are networks of communication. It is the communication systems on all levels that enable and limit alternatives of choice. Function systems establish and limit how events can be communicated according to specific logics – is an event, for instance, provided help, an economic exchange, or scientific research? Organisations, for their part, establish and limit routines of decision-making as well as rules for who has what authorisation to say what to whom. Interaction systems, finally, establish and limit systemic dynamics in real-time: who is present, who has said what, how can it be interpreted, whose contributions and viewpoints need to be considered and whose can be ignored, do relational or content aspects contradict each other?

The whole point of systems theory is to direct focus towards the relations between phenomena or people in the social world – not towards the separate parts and their properties. This is the core of *emergence*, one of the key words in this book. The whole is different than the sum of its parts. The whole is a reality *sui generis*, as Durkheim called it, and is therefore qualitatively different from its constitutive elements. Problems within a family cannot be understood adequately by looking at the parents' and children's behaviours alone. In order to bring about change, practitioners or therapists need to intervene in social systems, not in individual psychic systems.

We have argued that systems theory is relevant both for constructionist and realist research and practice. With tools from systems theory we can analyse how things *are*, i.e. we can see they are complex phenomena with emergent properties. At the same time, we can take systems seriously as generators, as constructors, of their own realities. This is a mix of realism and constructionism: we look at what systems actually and factually *do*, namely *construct*. Hence, it is correct to understand systems theory as a constructionist framework that examines how systems construct their environment. Systems are observers that can be specified empirically; their descriptions of the world are not representations of the world but *observer-dependent* descriptions. Without exception, everything that is said or written is said or written by somebody (this includes our book). A conscientious social worker and a rigorous researcher have to take into account who is the observer and which observational perspective is used (for example, from which function system), but also, what is this observer able and unable to see?

This brings us to a related concept that we believe should receive more attention in social work, namely *multiperspectivity*. The concept is based upon the assumption that the characteristic principle of modern society is *functional differentiation*, i.e. a differentiation in systems with functional logics and rationalities with distinct views on the world. A certain phenomenon has different properties observed from different systems' perspectives. For instance, an alcohol-abusing man can be seen as a case for social help, a cost factor, a research subject, a delinquent, an unreliable husband, etc. Multiperspectivity in practice means that a good social worker needs to avoid imposing his/her perspective on the client's situation without considering other perspectives from which the situation appears completely different. Both researcher and practitioner have to accept that there are several legitimate descriptions for every problem, even if these descriptions sometimes appear contradictory and incompatible.

Multiperspectivity, i.e. the circumstance that perspectives are diverse, separate, and sometimes in conflict with each other, should not be considered as a problem.

On the contrary, the differentiation in diverse perspectives is a characteristic of modern pluralist societies. If we try to deny or whitewash this structural characteristic, we end up in trouble. The claim that there is (or should be) one and only one valid perspective (such as the word of a prophet) is at its core intolerant and totalitarian.[1] The systems-theoretical emphasis on multiperspectivity protects us against both simplifications and one-eyed analyses (clients have their own perspective, which does not coincide, and often conflicts, with the perspective of social work; the social worker's perspective may conflict with that of the police; political perspectives may conflict with scientific perspectives, etc.). One added value of the concept of multiperspectivity is that researchers and practitioners can take in much more information for analysing and tackling a given problem, and it also allows them to see solutions to a given problem that they may have missed otherwise.

The more we take multiperspectivity and observer-dependence seriously, the less we can solely rely on normative theories that tell us what is good or bad, morally or politically desirable or detestable, as the sole source of information.[2] That is a different story in the practice of helping professions because it takes place in a context characterised by values and professional ethics in accordance with what the help system, its organisations, and the local political system prescribe. However, a scientific perspective, we should note, does not exclude criticism. We have argued that science, the drive to achieve cognition, to know something, to find out new things, already entails a critical potential insofar as it highlights contingency and questions the status quo, prevailing ideologies, taken-for-granted truisms, and normative systems.

Seen from the perspective of systems theory, a researcher is not critical by taking a stance against certain social conditions (which we can do as private persons) but by pointing out contingency (it can be different or can be done differently) and latency (who benefits from dominant descriptions, what is left out of official descriptions) as well as multiperspectivity (how other agents and systems look at things). All of this is criticism, and we consider it a central source of inspiration in a field such as social work. A social worker who, in a one-eyed manner, takes for granted what her employers, leading colleagues, the media, or politicians tell her cannot be a good social worker because she does not think autonomously. How can such an attitude be good for a client in urgent need? Social workers are not trivial machines either, who only follow orders and operate like cogs in a giant bureaucracy. Systems theory is a sort of guide to thinking autonomously, and this is something we consider to be a key competence in social work, in both practice and research.

Notes

1 On this matter see the outstanding story of Professor Caritat (Lukes, 1996).
2 Hence, pluralism within the reflection theories of function systems is an asset because it makes the whole field more tolerant, more open towards new developments that require cognitive expectations.

REFERENCES

Abbas, T. (2007). Muslim minorities in Britain: integration, multiculturalism and radicalism in the post-7/7 period. *Journal of Intercultural Studies, 28*(3), 287–300.

Abbott, A. (2014). *The system of professions: An essay on the division of expert labor.* Chicago, IL: University of Chicago Press.

Achterhuis, H. (2010). *De utopie van de vrije markt.* Rotterdam: Lemniscaat.

Ahrne, G. (1994). *Social organizations: Interaction inside, outside, and between organizations.* London: SAGE.

Ahrne, G. (2014). *Att se samhället.* Malmö: Liber.

Andersen, N. Å. (2003a). *Discursive analytical strategies.* Bristol: Policy Press.

Andersen, N. Å. (2003b). Polyphonic organisations. In T. Hernes & T. Bakken (Eds.), *Autopoietic organization theory* (pp. 151–182). Oslo: Liber.

Anderson, E. (1999). *Code of the street.* New York: Norton.

Ashby, W. R. (1962). Principles of the self-organizing system. In H. Von Foerster & G. Zopf (Eds.), *Principles of self-organization: Transactions of the University of Illinois Symposium* (pp. 255–278). London: Pergamon Press.

Baecker, D. (1994). Soziale Hilfe als Funktionssystem der Gesellschaft. *Zeitschrift für Soziologie, 23*(1), 93–110.

Bardmann, T., & Hermsen, T. (2000). Luhmanns Systemtheorie in der Reflexion Sozialer Arbeit. In R. Merten (Ed.), *Systemtheorie Sozialer Arbeit* (pp. 87–112). Opladen: Leske & Budrich.

Bateson, G. (1972). *Steps to an ecology of mind.* Chicago, IL: University of Chicago Press.

Bateson, G., Jackson, D., Haley, J., & Weakland, J. (1956). Toward a theory of schizophrenia. *Behavioral Science, 1*(4), 251–264.

Bauman, Z. (1990). Modernity and ambivalence. *Theory, Culture and Society, 7*, 143–169.

Bauman, Z. (2004). *Wasted lives: Modernity and its outcasts.* Cambridge: Polity Press.

Beck, U. (1992). *Risk society: Towards a new modernity* London/New Delhi: SAGE.

Becker, H. S. (1966). *Social problems: A modern approach.* New York: Wiley.

Bensman, J., & Gerver, I. (1963). Crime and punishment in the factory: the function of deviancy in maintaining the social system. *American Sociological Review, 28*(4), 588–598.

Bernstein, M. (2005). Identity politics. *Annual Review of Sociology*, 31(1), 47–74.

Beyer, P. (1998). Globalizing systems, global cultural models and religion(s). *International Sociology*, 13(1), 79–94.

Beyer, P. (2009). Religion as communication: on Niklas Luhmann. In M. Stausberg (Ed.), *Contemporary Theories of Religion* (pp. 99–114). Oxon: Routledge.

Blom, B. (2009). Knowing or un-knowing? That is the question in the era of evidence-based social work practice. *Journal of Social Work*, 9(2), 158–177.

Blom, T., & Van Dijk, L. (1999). A theoretical frame of reference for family systems therapy? An introduction to Luhmann's theory of social systems. *Journal of Family Therapy*, 21(2), 195–216.

Bommes, M., & Scherr, A. (2000a). Soziale Arbeit, sekundäre Ordnungsbildung und die Kommunikation unspezifischer Hilfsbedürftigkeit. In R. Merten (Ed.), *Systemtheorie Sozialer Arbeit* (pp. 67–86). Opladen: Leske & Budrich.

Bommes, M., & Scherr, A. (2000b). *Soziologie der sozialen Arbeit*. Weinheim/Basel: Beltz Juventa.

Bora, A. (2002). "Wer gehört dazu?" Überlegungen zur Theorie der Inklusion. In K.-U. Hellmann & R. Schmalz-Bruns (Eds.), *Therorie der Politik. Niklas Luhmanns politische Soziologie* (pp. 60–84). Frankfurt/Main: Suhrkamp.

Bourdieu, P. (2013 [1979]). *Distinction: A social critique of the judgement of taste*. New York: Routledge.

Braeckman, A. (2006). Niklas Luhmann's systems theoretical redescription of the inclusion/exclusion debate. *Philosophy & Social Criticism*, 32(1), 65–88.

Brante, T. (1987). Sociologiska föreställningar om professioner. In U. Bergryd (Ed.), *Den Sociologiska Fantasin – teorier om samhället* (pp. 124–154). Stockholm: Raben & Sjögren.

Brekke, J. S. (2012). Shaping a science of social work. *Research on Social Work Practice*, 22(5), 455–464.

Brekke, J. S. (2014). A science of social work, and social work as an integrative scientific discipline: have we gone too far, or not far enough? *Research on Social Work Practice*, 24(5), 517–523.

Bronfenbrenner, U. (1979). *The ecology of human development: Experiments by design and nature*. Cambridge, MA: Harvard University Press.

Brunczel, B. (2010). *Disillusioning modernity*. Frankfurt/Main: Lang.

Butler, J. (2002). *Gender trouble*. New York: Routledge.

Bryant, L. (2011). *The democracy of objects*. Ann Arbor, MI: Open Humanities Press.

Callon, M. (1986). Some elements of a sociology of translation: Domestication of the scallops and the fishermen of Saint Brieuc Bay. In J. Law & P. Kegan (Eds.), *Power, action and belief: A new sociology of knowledge?* (pp. 196–233). London: Routledge.

Calltorp, J. (1999). Priority setting in health policy in Sweden and a comparison with Norway. *Health Policy*, 50, 1–22.

Campbell, B. (2014). Anti-Minotaur: the myth of a sociological morality. *Society*, 51(5), 443–451.

Cappelen, A., & Norheim, O. F. (2005). Responsibility in health care: a liberal egalitarian approach. *Journal of Medical Ethics*, 31, 476–480.

Coleman, J. (1994). *Foundations of social theory*. Cambridge, MA: Harvard University Press.

Collins, R. (1982). *Sociological insight: An introduction to nonobvious sociology*. New York/Oxford: Oxford University Press.

Coyle, C. E., & Dugan, E. (2012). Social isolation, loneliness and health among older adults. *Journal of Aging and Health*, 24(8), 1346–1363.

Crawford, R. (1977). You are dangerous to your health: the ideology and politics of victim blaming. *International Journal of Health Services*, 7, 663–680.

Crenshaw, K. (1991). Mapping the margins: intersectionality, identity politics, and violence against women of color. *Stanford Law Review*, 43(6), 1241–1299.

Dahlberg, L., & McKee, K. (2014). Correlates of social and emotional loneliness in older people: evidence from an English community study. *Aging & Mental Health, 18*(4), 504–514. doi:10.1080/13607863.2013.856863

Dahlberg, L., Andersson, L., McKee, K., & Lennartsson, C. (2015). Predictors of loneliness among older women and men in Sweden: a national longitudinal study. *Ageing & Mental Health, 19*(5), 409–417. doi:10.1080/13607863.2014.944091

Darwin, C. (2011 [1859]). *The origin of species by means of natural selection.* Cambridge, MA: Harvard University Press.

Davis, K. (1937). The sociology of prostitution. *American Sociological Review*, 2(5), 744–755.

Davis, K., & Moore, W. E. (1945). Some principles of stratification. *American Sociological Review*, 10(2), 242–249.

Derlugian, G. (2013). What communism was. In I. Wallerstein, R. Collins, M. Mann, G. Derlugian, & C. Calhoun (Eds.), *Does capitalism have a future?* (pp. 99–129). Oxford: Oxford University Press.

Dominelli, L. (2002). *Anti-oppressive social work theory and practice.* Hampshire: Palgrave MacMillan.

Dore, R. P. (1961). Function and cause. *American Sociological Review*, 26(6), 843–853.

Durkheim, É. (1979 [1897]). *Suicide: a study in sociology.* New York: Free Press.

Durkheim, É. (2012 [1893]). *The division of labor in society.* Eastford, CT: Martino Fine Books.

Durkheim, É. (2014 [1895]). *The rules of sociological method: and selected texts on sociology and its method.* New York: Free Press.

Easton, D. (1967). *A systems analysis of political life.* New York: Wiley.

Echelbarger, C. (2007). Battling the siege of loneliness. *The Pillar*, 8(1). Retrieved from http://rcg.org/pillar/0801pp-btsol.html

Erikson, E. (1950). *Childhood and society.* New York: W.W. Norton & Co.

Etzioni, A. (2000). Creating good communities and good societies. *Contemporary Sociology*, 29(1), 188–195.

Fiske, J. (1990). *Introduction to communication studies.* London: Routledge.

Fook, J. (2002). *Social work: Critical theory and practice.* London: SAGE.

Fordham, S., & Ogbu, J. U. (1986). Black students' school success: coping with the "burden of 'acting white'". *The Urban Review*, 18(3), 176–206.

Försterling, F. (2001). *Attribution: An introduction to theories, research and applications.* Hove: Psychology Press.

Foucault, M. (2002 [1963]). *The birth of the clinic.* New York: Routledge.

Fraser, N., & Honneth, A. (2003). *Redistribution or recognition? A political–philosophical exchange.* London: Verso.

Freud, S. (2003). *An outline of psychoanalysis.* London: Penguin UK.

Fuchs, P. (1997). Adressabilität als Grundbegriff der soziologischen Systemtheorie. *Soziale Systeme*, 3(1), 57–79.

Fuchs, P. (2000). Systemtheorie und Soziale Arbeit. In R. Merten (Ed.), *Systemtheorie Sozialer Arbeit* (pp. 157–175). Opladen: Leske & Budrich.

Fuchs, S. (2001a). *Against essentialism.* Cambridge, MA: Harvard University Press.

Fuchs, S. (2001b). Beyond agency. *Sociological Theory*, 19(1), 24–40.

Fuller, R., & Myers, R. (1941). Some aspects of a theory of social problems. *American Sociological Review*, 6(2), 24–32.

Gadamer, H.-G. (2004 [1960]). *Truth and method.* London: Bloomsbury.

Gambrill, E. (1999). Evidence-based practice: an alternative to authority-based practice. *Families in Society: The Journal of Contemporary Social Services*, 80(4), 341–350.

Gambrill, E. (2001). Social work: an authority-based profession. *Research on Social Work Practice*, 11(2), 166–175.

Garfinkel, H. (1967). *Studies in ethnomethodology*. Englewood Cliffs, NJ: Prentice-Hall.

Gethin-Jones, S. (2012). Outcomes and well-being part 2: a comparative longitudinal study of two models of homecare delivery and their impact upon the older person self-reported subjective well-being: a qualitative follow up study paper. *Working with Older People*, 16(2), 52–60.

Glynn, J., Hohm, C., & Stewart, E. (1996). *Global social problems*. New York: HarperCollins College Publishers.

Goffman, E. (1952). On cooling the mark out: some aspects of adaptation to failure. *Psychiatry*, 15(4), 451–463.

Goffman, E. (1963). *Behavior in public places: Notes on the social organization of gatherings*. Glencoe, IL: Free Press.

Goffman, E. (1967). *Interaction ritual: Essays on face-to-face behavior*. Garden City, NY: Doubleday.

Goldstein, H. (1973). *Social work practice: A unitary approach*. Columbia: University of South Carolina Press.

Guntrip, H. (1995). *Personality structure and human interaction: The developing synthesis of psychodynamic theory*. London: Karnac Books.

Habermas, J. (1991). *The theory of communicative action Vol.1: Reason and the rationalization of society*. Cambridge: Polity Press.

Habermas, J. (1992a). *Between facts and norms: Contributions to a discourse theory of law and democracy*. Cambridge: Polity Press.

Habermas, J. (1992b). *The theory of communicative action Vol. 2: Lifeworld and system: A critique of functionalist reason*. Cambridge: Polity Press.

Habermas, J., & Luhmann, N. (1971). *Theorie der gesellschaft oder sozialtechnologie*. Frankfurt/Main: Suhrkamp.

Hagen, R. (2000). Rational solidarity and functional differentiation. *Acta Sociologica*, 43(1), 27–42.

Hagen, R. (2006). *Nyliberalismen og samfunnsvitenskapene: Refleksjonsteorier for det moderne samfunnet*. Oslo: Universitetsforlaget.

Haidt, J. (2012). *The righteous mind: Why good people are divided by politics and religion*. New York: Pantheon.

Hall, J., & Knapp, M. (2013). *Nonverbal communication*. Berlin: De Gruyter Mouton.

Harris, J. (1998). Scientific management, bureau-professionalism, new managerialism: the labour process of state social work. *British Journal of Social Work*, 28(6), 839–862.

Harste, G. (2004). Society's war: The evolution of a self-referential military system. In M. Albert & L. Hilkermeier (Eds.), *Observing international relations: Niklas Luhmann and world politics* (pp. 157–177). London: Routledge.

Havelock, E. (1996). *The muse learns to write*. New Haven, CT: Yale University Press.

Hayles, N. K. (1984). *The cosmic web: Scientific field models and literary strategies in the twentieth century*Ithaca, NY: Cornell University Press.

The Health and Medical Service Act. (1982). *Health and Medical Services Act 1982:763*. Stockholm: Swedish Code of Statutes. Retrieved from www.riksdagen.se/sv/dokument-lagar/dokument/svensk-forfattningssamling/halso–och-sjukvardslag-1982763_sfs-1982-763

Healy, L. (2001). *International social work: Professional action in an interdependent world*. Oxford: Oxford University Press.

Healy, L., & Link, R. (Eds.). (2012). *Handbook of international social work: Human rights, development, and the global profession*. New York: Oxford University Press

Hechter, M. (1986). Rational choice theory and the study of race and ethnic relations. In J. Rex & D. Mason (Eds.), *Theories of race and ethnic relations* (pp. 264–279). Cambridge: Cambridge University Press.

Hedström, P., & Swedberg, R. (1998). *Social mechanisms: An analytical approach to social theory.* Cambridge: Cambridge University Press.

Heisenberg, W. V. (2000). *Physics and philosophy: The revolution in modern science.* New York: Penguin Classics.

Helm, P. (1971). Manifest and latent functions. *The Philosophical Quarterly,* 21(82), 51–60.

Hempel, C. G. (1959). The logic of functional analysis. In L. Gross (Ed.), *Symposium on sociological theory* (pp. 271–307). Evanston, IL: Row, Peterson & Co.

Herz, J. (1950). Idealist internationalism and the security dilemma. *World Politics,* 2(2), 157–180.

Hill-Collins, P. H. (1998). It's all in the family: intersections of gender, race, and nation. *Hypatia,* 13(3), 62–82.

Hillebrandt, F. (1999). *Exklusionsindividualität.* Opladen: Leske & Budrich.

Høgsbro, K. (2011). Evidensbaseret praksis-forhåbninger, begrænsninger og muligheder. *Tidsskrift for Forskning i Sygdom og Samfund,* 8(15). Retrieved from https://doi.org/10.7146/tfss.v8i15.5737

Høgsbro, K. (2012). Social policy and self-help in Denmark: a Foucauldian perspective. *International Journal of Self Help and Self Care,* 6(1), 43.

Højlund, H., & Knudsen, M. (2003). *Organiseret Kommunikation-Systemteoretiske analyser.* Köpenhamn: Samfundslitteratur.

Holstein, J., & Miller, G. (1993). Social constructionism and social problems work. In J. Holstein & G. Miller (Eds.), *Reconsidering social constructionism* (pp. 151–172). New Brunswick, NJ: Aldine Transaction.

Homans, G. C. (1958). Social behavior as exchange. *American Journal of Sociology,* 63(6), 597–606.

Homans, G. C. (1967). *The nature of social science.* New York: Harcourt, Brace and World.

Honneth, A. (2007). *Disrespect.* Cambridge: Polity Press.

Horkheimer, M., & Adorno, T. W. (2002 [1947]). *Dialectic of enlightenment.* Palo Alto, CA: Stanford University Press.

Horton, P., Leslie, G., Lawson, R., & Horton, R. (1997). *The sociology of social problems.* Englewood Cliffs, NJ: Prentice Hall.

Hutchinson Strand, G. (2009). *Community work in the Nordic countries: New trends.* Oslo: Universitetsforlaget.

Ife, J. (2012). *Human rights and social work: Towards rights-based practice* (3rd.). Cambridge: Cambridge University Press.

Isacsson, G. (2006). Självmord har blivit allt ovanligare. *Läkartidningen,* 103(17), E24–25.

Jönhill, J. I. (2012). Inclusion and exclusion: a guiding distinction to the understanding of issues of cultural background. *Systems Research and Behavioral Science,* 29(4), 387–401.

Kahneman, D. (2011). *Thinking, fast and slow.* New York: Allen Lane and Penguin Books.

Kieserling, A. (2004a). Die Soziologie der Selbstbeschreibung: Über die Reflexionstheorien der Funktionssysteme und ihre Rezeption der soziologischen Theorie. In A. Kieserling (Ed.), *Selbstbeschreibung und Fremdbeschreibung: Beiträge zur Soziologie soziologischen Wissens* (pp. 46–108). Frankfurt/Main: Suhrkamp.

Kieserling, A. (2004b). *Selbstbeschreibung und Fremdbeschreibung: Beiträge zur Soziologie soziologischen Wissens.* Frankfurt/Main: Suhrkamp.

Kihlström, A. (2012). Luhmann's system theory in social work: criticism and reflections. *Journal of Social Work,* 12(3), 287–299.

King, M., & Thornhill, C. (2003). *Niklas Luhmann's theory of politics and law.* Basingstoke: Palgrave Macmillan.

Klassen, M. (2004). *Was leisten Systemtheorien in der sozialen Arbeit?* Bern: Haupt.

Kleve, H. (2007). *Postmoderne Soziale Arbeit. Ein systemtheoretisch-konstruktivistischer Beitrag zur Sozialarbeitswissenschaft.* Wiesbaden: VS-Verlag.

Kneer, G. (2001). Organisation und Gesellschaft: Zum ungeklärten Verhältnis von Organisations- und Funktionssystemen in Luhmanns Theorie sozialer Systeme. *Zeitschrift für Soziologie,* 30(6), 407–428.

Kneer, G., & Nassehi, A. (1993). *Niklas Luhmanns Theorie sozialer Systeme: Eine Einführung.* München: UTB.

Knorr-Cetina, K. (1983). The ethnographic study of scientific work: Towards a constructivist interpretation of science. In K. Knorr-Cetina & M. Mulkay (Eds.), *Science observed: Perspectives on the Social Study of Science* (pp. 115–140). Beverly Hills, CA: SAGE.

Knudsen, M. (2010). Surprised by method: functional method and systems theory. *Forum Qualitative Sozialforschung,* 11(3), Art.12.

Krahn, G. L., Walker, D. K., & Correa-De-Araujo, R. (2015). Persons with disabilities as an unrecognized health disparity population. *American Journal of Public Health,* 105(S2), S198–S206.

La Cour, A. (2002). *Frivillighedens pris: en undersøgelse af Niklas Luhmanns teori om sociale systemer og dens anvendelse på området for frivilligt socialt arbejde.* Copenhagen: Copenhagen University.

La Cour, A., & Højlund, H. (2008). Voluntary social work as a paradox. *Acta Sociologica,* 51(1), 41–54.

La Cour, A., & Philippopoulos-Mihalopoulos, A. (Eds.). (2013). *Luhmann observed: Radical theoretical encounters.* Basingstoke: Palgrave Macmillan.

Laermans, R., & Verschraegen, G. (2001). "The late Niklas Luhmann" on religion: an overview. *Social Compass,* 48(1), 7–20.

Latour, B., & Woolgar, S. (1979). *Laboratory life: The social construction of scientific facts.* Beverly Hills, CA: SAGE.

Lee, D. B. (2000). The society of society: the grand finale of Niklas Luhmann. *Sociological Theory,* 18(2), 320–330.

Lee, D. B., & Brosziewski, A. (2009). *Observing Society: Meaning, Communication, and Social Systems.* Amherst, NY: Cambria Press.

Lemert, E. (1972). *Human Deviance, Social Problems, and Social Control.* Englewood Cliffs, NJ: Prentice-Hall.

Lévi-Strauss, C. (1963). *Structural anthropology Vol. 1.* New York: Basic Books.

Lloyd, C., King, R., & Chenoweth, L. (2002). Social work, stress and burnout: a review. *Journal of Mental Health,* 11(3), 255–265.

Loseke, D. (2003). *Thinking about social problems* (2nd.). Hawthorne, NY: Aldine Transaction.

Loseke, D., & Best, J. (Eds.). (2011). *Social problems: Constructionist readings.* Hawthorne, NY: Aldine Transaction.

Luhmann, N. (1979). *Trust and power.* Chichester: Wiley.

Luhmann, N. (1981). *Politische Theorie im Wohlfahrtsstaat.* München: Olzog.

Luhmann, N. (1988). *Die Wirtschaft der Gesellschaft.* Frankfurt/Main: Suhrkamp.

Luhmann, N. (1989a). *Ecological communication.* Chicago, IL: University of Chicago Press.

Luhmann, N. (1989b). Ethik als Reflexionstheorie der Moral. In N. Luhmann (Ed.), *Gesellschaftsstruktur und Semantik. Studien zur Wissenssoziologie der modernen Gesellschaft 3* (pp. 358–447). Frankfurt/Main: Suhrkamp.

Luhmann, N. (1989c). Individuum, Individualität, Individualismus. In N. Luhmann (Ed.), *Gesellschaftsstruktur und Semantik. Studien zur Wissenssoziologie der modernen Gesellschaft 3* (pp. 149–258). Frankfurt/Main: Suhrkamp.

Luhmann, N. (1990a). *Die Wissenschaft der Gesellschaft.* Frankfurt/Main: Suhrkamp.

Luhmann, N. (1990b). *Paradigm lost: Über die ethische Reflexion der Moral.* Frankfurt/Main: Suhrkamp.

Luhmann, N. (1990c). *Political theory in the welfare state.* Berlin: Walter de Gruyter.

Luhmann, N. (1992). What is communication? *Communication Theory,* 2(3), 251–259.

Luhmann, N. (1993). *Risk: A sociological theory.* New Brunswick, NJ: Transaction Publishers.

Luhmann, N. (1995). *Social systems.* Palo Alto, CA: Stanford University Press.

Luhmann, N. (1997a). Globalization or world society: how to conceive of modern society? *International Review of Sociology,* 7(1), 67–79.

Luhmann, N. (1997b). Limits of steering. *Theory, Culture and Society,* 14(1), 41–57.

Luhmann, N. (1998). *Observations on modernity.* Palo Alto, CA: Stanford University Press.

Luhmann, N. (2000a). *Die Politik der Gesellschaft.* Frankfurt/Main: Suhrkamp.

Luhmann, N. (2000b). *Organisation und Entscheidung.* Opladen: Westdeutscher Verlag.

Luhmann, N. (2005a [1990]). Der medizinische Code. In N. Luhmann (Ed.), *Soziologische Aufklärung 5* (pp. 176–188). Wiesbaden: VS Verlag.

Luhmann, N. (2005b [1973]). Formen des Helfens im Wandel gesellschaftlicher Bedingungen. In N. Luhmann (Ed.), *Soziologische Aufklärung 2* (pp. 167–186). Wiesbaden: VS-Verlag.

Luhmann, N. (2005c [1964]). Funktionale Methode und Systemtheorie. In N. Luhmann (Ed.), *Soziologische Aufklärung 1: Aufsätze zur Theorie sozialer Systeme* (pp. 39–67). Wiesbaden: VS Verlag.

Luhmann, N. (2005d [1995]). Inklusion und Exklusion. In N. Luhmann (Ed.), *Soziologische Aufklärung 6* (pp. 226–251). Wiesbaden: VS-Verlag.

Luhmann, N. (2008). The autopoiesis of social systems. *Journal of Sociocybernetics,* 6(2), 84–95.

Luhmann, N. (2012). *Theory of society: Volume 1.* Palo Alto, CA: Stanford University Press.

Luhmann, N. (2013). *Theory of society: Volume 2.* Palo Alto, CA: Stanford University Press.

Luhmann, N. (2014 [1972]). *A sociological theory of law.* Oxon: Routledge.

Lukes, S. (1996). *The curious enlightenment of Professor Caritat: A comedy of ideas.* New York: Verso.

Malinowski, B. (1944). *A scientific theory of culture, and other essays.* Chapel Hill: University of North Carolina Press.

Mann, M. (2013). The end may be nigh, but for whom? In I. Wallerstein, R. Collins, M. Mann, G. Derlugian, & C. Calhoun (Eds.), *Does capitalism have a future?* (pp. 71–97). Oxford: Oxford University Press.

March, J. G., & Simon, H. A. (1967). *Organizations.* New York: John Wiley.

Marx, K., & Engels, F. (2014 [1847]). *The communist manifesto.* London: Penguin Classics.

Maturana, H., & Varela, F. (1987). *The tree of knowledge: The biological roots of human understanding.* Boston, MA: Shambala.

McNeece, C. A., & Thyer, B. A. (2004). Evidence-based practice and social work. *Journal of Evidence-Based Social Work,* 1(1), 7–25.

McNeill, T. (2006). Evidence-based practice in an age of relativism: toward a model for practice. *Social Work,* 51(2), 147–156.

Mead, G. H.. (1962 [1934]). *Mind, self and society: From the standpoint of a social behaviourist.* Chicago, IL: University of Chicago Press.

Mehrabian, A. (2007). *Nonverbal communication.* New Brunswick, NJ: Aldine Transaction.

Merten, R., Sommerfeld, P., & Koditek, T. (1996). *Sozialarbeitswissenschaft: Kontroversen und Perspektiven.* Neuwied: Luchterhand.

Merton, R. K. (1968). *Social theory and social structure.* New York: Free Press.

Merton, R. K., & Nisbet, R. (Eds.). (1971). *Contemporary social problems.* New York: Harcourt Brace Jovanovich.

Meyer, J. W., & Rowan, B. (1977). Institutionalized organizations: formal structure as myth and ceremony. *American Journal of Sociology*, 83(2), 340–363.

Michailakis, D. (2000). *Studie av arbetsplatsanpassningar med IT-baserade hjälpmedel för funktionshindrade personer.forskningsrapport*. Research report 2000(2). Uppsala: Institutet för arbetsmarknadspolitisk utvärdering (IFAU).

Michailakis, D. (2002). Autopoiesis och styrning: En studie av handikappolitiska program. *Sociologisk forskning*, 39(1), 90–121.

Michailakis, D. (2008). *Sjukdom och sjukskrivning*. Malmö: Gleerups.

Michailakis, D., & Schirmer, W. (2010). Agents of their health? How the Swedish welfare state introduces expectations of individual responsibility. *Sociology of Health & Illness*, 32(6), 930–947.

Michailakis, D., & Schirmer, W. (2012). *Solidaritet som finansieringsform och som prioriteringsprincip*. Retrieved from Linköping: http://urn.kb.se/resolve?urn=urn:nbn:se:liu:diva-75196

Michailakis, D., & Schirmer, W. (2014a). Social work and social problems: a contribution from systems theory and constructionism. *International Journal of Social Welfare*, 23(4), 431–442.

Michailakis, D., & Schirmer, W. (2014b). Vad händer när teori och praktik i socialt arbete integreras? [What happens if social work theory and practice are integrated?]. *Socialvetenskaplig tidskrift*, 21(2), 127–141.

Michailakis, D., & Schirmer, W. (2015). Välfärdsstatens manifesta och latenta problem med den ökande psykosociala ohälsan i arbetslivet. *Socialvetenskaplig tidskrift*, 22(2), 64–81.

Mik-Meyer, N., & Villadsen, K. (2013). *Power and welfare: Understanding citizens' encounters with state welfare*. London: Routledge.

Miller, T. (2001). *Systemtheorie und soziale Arbeit: Entwurf einer Handlungstheorie*. Stuttgart: Lucius & Lucius.

Mills, C. W. (1959). *The sociological imagination*. New York: Oxford University Press.

Minkler, M. (1999). Personal responsibility for health? A review of the arguments and the evidence at century's end. *Health Education and Behavior*, 26(1), 121–140.

Moe, S. (2003). *Den moderne hjelpens sosiologi: Velferd i systemteoretisk perspektiv*. Sandnes: Apeiros Forlag.

Moeller, H.-G. (2012). *The radical Luhmann*. New York: Columbia University Press.

Mortensen, N. (2004). *Det paradoksale samfund: Undersøgelser af forholdet mellem individ og samfund*. Kopenhagen: Hans Reitzels Forlag.

Mumford, L. (2010). *Technics and civilization*. Chicago, IL: University of Chicago Press.

Munn, M. H. (2006). *The mother of the gods, Athens, and the tyranny of Asia: A study of sovereignty in ancient religion*. Berkeley/Los Angeles: University of California Press.

Nassehi, A. (2002). Exclusion individuality or individualization by inclusion. *Soziale Systeme*, 8(1), 124–135.

Nassehi, A. (2005). Organizations as decision machines: Niklas Luhmann's theory of organized social systems. *The Sociological Review*, 53(1), 178–191.

Nassehi, A. (2008a). Rethinking functionalism. Zur Empiriefähigkeit systemtheoretischer Soziologie. In H. Kalthoff, S. Hirschauer, & G. Lindemann (Eds.), *Theoretische Empirie – Zur Relevanz qualitativer Forschung* (pp. 79–106). Frankfurt/Main: Suhrkamp.

Nassehi, A. (2008b). *Soziologie*. Wiesbaden: VS Verlag für Sozialwissenschaften.

Nevo, I., & Slonim-Nevo, V. (2011). The myth of evidence-based practice: towards evidence-informed practice. *British Journal of Social Work*, 41(6), 1176–1197.

Nissen, M. A. (2014). In search for a sociology of social problems for social work. *Qualitative Social Work*, 13(4), 555–570. doi:10.1177/1473325013506928

Obrecht, W. (1996). Sozialarbeitswissenschaft als integrative Handlungswissenschaft. Ein metawissenschaftlicher Bezugsrahmen für eine Wissenschaft der Sozialen Arbeit. In R.

Merten, P. Sommerfeld, & T. Koditek (Eds.), *Sozialarbeitswissenschaft: Kontroversen und Perspektiven* (pp. 121–183). Neuwied: Luchterhand.

O'Luanaigh, C., & Lawlor, B. (2008). Loneliness and the health of older people. *International Journal of Geriatric Psychiatry*, 23(12), 1213–1221.

Orlik, P. (2016). *Media criticism in a digital age: Professional and consumer considerations*. New York: Routledge.

Otto, H.-U., Polutta, A., & Ziegler, H. (Eds.). (2009). *Evidence-based practice: Modernising the knowledge base of social work*. Opladen/Farmington Hills, MI: Barbara Budrich.

Parsons, T. (1951). *The social system*. Glencoe, IL: Free Press.

Parsons, T. (1963). *Sociological theory and modern society*. New York: The Free Press.

Parsons, T., & Smelser, N. (1956). *Economy and society*. London: Routlege.

Parton, N. (2000). Some thoughts on the relationship between theory and practice in and for social work. *British Journal of Social Work*, 30(4), 449–463.

Payne, M. (2005). *Modern social work theory*. Basingstoke: Palgrave Macmillan.

Piaget, J. (1971). *Structuralism*. London: Routledge.

Pincus, A., & Minahan, A. (1973). *Social work practice: Model and method*. Itasca, IL: Peacock.

Pinker, S. (2002). *The blank slate: The modern denial of human nature*. New York: Penguin.

Pinker, S. (2007). The evolutionary social psychology of off-record indirect speech acts. *Intercultural Pragmatics*, 4(4), 437–461.

Prioriteringscentrum. (2008). *Resolving health care's difficult choices*. Linköping: Prioriteringscentrum.

Radcliffe-Brown, A. (1940). On social structure. *The Journal of the Royal Anthropological Institute of Great Britain and Ireland*, 70(1), 1–12.

Reich, W., & Michailakis, D. (2005). The notion of equal opportunity in political communication. *Revue française des affaires sociales*, 2(2), 49–60.

Riksrevisionen. (2004). *Riktlinjer för prioriteringar inom hälso- och sjukvård. RiR 2004:9*. Stockholm: Riksdagstryckeriet.

Roose, R., Roets, G., & Bouverne-De Bie, M. (2012). Irony and social work: in search of the happy Sisyphus. *British Journal of Social Work*, 42(8), 1592–1607.

Ross, S. D., & Lester, P. M. (Eds.). (2011). *Images that injure: Pictorial stereotypes in the media*. Santa Barbara, CA: Praeger.

Roth, S. (2014). The multifunctional organization: two cases for a critical update for research programs in management and organization. *TAMARA: Journal for Critical Organization Inquiry*, 12(3), 37–54.

Roth, S., & Schütz, A. (2015). Ten systems: toward a canon of function systems. *Cybernetics & Human Knowing*, 22(4), 11–31.

Saake, I. (2003). Die Performanz des Medizinischen: Zur Asymmetrie der Arzt-Patienten-Interaktion. *Soziale Welt*, 54(4), 429–459.

Sackett, D., Rosenberg, W., Gray, J., Haynes, R., & Richardson, W. (1996). Evidence based medicine: what it is and what it isn't. *BMJ: British Medical Journal*, 312(7023), 71–72.

Sanderson, S. (2001). *The evolution of human sociality*. Lanham, MD: Rowman & Littlefield.

Scherr, A. (1999). Transformations in social work: from help towards social inclusion to the management of exclusion. *European Journal of Social Work*, 2(1), 15–25.

Schimank, U. (1999). Funktionale Differenzierung und Systemintegration der modernen Gesellschaft. In J. Friedrichs & W. Jagodzinski (Eds.), *Soziale Integration. Sonderheft 39 der Kölner Zeitschrift für Soziologie* (pp. 47–65). Opladen: Westdeutscher Verlag.

Schirmer, W. (2007). Addresses in world societal conflicts: A systems theoretical contribution to the theory of the state in international relations. In S. Stetter (Ed.), *Territorial conflicts in world society: Modern systems theory, international relations and conflict studies* (pp. 125–148). London/New York: Routledge.

Schirmer, W., & Hadamek, C. (2007). Steering as paradox: the ambiguous role of the political system in modern society. *Cybernetics and Human Knowing*, 14(2–3), 133–150.

Schirmer, W., & Michailakis, D. (2008). Intersektionalitet och systemteori. In M. Söder & L. Grönvik (Eds.), *Bara funktionshindrad?* (pp. 185–214). Lund: Gleerups.

Schirmer, W., & Michailakis, D. (2011). The responsibility principle: contradictions of priority-setting in Swedish healthcare. *Acta Sociologica*, 54(3), 267–282.

Schirmer, W., & Michailakis, D. (2012). The latent function of "responsibility for one's health" in Swedish healthcare priority-setting. *Health Sociology Review*, 21(1), 36–46.

Schirmer, W., & Michailakis, D. (2014). Two ways of managing polycontexturality in priority setting in Swedish healthcare. In M. Knudsen & W. Vogd (Eds.), *Systems Theory and the Sociology of Health and Illness. Observing Healthcare* (pp. 63–80). London: Routledge.

Schirmer, W., & Michailakis, D. (2015a). The help system and its reflection theory: a sociological observation of social work. *Nordic Social Work Research, 5* (Supplement 1), 71–84. doi:10.1080/2156857X.2015.1012106

Schirmer, W., & Michailakis, D. (2015b). The Luhmannian approach to exclusion/inclusion and its relevance to social work. *Journal of Social Work*, 15(1), 45–64. doi:1468017313504607

Schirmer, W., & Michailakis, D. (2016). Loneliness among older people as a social problem: the perspectives of medicine, religion and economy. *Ageing & Society*, 36(8), 1559–1579. doi:10.1017/S0144686X15000999

Schirmer, W., & Michailakis, D. (2018a). Inclusion/exclusion as the missing link: a Luhmannian analysis of loneliness among older people. *Systems Research and Behavioral Science*, 35(1), 76–89. doi:10.1002/sres.2441

Schirmer, W., & Michailakis, D. (2018b). Luhmann's sociological systems theory and the study of social problems. In J. Treviño (Ed.), *The Cambridge handbook of social problems* (Vol. 1, pp. 221–240). Cambridge: Cambridge University Press.

Schirmer, W., Weidenstedt, L., & Reich, W. (2012). From tolerance to respect in interethnic contexts. *Journal of Ethnic and Migration Studies*, 38(7), 1049–1065.

Schmidt, V. G. (2005). Die Systeme der Systemtheorie. Stärken, Schwächen und ein Lösungsvorschlag. *Zeitschrift für Soziologie*, 34(6), 406–424.

Schneider, W. L. (2005). *Grundlagen der soziologischen Theorie Band: Sinnverstehen und Intersubjektivität: Hermeneutik, funktionale Analyse, Konversationsanalyse und Systemtheorie*. Wiesbaden: VS Verlag.

Seidl, D., & Becker, K. H. (2006). Organizations as distinction generating and processing systems: Niklas Luhmann's contribution to organization studies. *Organization*, 13(1), 9–35.

Selvini-Palazzoli, M. S., Boscolo, L., Cecchin, G., & Prata, G. (1994). *Paradox and counterparadox: A new model in the therapy of the family in schizophrenic transaction*. Lanham, MD: Jason Aronson.

Shaked, H., & Schechter, C. (2017). Systems thinking among school middle leaders. *Journal of Educational Management Administration & Leadership*, 45(4), 699–718.

Shannon, C., & Weaver, W. (1972). *The mathematical theory of communication*. Urbana: University of Illinois Press.

Shaw, A. (2013, Dec 12). Could inheritance tax reform help combat loneliness among older people? *Saga*. Retrieved from www.saga.co.uk/money/experts/could-inheritance-tax-reform-help-combat-loneliness.aspx?pid=mn

Shaw, I. (2005). Practitioner research: evidence or critique? *British Journal of Social Work*, 35(8), 1231–1248.

Simmel, G. (2009). *Sociology: Inquiries into the construction of social forms*. Leiden: Brill.

Sjöberg, S., & Turunen, P. I. (Eds.). (2007). *Samhällsarbete i rörelse: aktörer, arenor och perspektiv*. Lund: Studentlitteratur.

Smale, G., Tuson, G., & Statham, D. (2000). *Social work and social problems: Working towards social inclusion and social change*. Basingstoke: Palgrave Macmillan.

Socialstyrelsen. (2006). Etisk plattform för prioriteringar i vården. Retrieved from www.socia lstyrelsen.se/halso-ochsjukvard/prioriteringar/etiskplattform

Socialstyrelsen. (2011). Ojämna villkor för hälsa och vård Jämlikhetsperspektiv på hälso- och sjukvården. Retrieved from www.socialstyrelsen.se/lists/Artikelkatalog/Attachments/18546/2011-12-30.pdf

Söder, M., & Hugemark, A. (2016). *Bara funktionshindrad? Funktionshinder och intersektionalitet* (2nd.). Malmö: Gleerup.

Soffer, O. (2016). The oral paradigm and Snapchat. *Social Media + Society*, 2(3), 1–4.

Sokal, A. (1998). What the social text affair does and does not prove. *Critical Quarterly*, 40(2), 3–18.

SOU [Swedish Government Official Reports]. (1993). *Vårdens svåra val*. Stockholm: Allmänna Förlaget.

SOU [Swedish Government Official Reports]. (1995). *Vårdens svåra val (Del II)*. Stockholm: Allmänna Förlaget.

SOU [Swedish Government Official Reports]. (2010). *SOU 2010:80. Skolan och ungdomars psykosociala hälsa*. Stockholm: Utbildningsdepartementet.

Soydan, H. (2008). Applying randomized controlled trials and systematic reviews in social work research. *Research on Social Work Practice*, 18, 311–318.

Spector, M., & Kitsuse, J. (1987 [1977]). *Constructing social problems*. Hawthorne, NY: de Gruyter.

Spencer, H. (2010 [1876]). *The principles of sociology*. Charleston, SC: Nabu Press.

Staub-Bernasconi, S. (2007). *Soziale Arbeit als Handlungswissenschaft, Systemische Grundlagen und professionelle Praxis: Ein Lehrbuch*. Bern: Haupt.

Staub-Bernasconi, S. (2010). Soziale Arbeit und soziale Probleme. In W. Thole (Ed.), *Grundriss Soziale Arbeit. Ein einführendes Handbuch* (pp. 267–282). Wiesbaden: VS-Verlag.

Stichweh, R. (1988). Inklusion in Funktionssysteme der modernen Gesellschaft. In R. Mayntz, B. Rosewitz, U. Schimank, & R. Stichweh (Eds.), *Differenzierung und Verselbständigung* (pp. 261–294). Frankfurt/Main: Campus.

Stichweh, R. (2000). *Die Weltgesellschaft*. Frankfurt/Main: Suhrkamp.

Swedish Government. (1996). *Government Bill 1996/97:60: Priority settings within health and medical care*. Stockholm: Ministry of Health.

Swedish Government. (2008). *Government Bill 2007/08:110: A renewed public health policy*. Stockholm: Ministry of Health.

Thyer, B. (2008). The quest for evidence-based practice? We are all positivists! *Research on Social Work Practice*, 18(4), 339–345.

Tönnies, F., & Loomis, C. (1964 [1887]). *Community and society: Gemeinschaft und Gesellschaft*. East Lansing: Michigan State University Press.

Trevett, J. (2011). Statistik som skrämmer. *Revansch*, 31(4), 2.

Turkle, S. (2011). *Alone together: Why we expect more form technology and less from each other*. New York: Basic Books.

Turner, S. (2002). *Brains/practices/relativism: Social theory after cognitive science*. Chicago, IL: University of Chicago Press.

Udéhn, L. (2001). *Methodological individualism: Background, history and meaning*. London: Routledge.

Van den Berghe, P. (1990). Why most sociologists don't (and won't) think evolutionarily. *Sociological Forum*, 5(2), 173–185.

Van Dijck, J. (2013). *The culture of connectivity: A critical history of social media*. Oxford: Oxford University Press.

Van Ewijk, H. (2018). *Complexity and social work*. London: Routledge.

Vandenbroeck, M., Roets, G., & Roose, R. (2012). Why the evidence-based paradigm in early childhood education and care is anything but evident. *European Early Childhood Education Research Journal*, 20(4), 537–552.

Victor, C., Scambler, S., & Bond, J. (2009). *The social world of older people: Understanding loneliness and social isolation in later life*. New York: Open University Press.

Villadsen, K. (2008). Polyphonic welfare: Luhmann's systems theory applied to modern social work. *International Journal of Social Welfare*, 17(1), 65–73.

Von Bertalanffy, L. (1968). *General system theory: Foundations, development, applications*. New York: Braziller.

Von Foerster, H. (1984). *Observing systems*. Seaside, CA: Intersystems Publications.

Von Foerster, H. (1995). *Cybernetics of cybernetics: The control of control and the communication of communication*. Minneapolis, MN: Future Systems.

Wagner-Tsukamoto, S. (2003). *Human nature and organization theory*. London: Edward Elgar.

Watzlawick, P. (1983a). *Anleitung zum Unglücklichsein*. München: Piper.

Watzlawick, P. (1983b). *The situation is hopeless, not serious*. New York: Norton.

Watzlawick, P. (1984). *The invented reality: How do we know what we believe we know? Contributions to constructivism*. New York: Norton.

Watzlawick, P. (1993). *The language of change*. New York: W. W. Norton.

Watzlawick, P., & Weakland, J. (Eds.). (1977). *The interactional view*. New York: Norton.

Watzlawick, P., Beavin, J., & Jackson, D. (1967). *Pragmatics of human communication: A study of interactional patterns, pathologies, and paradoxes*. New York: Norton.

Webb, S. (2001). Some considerations on the validity of evidence-based practice in social work. *British Journal of Social Work*, 31(1), 57–79.

Weber, M. (1946). Politics as a vocation. In H. Gehrt & C. W. Mills (Eds.), *From Max Weber* (pp. 77–128). New York: Oxford University Press.

Weber, M. (1958 [1922]). Science as a vocation. *Daedalus*, 87(1), 111–134.

Weber, M. (1968). *Economy and society: An outline of interpretive sociology*. New York: Bedminster P.

Weber, M. (2009 [1904]). *The protestant ethic and the spirit of capitalism*. New York: Norton.

Weiner, B. (1974). *Achievement motivation and attribution theory*. Morristown, NJ: General Learning Press.

Wikler, D. (1987). Who should be blamed for being sick? *Health Education & Behavior*, 14(1), 11–25.

Wikler, D. (2002). Personal and social responsibility for health. *Ethics & International Affairs*, 16(2), 47–55.

Willis, P. (1993). *Learning to labour: How working class kids get working class jobs*. Hampshire: Ashgate.

Willke, H. (1991). *Systemtheorie*. Stuttgart/New York: Fischer.

Willke, H. (1992). *Ironie des Staates*. Frankfurt/Main: Suhrkamp.

Willke, H. (2001). *Systemtheorie III: Steuerungstheorie*. Stuttgart: Lucius & Lucius.

Wirth, J. (2009). The function of social work. *Journal of Social Work*, 9(4), 405–419.

Wodarski, J., & Thyer, B. (Eds.). (1998). *Handbook of empirical social work practice: Social problems and practice issues Vol 2*. New York: Wiley.

INDEX

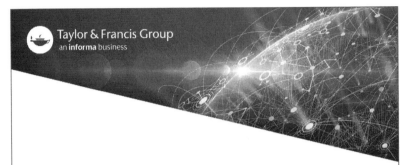